AFTER EVERY *Wedding*

COMES A *Marriage*

Florence & Fred Littauer

HARVEST HOUSE PUBLISHERS
Eugene, Oregon 97402

AFTER EVERY WEDDING COMES A MARRIAGE

Copyright © 1981, 1997 by Harvest House Publishers
Eugene, Oregon 97402

Library of Congress Cataloging-in-Publication Data

Littauer, Fred
    After every wedding comes a marriage / Fred Littauer and Florence Littauer.
        p. cm.
    "Revised and Expanded."
    ISBN 1-56507-552-8
    1. Marriage—Religious aspects—Christianity. I. Littauer, Florence. II. Title.
BV835.L54 1997
248.4—dc21   96-45430
                                                                                       CIP

Printed in the United States of America.

    98   99   00   01   02   / BC /   10   9   8   7   6   5   4   3

I dedicate my portion of this book to Fred, who has been patient and longsuffering with me as I have chased dreams and neglected to check off the charts he has dutifully set up for me. He has allowed me to use him as a humorous example, never demanding equal time for rebuttals. Fred has always been a gentleman, and the worst he ever did was to work a little too hard at trying to make me perfect. He has brought stability and order to my life, and was willing to give up his business many years ago to join me in bringing hope to the discouraged and healing to those in pain.

I also dedicate this book to our children, who have been used over the years as prize examples for our teaching. They have given up much of their personal privacy and have taken our openness in stride. Their lives are in over 20 open books! A special tribute to Lauren, who has been an exemplary mother to our three grandsons. She has taught us many lessons on running a busy household and disciplining children with consistency, love, and a light touch.

—Florence Littauer

I dedicate my portion of this book first to my Lord Jesus Christ, without whom the marriage between two self-willed, independent individuals could never have become the unity between a man and a woman that it was designed to be. He gave us the principles and truths to direct our journey through life together. When we listened, when we obeyed, when we submitted our lives to His will for us, miraculous changes became evident. Today, after 44 years of living together, we enjoy a daily oneness in spirit and purpose, a life totally without friction between those same two strong personalities. The relationship which our Lord always intended for us has become a reality.

Secondly, I dedicate this book to my wife, beautiful in sight and spirit, who has always been, despite her sparkling Sanguine nature, the stabilizing, patient, and faithful partner when the waters were deep and the seas rough. Thank you, Florence, for always believing tomorrow could be better . . . and now it is!

To you, our reader, we offer God's truths and our experiences to better enable you to enjoy the very same success which God has given to us.

—Frederick J. Littauer

CONTENTS

1

GI GENERATION, BABY BOOMERS, OR GENERATION X-ERS?

When Fred and I were asked to teach a Sunday school class on marriage in the fall of 1969, we joyfully accepted. We had been dedicated Christians for several years and had seen miraculous changes in our attitude toward each other and our ability to communicate without hostility. We felt we were normal people, and we wanted to help other couples improve their own relationships as well.

Labels for age groups had not yet been invented, so we didn't know we were the GI Generation, the traditionalists who expected to follow the marriage patterns of our parents. Nor did we realize we had willingly participated in producing children who would become Baby Boomers, rebelling against conformity and wanting to do their own thing. Those Boomers who didn't focus on dating, drinking, and disco often became "Jesus Freaks," wearing bold T-shirts and witnessing to their worldly classmates. Our Lauren led prayer meetings in the junior high parking lot before school each morning, Marita went on Jesus marches, and young Fred joined in the excitement at the new Calvary Chapel on Sunday evenings.

As our family was involved in church and ministry outreach, we never thought that one day we would have grandchildren labeled Generation X-ers, who, if conforming to the nonconformity, would feel the world owed them a living and responsibility was a relic of the past.

Was it possible in 1969 to create a class on marriage that could stand the test of time? Yes, if it was based on a Book that never goes out of date, on eternal truth that will never change.

Fred and I started combing through God's Word, seeking instruction that we could pass on in confidence. We added examples from our own experience and began to teach. Couples were hungry for truth that could change their lives, and our class grew each time it was offered, until after four semesters almost everybody in our church had participated. We wrote homework assignments, started study groups, and personally ministered to many couples in need.

Because there was such demand, we started classes in our home that grew so large we used the two houses next door for the small group-activity hour. Fred and I alternated teaching and spent countless hours each week in the study of Scripture, constantly updating our material. Soon we were invited to speak at couple's retreats, and then we were asked to write a book on marriage. Over the years this book has given hope to thousands of couples. In this edition we have updated some of our examples and added new material, but the everlasting principles remain the same.

Fred and I believe that marriage is a sacred institution blessed by God and meant to be lived in harmony, not chaos. We have lived "richer and poorer, in sickness and in health." We have raised two beautiful daughters and suffered through the illness and death of two sons. We have learned God's principle of adopting us into His family by adopting our Fred, who is now over 30. We are grandparents, authors, and speakers who want to share with others how to have a happy and meaningful home life.

We don't pretend to be psychologists, but we share from the heart God's principles as we have learned to live them.

So if you are of the GI Generation of traditionalists, you can use this information to add excitement and a light touch of fresh love to your life. If you are Baby Boomers, like our children, you have already found that a family can't function with each one doing his or her own thing. This book will bring some consistency and a proven pattern to your busy schedules. And if you happen to be a Generation X-er whose parents have thrust this book upon you, relax and enjoy the time we'll spend together. Responsibility may drop upon you any day, and won't it be great when you can say "I'm ready!"

2

First the Wedding

I always wanted to be a bride. From the time I was a flower girl in a Tom Thumb wedding, I liked walking down aisles amid a drift of rose petals. As I fantasized about my future, the aisles got longer, the crowds thicker, and the rose petals deeper.

Even though I lived in three little rooms behind my father's store, I believed in the all-American dream of rags-to-riches, of charity hand-me-downs to designer dresses. The night after I saw the Wendell Willkie campaign on a hastily constructed platform in front of the post office at Washington Square in my hometown of Haverhill, Massachusetts, I had a dream that I got married on that stage. Everyone in Haverhill showed up as I marched across the square from Gerros' Men's Shop with one of the mannequins from the store window as my groom. The school band played "We're Going to Win for Dear Old Haverhill" as we stood on the platform, draped with red-white-and-blue bunting. My groom and I waved American flags while the crowds cheered and threw confetti.

As I took a regal curtsy, my heavy gold crown, twinkling with patriotic stars, fell off my head, the mannequin moved toward me, and I woke up. I tried so hard to go back to sleep to see if I lived happily ever after, but I never did find out.

From that moment on I began to plan my wedding. For reference material I went to every wedding at our church and always volunteered to model in the annual bride's fashion show put on by the Ladies' Circles. I bought bride paper dolls and cut out pictures of brides from glossy magazines. I read romantic Cinderella novels and always pictured myself in a gossamer gown, pulled out of thin air by an indulgent fairy godmother as I rode off in a gold carriage toward the turreted castle on the hill.

When things were dull in the summer I would stage neighborhood plays on the church lawn, often writing in a bride part for myself. Once I used the lace curtains from the ladies' parlor as my veil. My brother James was always the minister, accurately predicting his future profession, and little Ron was the ringbearer from the moment he could walk.

Through all this preoccupation with mock weddings, I never thought that after every wedding comes a marriage. Weddings were clear-cut, but marriage was vague. You could see portraits of weddings, but was there ever a picture of a marriage?

When I graduated from high school, several of my friends got married, and I was a bridesmaid for one of them.

During college my zeal for nuptials faded because there were few men around and I was determined to graduate and have a career. I went back to Haverhill High School as a teacher and found myself in a profession where a wedding was a rarity. The school was full of spinsters of assorted ages and was dotted with a few men, who were almost all married. Mr. Nelsen, the band leader, was available and looked like Van Johnson, the movie idol of the moment, but he joined the Navy, never to be seen again. The only single man left was my brother's typing teacher, Mr. Sasso, whom I dated long enough to get Ron through the class.

By the time I met Fred Littauer from New York, I was more than ready for romance. The first picture Fred gave me was a portrait of him in a cutaway suit at his sister's wedding. Fred was so storybook handsome that I thought they should shrink him down and set him on top of a wedding cake.

Soon after we began dating, Fred's brother Dick got married and Fred was an usher in formal attire. I wore a white gown trimmed with black bugle beads and rhinestones and felt dramatic in a large black velvet hat as Fred led me to my seat in the church. His Aunt Stella turned around and said, "You two looked good coming down the aisle together. Maybe you'll be next."

What a thought—"Maybe you'll be next." Fred's family seemed to have beautiful weddings, lavish receptions, extravagant gifts, and honeymoons in Bermuda. I was ready to be next.

Fred had romantic ideas too, and he proposed to me in a horse-drawn surrey in Central Park. He presented me with an orchid and a diamond ring that he had designed himself. We both began to plan for the wedding of the century. Fred loved to organize, so he went to work on the details for our honeymoon while I, having a real feel for the stage, began to mount a spectacular that Haverhill would never forget—and they didn't.

My high school speech and drama pupils all loved weddings as much as I did, and they volunteered to help stage the production. This would be no Tom Thumb wedding, but a coronation with me as the queen. Four of my leading ladies were to be bridesmaids in yellow gowns, and every girl who had a strapless fluffy-net evening dress and was willing to show up at the wedding became part of the court. My college roommate, Hazel, was chosen as maid-of-honor and was draped in aqua silk. I found twins with Shirley Temple curls for flower girls and an adorable little boy for the ringbearer in a rented tuxedo.

Every Monday after school we had committee meetings on the high school stage for those anxious to participate, and their creative ideas caught up with mine. The girls planned the royal buffet, the home ec teacher made my crown, the woodshop boys made scepters out of broomsticks, the metal shop built display racks for the gifts, the autoshop boys borrowed a long white Cadillac from the owner of a shoe factory, and the high school band began practicing the wedding march with my brother Ron at first trumpet.

Wedding fever swept the high school as Cinderella got ready to meet Prince Charming at the altar and live happily ever after. As a creative writing project one of my pupils summed up the excitement of the entire student body in a letter to *Life* magazine, and the editor caught the youthful spirit right off the paper. Since they were already looking for a bride for a bride-of-the-year, *Life* thought my wedding offered a new twist and they decided to hurry up to Haverhill.

To have *Life* come to my wedding was beyond even my exaggerated dreams, and my royal court was ecstatic. Imagine, Miss Chapman and her followers spread across the pages of the most popular magazine in the country! We held emergency meetings to intensify our efforts and dramatize the details.

For the two weeks before the wedding my every move was photographed. I lay awake at night creating clever ad libs for the next day and practicing how to look surprised at a shower I had planned for myself. My brother Ron, now the top radio personality in Dallas, swept ahead of me as I made entrances and he kept everyone laughing in the role of court jester. We were on stage from the moment we got up each day, and we both loved it.

14

By the night of the wedding everyone in Haverhill knew that Miss Chapman was getting married. Young men in tuxedos helped me in and out of the long white Cadillac, and the police blocked off the entire square with long white wooden horses usually reserved to hold back crowds at parades. There *were* crowds and this was *more* than a parade.

I walked the length of the church driveway through the rows of cheering students who formed archways for me to walk through. I held my crowned head high as I had seen the new Queen Elizabeth do at her coronation.

Temporary floodlights were beaming on me from the church rafters, and my college music professor was playing the organ with all the stops pulled out. As he hit those chilling notes preceding "Here Comes the Bride," the audience rose in unison and turned their heads in my direction. I marched down the aisle on my brother Jim's arm as the twins threw rose petals in my path.

It was a perfect night: the wedding of two perfect people in a perfect setting. *But*—after every wedding comes a marriage.

3

✿

REALITY SETS IN

Fred and I had much going for us. We were both well-meaning, positive, and attractive people. We were college graduates with identical I.Q.'s. Fred had checked that out. I had taught English, speech, and drama for four years and knew how to make a living. Fred had served in the Army and was a promising assistant manager for Stouffer's Restaurants in New York City. We were both goal-oriented and were united in wanting every good thing that life had to offer. Before we were married, we focused on each other's strengths and assumed that two perfect people would produce a perfect marriage, and later perfect children. We both were idealistic and ready to live happily ever after.

How could such a promising union possibly lead to problems? Even though we had many similarities, we were unprepared for the conflict our differences would bring—differences in:

Background

Religion

Personality

Differences in Background

Although Fred and I were the same age and of equal intelligence, our backgrounds were very different. We had been brought up in the Depression, and both our families had worked hard for a living. My father owned the Riverside Variety Store, and by laboring from 6:30 in the morning until 11:00 at night, seven days a week, he was barely able to make a living. My frail mother, who had been a violinist and orchestra conductor before marriage, had to work at my father's side, in addition to raising us children in three rooms behind the store, feeding us all in full view of the customers, and doing all the laundry by hand in the kitchen sink. Times were tough, but we all determined to succeed.

Fred's grandfather had risen from sweeping streets in New York to owning a chain of millinery stores. By shrewd investments at the right moments he had been able to make money on other people's losses. Fred's mother and father both worked with him, and the family business prospered. Fred's mother took time out to have five children, who were raised in a large English Tudor home by a German nursemaid. Fred spent so much time with Freda that he spoke only German until he was three. Anna, the German maid, baked pies and cakes, polished furniture and silver, and served family meals in the large, formal dining room.

The Chapmans lived a casual life among the customers, whereas the Littauers conversed between the candelabra. The Chapmans made fun out of the trivia of life. My father encouraged us to be creative, to memorize tongue-twisters, and to develop a sharp sense of humor. Fred's family felt that anything but business was a waste of time, and their discussions were serious and purposeful. They analyzed the day's profits during dinner and balanced columns for dessert.

Because of our differences in background we had divergent expectations. I thought marriage would be fun, but Fred wanted me to get down to business. When we returned from our honeymoon, Fred put me on a training program. He wanted me to be the perfect wife, and he worked to teach me how to walk, talk, look, and cook. I thought I knew enough already, so I quietly rebelled at his instructions. But he persevered and felt that I should be grateful to be so well-trained.

Once while watching me do dishes, he noted that I made 42 unnecessary moves. I had never heard of anyone counting the moves at the sink. I threw a sponge at him. He returned it to me with dignity and looked down at me as a poor fallen angel. In deep tones he stated, "I feel it is only right for one with superior knowledge to share it with those less gifted." I was aghast, but I stopped throwing sponges. My alternative was to go back to Haverhill, so I decided to make the best of my training program. Slowly but systematically Fred suppressed my talkative personality and made me into a puppet with big eyes but no voice. I moved when he pulled the strings, I nodded in response, and I was constantly pressured to improve.

As we had children, Fred added to my responsibilities. I was to be a full-time mother performing all the duties of a full-time Freda. I was to bake streusel and keep a perfect house, like Anna, and I was to look lovely at all times and be a gracious hostess, like his mother.

I was stretched beyond my abilities, but I determined to be all things to Fred. Underneath I resented having no fun and being looked down upon as a dummy. Fred couldn't understand why I wanted to socialize without him and why I left him quickly at parties to circulate with those who found me witty and attractive. He was jealous of my friends and very possessive.

Fred wanted me to be a robot. He wanted to program me with positive information and to know that I would behave in an acceptable pattern, spewing forth only the correct responses with little emotion.

I found it difficult to love Fred, and I performed my conjugal duties as mechanically as a robot and with as much feeling. I expected marriage to be fun, but Fred wanted it perfect. For me perfect was no fun.

The *differences in background* leading to unrealistic expectations drove a wedge into the heart of our marriage.

Differences in Religion

Our local church had been the center of our social lives. My father often taught the adult Sunday school, and mother sang in the choir and played the violin. We all attended the proper classes and won Bibles in sixth grade, geraniums on Children's Day, and perfect-attendance buttons each June. We were taught to be moral and pure, to stay out of trouble, and to grow up to be good citizens. We were never encumbered by much heavy doctrine, and we were all going to heaven on our good works.

The Littauers were avid members of a religion outside the mainline denominations. They had what appeared to me as strange beliefs. Everyone who belonged was God's perfect child, there was no sin in the world, and illness was only a manifestation of mortal mind.

Fred and I were married in my church, but I had never dared ask where we would choose to attend. Since we lived in New York near his family, it appeared automatic that we would go to his church. I was offended by their offbeat theories, but Fred insisted that I join him each week. There was tension every Sunday as we headed out for church, and I would be incensed as Fred slept through the weekly monotonal readings. I felt that if I had to listen, he should also.

Differences in religion divided us from the beginning, but the problems came to a boil when we faced tragedy. We had two daughters, Lauren and Marita, four years apart. Since Fred wanted a son, we tried again, and when Marita was 1½, I gave birth to Frederick Jerome Littauer III. When he was about seven months old he seemed to regress. He could not sit up, and he began to stiffen out and scream. I took him to my pediatrician, who examined him and said, "Florence, I don't know how to tell you this, but I'm afraid he's hopelessly brain-damaged. You had better prepare yourself to put him away, forget him, and have another one."

I was stunned, aghast, sick to my stomach. Fred and I couldn't believe that two perfect people could possibly produce an imperfect son. Fred's family suggested that we take him to a healer from their religion, and once a week we went by train to New York City for spiritual counsel. The dignified gentleman informed me that *I* was the problem. If I could embrace their faith and look at this child as whole, he would be healed. I tried my best, but each time my Freddie went into a convulsion I lost my firm resolve. I was already pregnant with my next child, and I finally gave up in disgrace, bearing the guilt of responsibility for his ultimate death.

One week after Freddie died in a small private hospital in Connecticut, I sensed a problem with little Larry. I took him quickly to the same doctor I had with Freddie, and he said, "Florence, I'm afraid it's the same thing."

This time I took him to specialists at Johns Hopkins in Baltimore, and they operated on Larry, only to find he didn't have a normal brain. We brought him home bandaged, swollen, and hopeless. We knew there was no God who would bring tragedy to good churchgoing people like us.

Our differences in religion, coupled with the double deaths, split us apart and left us with no faith in God, church, or ourselves.

Is it possible for two people with different backgrounds and different religions to ever get together? What happens when those with fairy-tale expectations are brought to the harsh realities of hopelessness and death? Is there any force on earth to bind up the wounded and revive those with no love of life?

Perhaps you have problems which seem hopeless too. Let us give you courage and strength.

Fred and I were at the bottom. Our marriage was meaningless. Our two sons were hopeless. We had given up on making each other perfect and we had given up on God.

At this point I went to a Christian women's club, where I heard a speaker, Dr. Roy Gustafson, tell of a lady just like me. She had started out with lofty goals and had achieved them. She had married a handsome man and planned a perfect marriage. But tragedy fell upon her and she had no inner strength.

Dr. Gustafson went on, "There may be someone like this woman here today—someone who is good, has gone to church, has done the right things in life. She may look beautiful on the outside, but she knows she's miserable underneath."

He pointed right at me. I was dressed in a ruby-red ensemble with a satin turban on my head. I looked good on the outside, but he was right—I was miserable underneath. He asked those who identified with what he had said to pray with him and dedicate our lives to the Lord Jesus. We were to give ourselves to the Lord and ask Him to make us into what He knew we should be.

I remember thinking, "If you can do anything with me God, good luck."

Dr. Gustafson quoted Romans 12:1,2 and said that we were to present our bodies to the Lord, not be conformed to the world (as I had spent my life doing), and instead be transformed by the renewing of our minds. I didn't know that God was in the business of dealing with our minds. I didn't know there was anything to religion but going to church.

As he repeated the verse, I felt a peace come over me, and I followed him in prayer.

"Lord Jesus, I need You. I've tried to do everything in my own power and I've failed. Come into my heart. Change me. Make me into what You want me to be. Thank You ahead of time for what You are going to do with my life. Amen."

A few weeks later a young pastor came to our home and invited us to church. Since religion had been a problem with us, I didn't want to try another church, but he was both attractive and sincere. I told him why I didn't go to church anymore, and after I finished telling the sad tale of my two sons he said, "I don't blame you. If I'd had those things happen to me, I probably wouldn't go to church either."

Somehow that comment broke down the barriers. Then he added, "But if you ever change your mind, come to my church. At least you'll know I understand."

What beautiful words: "I understand." Those of us in hard times don't think anyone really understands.

The next Sunday I took my two girls to the Evangelical Baptist Church, which met in a school gymnasium, where the pastor stood under a basketball hoop. Once I got over the unspiritual surroundings and put my focus on the pastor, I was moved by what he said. He opened up the Bible and taught us how to apply scriptural truths to our everyday lives. I was fascinated. The Bible took on new meaning. It was not dull and old; it was fresh and new.

The next week the girls asked Fred to come to church, and he did. As we sat together in this loving group of people, we both felt a warmth we needed. Week by week the lessons learned and verses quoted became increasingly important to us, and within one year

Fred raised his hand one Sunday morning to signify that he had asked the Lord Jesus into his life.

The Lord did not restore our sons, but He did bring a new baby into our lives. We adopted Frederick Jeffrey Littauer and we began to rebuild our family life.

When this Fred was 12 years old he said to me, "I'm sorry you had those problems with your boys, but if it hadn't been for that I wouldn't be your son today. I would have been born anyway and somebody would have had me, but it wouldn't be you and I might not even be a Christian today."

The Bible tells us not that everything *is* good but that all things *work together* for good to those who love the Lord and are called according to His purpose (Romans 8:28).

Where do you stand today? Do you have some marriage problems? Do you need some uplifting and encouragement? This book will show you the steps we went through and how you can apply the same principles to your life.

4

Let's Examine Ourselves

As Fred and I set out to rebuild our marriage, we began to study the Bible and apply it to our lives. We found that we are not responsible for each other's conduct and that we are to accept each other as we are. After years of dedicated wife-training, Fred found it difficult to stop badgering me, but I was encouraged that he even cared. After years of building cold walls between us, I could not become instantly warm and loving, but Fred was grateful that I was trying.

Differences in Personality

One of the first major steps in our new understanding came when we attended a seminar on Christian living and were given Tim LaHaye's book *The Spirit-Controlled Temperament*. In this book we found four different types of people, and each of us could identify ourselves. I saw myself as Sparky Sanguine: talkative, fun-loving, life-of-the-party. Fred was Melancholy: thoughtful, analytical, perfectionist. Up to this point I had felt that Fred was the only person on earth like this, and that he was out to ruin me, obliterate my personality, and remove any fun from my life.

Fred had felt that I was the only person who was more interested in having a good time than in doing things in perfect order. Just seeing that we were not odd and that one-fourth of the world's population was like each of us removed some pressure from both of us. We were opposites; no wonder we didn't see things eye-to-eye! As we studied further we discovered that we were also somewhat alike but in a way that caused more conflict: We both identified with the Choleric—strong-willed, decisive, good leaders. But neither of us had ever wanted to follow. We desired to lead, but in opposite directions. What a mess we were in!

We began to examine our own weaknesses realistically for the first time. Instead of trying to change each other, we began to work on ourselves. My type of personality, the Popular Sanguine "Let's have a party," combined with the Powerful Choleric "I'll be in charge," likes to entertain and control events, so I invited ten couples from our new church into our home and began to teach the personalities like a parlor game. They were all so excited as they found themselves, and the Sanguines asked if they could come back next week. I didn't know what to say because I had already taught them all I knew, but I had a week to learn more so I invited them back. Between the first and second weeks Fred made charts, and by the next Friday he was in charge and trying to make the event perfect!

He divided us up into personality groups and sent me to the bedroom with the Sanguines. I was supposed to go down the Sanguine list and see how many of us fit those traits. Our first item said "talkative." Guess what we did with our time—we talked, we told stories, we laughed! Fred was in the living room with the

Melancholies. In one hour they went through the list perfectly. They weren't early or late; they were exactly on time. When Fred came to check on us, we looked up in surprise and said in unison, "Is our time up already?"

There were no Cholerics that night; they were all out running other organizations, but we did have a large group of Phlegmatics, and Fred had made the mistake of putting them in the family room with all the couches. When he went in to see them, guess how he found them? They were all asleep! When Fred asked what they had done with their list, one said, "I read down the list once and they all said 'uh huh, uh huh.' We got done so quickly we were able to take a rest."

We learned that very first night that the Melancholies did it perfectly and on time, the Sanguines had fun and didn't do the list at all, the Cholerics knew so much they didn't need to come, and the Phlegmatics did it the easy way and took a nap.

We saw living proof in our living room that a basic understanding of our strengths and weaknesses is a start toward changed individuals and improved marriages.

Many books have been published on this subject, and we have now written several different books that deal with various aspects of this fascinating and life-changing subject.

Four hundred years before Christ was born, Hippocrates first presented the concept of the temperaments to the world. As a physician and philosopher, he dealt closely with people and saw that there were extroverts and introverts, optimists and pessimists. He further categorized people according to their body fluids as Sanguine, blood; Choleric, yellow bile; Melancholy, black bile; and Phlegmatic, phlegm. While modern psychologists do not hold to the theory of the fluids, the terms and characteristics have proven over 24 centuries to be consistently valid. Virtually all modern personality-testing systems and instruments are based on these original concepts of Hippocrates.

Dr. Quentin Hyder, a Madison Avenue psychiatrist, says in writing on the temperaments, "For almost 25 centuries, men have recognized four basic temperamental types. No individual is completely of one type without having some tendency toward another. There is much overlap of characteristics, but nevertheless the one that predominates is not only descriptively helpful but can indicate the basic way the individual will react to different circumstances, opportunities, and interpersonal relationships."

Dr. Tim LaHaye, author of *The Spirit-Controlled Temperament,* wrote in a letter to me, "I am more convinced now than when I wrote the book that the four-temperament theory is the best explanation of human behavior there is."

In our past 25 years of Christian, public, and corporate speaking and teaching, the one subject most frequently requested of us by those planning the programs is The Four Basic Personalities. Rarely does a week go by that we don't receive letters in our office or comments from someone at a conference that one of our books on the personalities or one of our personality seminars changed someone's life. For example, "We wouldn't still be married today if we hadn't read your book." Recently a young mother came up to Fred at a conference and said, "My daughter wants to write a letter to your wife to tell her how much she appreciates her book *Personality Plus.** Understanding our personality differences has kept me from killing her."

"How old is your daughter?" I asked.

"She's 7½!"

It wasn't made clear to me whether the daughter had also read the book or merely wanted to write the thank-you letter!

---

* Florence Littauer, *Personality Plus* (Grand Rapids: Baker, 1983).

In our seminars and marriage counseling we use the knowledge of the Four Basic Personalities for two purposes:

1. To examine our own strengths and weaknesses and learn how to accentuate the positive and eliminate the negative.

2. To help us understand other people and realize that just because someone is different that doesn't make him wrong.

The complete personality profile test may be found in Appendix A beginning on page 294.

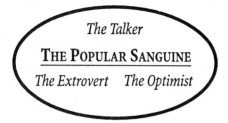

The Talker

THE POPULAR SANGUINE

The Extrovert   The Optimist

The Popular Sanguine's Emotions

STRENGTHS	WEAKNESSES
Talkative, storyteller	Compulsive talker
Life-of-the-party	Exaggerates and elaborates
Good sense of humor	Dwells on trivia
Memory for color	Can't remember names
Holds on to listener	Scares others off
Emotional and demonstrative	Too happy for some
Enthusiastic	Has restless energy
Cheerful and bubbling over	Egotistical
Animated and expressive	Blusters and complains

Good on stage
Wide-eyed and innocent
Lives in the present
Changeable disposition
Sincere at heart
Always a child

Has loud voice and laugh
Naïve, gets taken in
Controlled by circumstances
Gets angry easily
Seems phony to some
Never grows up

The Popular Sanguine at Work

Volunteers for jobs
Thinks up new activities
Looks great on the surface
Means well
Has energy and enthusiasm
Decides by feelings
Starts in a flashy way
Inspires others to join
Charms others to work

Would rather talk
Forgets obligations
Doesn't follow through
Confidence fades fast
Undisciplined
Priorities out of order
Easily distracted
Wastes time talking

The Popular Sanguine as a Friend

Makes friends easily
Loves people
Thrives on compliments
Seems exciting
Envied by others
Doesn't hold grudges
Apologizes quickly
Prevents dull moments
Likes spontaneous activities

Hates to be alone
Needs to be center stage
Wants to be popular
Looks for credit
Dominates conversations
Interrupts and doesn't listen
Answers for others
Fickle and forgetful
Makes excuses
Repeats stories

The Popular Sanguine as a Parent

Makes home fun	Keeps home in a frenzy
Turns disaster into humor	Doesn't listen to the whole story
Is the circus master	Forgets children's appointments
Is liked by children's friends	Disorganized

The Thinker
THE PERFECT MELANCHOLY
The Introvert   The Pessimist

The Perfect Melancholy's Emotions

STRENGTHS	WEAKNESSES
Deep and thoughtful	Remembers the negatives
Genius-prone	Moody and depressed
Talented and creative	Enjoys being hurt
Artistic or musical	Has false humility
Philosophical and poetic	Off in another world
Appreciative of beauty	Low self-image
Sensitive to others	Has selective hearing
Self-sacrificing	Self-centered
Analytical	Too introspective
Conscientious	Guilt feelings
Serious or purposeful	Tends to hypochondria

The Perfect Melancholy at Work

Schedule-oriented	Not people-oriented
Perfectionist	Depressed over imperfections

31

Detail-conscious
Persistent and thorough
Orderly and organized
Loves research
Senses needs
Sees the problems
Finds creative solutions
Likes charts, graphs, figures
Needs to finish what he starts

Chooses difficult work
Hesitant to start projects
Spends too much time planning
Prefers analysis to work
Self-deprecating
Hard to please
Standards often too high
Deep need for approval

The Perfect Melancholy as a Friend

Makes friends cautiously
Content to stay in background
Avoids causing attention
Faithful and devoted
Will listen to complaints
Can solve others' problems
Deep concern for other people
Moved to tears with compassion
Seeks ideal mate

Lives through others
Insecure socially
Withdrawn and remote
Critical of others
Holds back affection
Dislikes those in opposition
Suspicious of people
Antagonistic and vengeful
Full of contradictions
Unforgiving
Skeptical of compliments

The Perfect Melancholy as a Parent

Sets high standards
Wants everything done right
Keeps home in good order
Picks up after children
Sacrifices own will for others
Encourages scholarship and talent

Puts goals beyond reach
May discourage children
May be too meticulous
Becomes martyr
Sulks over disagreements
Puts guilt upon children

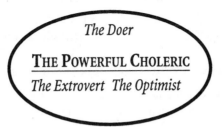

The Powerful Choleric's Emotions

STRENGTHS	WEAKNESSES
Born leader	Bossy
Dynamic and active	Impatient
Must correct wrongs	Quick-tempered
Strong-willed and decisive	Compulsive need for change
Enjoys controversy and argument	Can't relax
Exudes confidence	Too impetuous
Not easily discouraged	Unemotional
Can run anything	Won't give up when losing
Independent and self-sufficient	Is unsympathetic
	Inflexible
	Comes on too strong
	Is not complimentary
	Dislikes tears and emotions

The Powerful Choleric at Work

Goal-oriented	Little tolerance for mistakes
Sees the whole picture	Doesn't analyze details
Organizes well	Bored by trivia
Seeks practical solutions	May make rash decisions
Moves quickly to action	May be rude or tactless
Delegates work	Manipulates people
Insists on production	Demanding of others
Makes the goal	End justifies the means

Stimulates activity

Thrives on opposition

Work may become his god

Demands loyalty in the ranks

The Powerful Choleric as a Friend

Has little need for friends

Will work for group activity

Will lead and organize

Is usually right

Excels in emergencies

Tends to use people

Dominates others

Decides for others

Knows everything

Possessive of friends and mate

Is too independent

Can't say "I'm sorry"

May be right, but unpopular

Can do everything better

The Powerful Choleric as a Parent

Exerts sound leadership

Establishes goals

Motivates family to action

Knows the right answer

Tends to over dominate

Too busy for family

Gives answers too quickly

Impatient with poor performance

May send children into depression

Won't let children relax

The Watcher

THE PEACEFUL PHLEGMATIC

The Introvert   The Pessimist

The Peaceful Phlegmatic's Emotions

STRENGTHS

Low-key personality

Easygoing and relaxed

WEAKNESSES

Unenthusiastic

Fearful and worried

Calm, cool, collected
Well-balanced
Consistent life
Quiet, but witty
Sympathetic and kind
Keeps emotions hidden
Happily reconciled to life

Indecisive
Avoids responsibility
Quiet will of iron
Selfish
Too shy and reticent
Too compromising
Self-righteous

The Peaceful Phlegmatic at Work

Competent and steady
Peaceful and agreeable
Has administrative ability
Mediates problems
Avoids conflicts
Good under pressure
Finds the easy way

Not goal-oriented
Lacks self-motivation
Hard to get moving
Resents being pushed
Lazy and careless
Discourages others
Would rather watch

The Peaceful Phlegmatic as a Friend

Easy to get along with
Pleasant and enjoyable
Good listener
Dry sense of humor
Enjoys watching people
Has many friends
Has compassion and concern

Dampens enthusiasm
Stays uninvolved
Indifferent to plans
Judges others
Sarcastic and teasing
Resists change

The Peaceful Phlegmatic as a Parent

Makes a good parent
Takes time for the children
Is not in a hurry
Can take the good with the bad
Doesn't get upset easily

Lax on discipline
Doesn't organize home
Takes life too easy

As you have looked over these charts, have you found some areas of your life that need changing? We can't improve until we understand our weaknesses. The Bible encourages us to examine ourselves.

Galatians 6:4: Each one should judge his own conduct for himself (TEV).

1 Corinthians 11:28: Everyone should examine himself (TEV).

2 Corinthians 13:5: Put yourselves to the test and judge yourselves (TEV).

Psalm 26:1,2: Judge me, O LORD. . . . Examine me, O LORD, and prove me; try my reins and my heart.

Psalm 139:23,24: Search me, O God, and know my heart; try me, and know my thoughts; and see if there be any offensive way in me, and lead me in the way everlasting (NIV).

As you meditate over your own characteristics, there are a few key points to remember.

1. Labels are not important.

Our objective is to understand ourselves, to see that we have certain God-given strengths and weaknesses. We are not trying to categorize everyone into neat packages, but we have learned that presenting these traits in personality groups helps people to identify themselves.

2. Each of us is different.

We are unique individuals. God created us according to His master plan. As we all have different thumbprints, so we all have different temperament blends. Though two of us may identify ourselves as

Sanguines, we each have different strengths and weaknesses. We may have certain similarities, but we also have certain differences. We are each unique in our composition.

3. No one is 100 percent.

Each one of us is a combination of these traits. I am 50-50 Sanguine-Choleric, and our daughter Marita is the same. Fred is 50-50 Melancholy-Choleric, and our first daughter Lauren is the same. Young Fred has Melancholy traits with some Choleric. It doesn't matter what we are as long as we work to accentuate our positives and eliminate our negatives.

4. Testing is for self-analysis only.

We study our personality traits to understand ourselves, to learn about our own individual characteristics, to recognize our strengths and how God intends to use them, and to become aware that we may have weaknesses that could be annoying or offensive to our partner. Our function is *not* to label each other or become junior psychiatrists of other people, but to analyze ourselves. Recognition and understanding is the goal, and this can lead to change...change in ourselves.

5. No one personality is better than any other.

Our personalities are natural, inborn, God-given traits. No one pattern is better than another or held in higher esteem by God. Just as God put different parts in our human body and gave each of us different spiritual gifts, so He has distributed our temperament traits that we may use them for His glory.

6. We do not seek to change our personality to another one.

Since no personality is better than another, we should not try to become something else or to jump categories. What we can do, however, by understanding our weaknesses, is to work prayerfully to obliterate them from our lives.

7. Opposites attract.

When we focus on our partner's strengths we are complementary to each other, but when we look at our differences we have trouble. The frivolous Sanguine is attracted to the serious Melancholy. The Choleric, who wants to lead, is drawn to the Phlegmatic, who is willing to follow.

8. The Holy Spirit is at work in us.

It is the Holy Spirit of God who is constantly at work in us to transform us into the image of what He wants us to be. When we study the life of Jesus we find that He had the strengths of all four personalities but none of the weaknesses that encumber you and me! The Holy Spirit can enhance our strengths and overcome our weaknesses.

9. God uses all four.

As we study Scripture we see the personality traits of the men whom God used—Melancholy Moses, Phlegmatic Abraham, Choleric Paul, and Sanguine Peter. Each was different, but each was mightily used by God. And so it is today: God uses men and women of all these personalities to accomplish His work according to His plan.

Once we examine ourselves and stop trying to shape up others, we open our hearts to change. When we realize that others can be different and yet not be wrong, our relationships improve. God created all of us to be unique. If we were all Sanguines, we would have a lot of fun but would never get organized. If we were all Cholerics, we would have an abundance of leaders but no one willing to take direction. If we were all Melancholies, all things would be done decently and in order, but what would happen if we all got depressed on the same day? If we were all Phlegmatics, we could take life easy, but nothing would get done.

Whether we have studied the personalities or not, we function in our birth personalities by nature. One night Fred and I were in a hotel when at 2:00 in the morning an alarm rang and a voice said "The hotel is on fire. Please proceed in an orderly manner down the stairs to the lobby. Do *not* take the elevator."

We jumped out of bed, and while Fred grabbed important items, I went into the bathroom to fix my hair and put on lipstick. (How do you look at 2:00 in the morning?) Fred came by and stated simply "You can burn to death just as well without lipstick." We walked quietly down the stairs for 12 floors with all the others, somewhat like a death march. Hundreds of us stood around the lobby, ashamed of how we looked and hoping desperately that we wouldn't see anyone we knew. There was a large Phlegmatic security guard dressed like a Canadian Mountie. He was single-handedly blocking the entry to the elevators. A weepy Melancholy lady was begging him to let her take the elevator up to her room to get her jewelry. "It's my mother's gold and diamonds. I can't let them burn up," she cried.

Unmoved by her tears, the Phelgmatic looked straight ahead and replied, "I only do what I'm told, Ma'am, and I can't let anyone on that elevator." Arms outstretched, he blocked the passage and ignored the lady's sobbing requests.

Next came a Choleric woman pushing her ailing father in a wheelchair. Beware of Cholerics with wheelchairs! The poor father had bottles swaying over his head and tubes inserted in various places. His head was off to one side and he seemed one step ahead of death. The Choleric slammed his chair into the wall, jiggling his bottles and causing him to droop even further to one side. As she put his brake on, she turned to me and said, "Can you believe there is not one person on this hotel staff that can do CPR!" I hardly knew what CPR was at that time of the morning. She continued, "Everyone in my hometown of 7000 people knows CPR. We had a man come in and train us all, but when I asked here they said no one knew how to do it." She moved in closer to me and pointed her finger into my face. "My poor old father could die right before our eyes and they wouldn't care!" She turned in disgust and went to check her father's tubes.

At that point we were told to go back to our rooms. The fire was out. As I approached the elevator, an adorable Sanguine lady with bright lipstick and false eyelashes looked at me and said, "I love your robe! I got a new robe for Christmas. It's white eyelet with blue rosebuds embroidered on it. There's a blue ribbon at the waist with a little cluster of forget-me-nots. It's so pretty. If I'd only known we were going to be in a fire, I'd have brought my new robe!"

Here we were in a spontaneous gathering, and without any instruction we were all functioning in our true personalities.

The variety of natures is what adds spice to life as each of us sees the same event from a different point of view.

One winter when my mother was visiting us in California, she received a letter from a friend. It was such a perfect Melancholy note that I copied it to use as a humorous example.

> *Dear Katie,*
>
> *You picked a good winter to be away. Another snow storm yesterday and another today. You probably know your two next-door neighbors are gone—glory be! Maude is at home convalescing with her broken hip. Miss Lawton, upstairs from Maude, also came home a couple of days ago. Both Kane girls have been—and aren't over it yet—miserable. Mary fell and broke her nose some time ago! Then Katherine fell and fractured a vertebra—is in a corset-like brace, but back to work.*
>
> *Harold had a heart attack January 23 and was in intensive care for five days. He is in the regular hospital now—future unforeseeable, but improving. Mrs. Kelley had operations on both*

eyes and is much better now.

I'm on both feet and hope to stay there. Our heat has mostly been adequate. Spring is just around the corner and we'll see you when it gets here.

—Martha Melancholy

After I read this letter I realized that there must be people of each personality in Mother's apartment, and so I wrote corresponding letters showing how different people view the same winter in the same building.

Dear Katie,

You picked a good year to be away because it's been a long, dull winter. Nothing much has happened and I've been just sitting around most of the time. When I look at the bad weather, I almost wish I'd taken the trip with you, but when you get right down to it, it's just too much work to pack. Several of your friends have been sick and one or two even died, but when you get home there will be time enough to find out the details. I should have visited Miss Lawton when she was in the hospital, but by the time I get home at night all I feel like doing is watching TV. Mrs. Kelly used to come over and watch with me before she lost her eyes, and Katherine can't sit long in that brace so I just spend the evenings alone. I'm feeling pretty good myself under the circumstances, and I know I'll get out more when spring comes and you return to perk me up.

—Phyllis Phlegmatic

Hi Kate!

Just a quick note in the midst of another busy day. I thought you'd want to know that Agnes Kane died, so you could send a card. Don't get one that's too religious since half of her family are atheists. It's a little late for flowers, but poor Agnes won't know now anyway. Be sure you get a present for Harold before you return. He's been in intensive care, but he's making progress and will

41

probably be back in the apartment by the time you are. He has always had a soft spot for you, and if you bring him a nice gift while he's down, who knows what might happen. Let me know when your plane arrives and I'll be there to get you on time.

—Cora Choleric

Dear Katie,

You should never have gone away this winter because there has been something going on every minute. We had a great church supper in November in the left wing of the new addition in the room with the Paisley wallpaper. In between the turkey and the pumpkin pie, Maude slipped on a pat of butter and broke her hip. Isn't that hysterical! I rushed her to the hospital immediately and called all her relatives. The doctor was really handsome, and I found out he isn't even married. Let's hope I have more hospital visits. Right? One of the Kane girls (I can't remember which one) passed away the day after bridge group, and I signed your name in the guestbook at the funeral. They will never know you weren't there. The funeral was one of the best I've ever been to, with gorgeous floral arrangements. They even had a six-foot-high display of bird of paradise flown in from Hawaii. I'll give you more details when I see you in the spring.

—Sally Sanguine

5

Did You Marry a Red Volkswagen?

Many of you men allow more time for choosing a new car than you spent in selecting your wife. At the dealership you make sure the seats are properly contoured, the steering works the way you want it to, and the wheels are just the right kind. But when you choose a bride, you soon see that her seat is overstuffed, she refuses to be steered in any direction, and her wheels seem to be going around in circles.

If your lifelong dream is to own a long black Cadillac, you don't run out and buy a chubby little red Volkswagen and then take it home and bang it, stretch it, repaint it, and try to make it into a long, sleek, black Cadillac. Yet that is what many of you did in choosing a wife. You wanted a long black Cadillac, but instead you married a chubby little red Volkswagen—and you've spent the last 20 years trying to beat it, pull it, and remake it into a black Cadillac.

Unfortunately, we just can't remake each other; we must accept each other as we are and not try to construct a new image of what the perfect mate should be. So, men, if you wanted a Cadillac with class and you got a Volkswagen with dents, accept her as she is. Ladies, if you thought you were getting a charging Cougar but ended up with a powerless Pinto, be glad you've got anything in the garage, and drive it carefully.

Accepting each other as we are is the hardest principle to learn in marriage. We can always see how much better our partner would be if only he or she would follow our well-meaning and constructive suggestions. Yet each of us chafes under constant criticism, and we either march defiantly off in the opposite direction or else build a wall around ourselves and refuse to budge.

If ever two people could have remade each other it would have been Fred and I, for we tackled the repairs with such positive determination and youthful vigor. I knew that if Fred would only relax and have fun with me, we could be happy. But the cuter I got, the more disgusted were his glances and the more severe were his reprimands.

Fred knew that if only I would get serious and purposeful he could be happy, but as he nailed up the organizational charts on the wall I refused to fill in the blanks. We were two Mustangs bucking in opposite directions and refusing to be reined in.

One of the earliest problems in any marriage comes because we buy an attractive package without evaluating the contents. Then, when we get it home and live with it awhile, we want to take it back for a cash refund. But there is no clearinghouse for mismatched marriages—we can't turn each other in—so we do the only other logical thing: We try to remake our new mates.

For those of you still busy with attempted reconstruction, still holding the hammer and nails, still mixing the patching plaster, I have bad news for you: It just won't work. Fred and I are living proof that two positive people with sincere purpose could not remake each other in our first 15 long years.

Fred persistently worked on me to eliminate my Boston accent, to walk with my feet straight ahead, and to preheat the dinner plates, but he couldn't change my defensive attitude. He was able to fix up some of my exterior, but he could never overhaul the engine. While he chipped at me, I worked on him. But the more I tried to drag him to parties, the more he withdrew into business and left me to socialize alone.

We could not transform each other no matter how hard we tried. Why do we put forth such tremendous effort on such a losing cause? Because we are each born with a selfish nature, and we are determined to manipulate our circumstances until they suit our desires.

When I married Fred, I thought he would fulfill and surpass my single status. Since I had never lived in a real house, I put a major emphasis on fine furniture and drapes. I took much of the money he earned and decorated everything to suit me. Our first bedroom I swathed in pink organdy with embroidered eyelet ruffles. The walls swished with the rustle of pink taffeta hung from rods on the ceiling, and pink lightbulbs gave the room a rosy glow from behind sculptured sconces.

This bedroom would have delighted the heart of any 13-year-old girl, and it fulfilled the desires of my youth—the dream I'd had as I slept stashed behind the store.

But was it Fred's desire to come home from a hard day at work and sink into pink?

Fred married me in the expectation that I would spend the rest of my life pleasing him, but I was racing in a frenzy of self-indulgence to make up for lost time. He soon found that I was looking out for number one and he was footing the bills. As he found that his opinion was not important to me, he became moody and depressed and I could see he was not fun like my brothers.

Fred and I were both self-centered, and we did not live up to each other's expectations. Is that possibly where you are today? Are you still watching for your "if onlys" to come true? Are you stuck with a Subaru when you wanted a Seville? Oh, what's a person to do?

While the world is busy seeking alternate lifestyles, the author of the bestseller *Open Marriage* urges personal freedom and a loosening of the shackles of tradition. At a convention in New York she stated, "We have laid out a conceptual framework. We have no answers or solutions for individual marriage problems." If Nena O'Neil, the expert on modern marriage, has no answers, where can we look? There is only one place to look if we are seeking truth and validity—in the Good Book!

Once again let us repeat the perfect advice Paul gives us in Philippians 2:3,4: "Don't do anything from selfish ambition or from a cheap desire to boast, but be humble toward one another, always considering others better than yourselves. And look out for one another's interests, not just for your own" (TEV). If this one verse could be prayerfully applied to each family, what great changes could take place! When Fred decided to accept me as I was and gave me approval and even admiration, I began to improve. When I stopped telling Fred how great I was and instead started to cook, he began to appreciate me. When each of us started to put the other's needs and interests first, we started to get the results we had been seeking for years.

How can you improve your marriage? Stop trying to change your partner, and get to work on yourself. But you're not the problem, you say?

One night Fred and I were driving to the theater with another couple. The wife was grumbling with dissatisfaction, and the man said, "What can I do with her?"

Fred answered, "Start working on yourself."

"But there's nothing wrong with me. She's the one that's unhappy. I don't have a problem."

Fred said quietly but firmly, "If you have an unhappy wife, *you have* a problem."

It is so much easier to put the blame for discord on the other person than to take action ourselves. Think now of some problem in your marriage relationship and apply the following steps directly to yourself. Yes, take a moment now, and verbalize to yourself some aspect of your marriage relationship that is a source of deep disappointment or frustration to you.

6

The Cure for
Marriage Problems

1. Decide if you want to improve the situation.

I used to think that every woman with a problem wanted an answer. I assumed that if I threw out a solution to a man, he would snap it up and run home with it tucked under his arm, eager to put it into play. In fact, I was so sure that all troubled people would jump for my remedies that we originally wrote this lesson for our marriage class without this first step.

But the more we worked with real live people with real live problems, the more we began to see how few of them wanted to do something to improve the situation. I soon realized that if they couldn't grab hold of step number 1 and decide to take action no matter what the partner did, there was no point in bothering with the rest of the steps at all.

49

I found that if I laid out brilliant plans for a life, but the person before me had no desire to move, the thoughts and the time were wasted. All too often a person is unwilling to take the first step until he or she sees that his partner has already started down the journey of change. Consequently, neither one improves and both of them sit in a series of stalemates.

Harold and Missy came to our marriage classes because they were miserable together. He was a meticulous nitpicker and she was a casual housekeeper. "Messy Missy," he called her. He wanted everything perfect, but she couldn't care less. He not only lined up all his shoes in military order in the closet, but he tied all the laces into neat bows before he put the shoes away. He had wanted a Cadillac but he had married a bicycle.

Because they both liked animals, they bought a little farm and agreed to work it together even though they each had full-time jobs and couldn't get along on the simplest of projects.

On the last night of our marriage class we had a party in our home, and Harold came charging over to me with this thought: "How can you expect *me* to be romantically interested in *her* when she comes to bed at night straight from the barn, drops her overalls and smelly boots on the floor, and hops right in without taking a shower!"

As this clear picture flashed before my eyes, Missy retorted, "I wouldn't get into bed dirty if he'd help me milk the cows, but he makes me do all the work while he takes a long shower and spends an hour getting ready for bed! When I come in from the barn, he's lying there gorgeous and perfumed and I get furious."

When I tell this story at a seminar I usually ask, "What advice would you give this couple?" Invariably some wise guy in the audience yells out, "Sell the cows."

But are the cows their problem? If they sold the cows, wouldn't they fight over the goats? Yet how many of us, when faced with a problem, want to sell the cows. It's always easier to run away than to deal with the difficulties. Too often we find ourselves dealing with the symptom rather than the source of the problem.

When Harold and Missy finally took a breath and I had a chance to step in, I came up with a logical solution. (Any one of you could have done as well.) I suggested that they each spend a half-hour each night milking the cows and then both spend the next half-hour getting ready for bed. It seemed so simple that I smiled with the solution and sent them home to start.

A few weeks later I met Missy at the supermarket and asked optimistically, "How's the overall game going?" She answered, "Just the same. He won't milk the cows so I won't take a shower."

Without selling the cows there were three possible solutions to this situation. She could have gone all the way and milked the cows and then cheerfully showered before going to bed. He could have gone all the way and milked the cows alone while giving her plenty of time to get ready for bed. Or they could have compromised, as I had suggested. But neither one was willing to take the first step and they never did learn to walk together. Regretfully, neither one seemed to be willing. After five years of taunting each other with the "overall game" their marriage ended in divorce.

When *neither side* is willing, there is little hope that a marriage can be put back together.

When *one side* is willing, there is some hope. Jerry brought Dee to my office. He explained how depressed she was and asked me to cheer her up. "I can't stand one more day of her gloom," he said. As I talked with her alone, I learned that charming Jerry was an alcoholic and she was constantly worried about his behavior.

I called him back in and asked about his drinking problem. He said he didn't have one. He only stops at the bar on the way home because she's so depressed he can't face her without a few drinks.

I asked if he could stop drinking if it would help Dee and he said he could, but he wouldn't because the problem was not his drinking but her depression. "I'm happy as a lark as long as I stay away from her."

It was obvious that dealing with him was a waste of time, so I started with Dee and showed her how her gloom, understandable though it was, contributed to Jerry's desire to drink. She admitted to tantrums when he came home drunk, and so we started there—a loving, warm greeting no matter what. We worked on her living a consistent Christian life before him and accepting him as he was, regardless of his behavior.

One principle the Lord clearly taught me is that *God holds you accountable for your own actions, not your mate's reactions.*

When Dee left the office that day she was far from happy. A few days later she called me up and said, "I was really mad at you when you told me I had to do it all, but I prayed about it and God showed me there wasn't much other hope. Everyone else I've talked to about this problem has taken my side and agreed that I could be happy if only Jerry stopped drinking, but he never did. No one ever suggested that I should ignore his drinking and work on myself. I didn't like what you said, but I guess it's the only way."

Dee began attending Al-Anon meetings, where she found comfort from others in similar situations and learned how to handle Jerry in a positive way. One booklet, "The Merry-Go-Round Called Denial," was particularly helpful. We don't know if Jerry will improve, but Dee's mental health is stable and there is hope.

Again, if *neither side* is willing, there is *little hope*. If *one side* is willing, there is *some hope*.

What if *both sides* are willing? Praise the Lord, then there is *always real hope.*

Bob and Judy came in together "at the end of the rope." Judy was a beautiful woman—intelligent, articulate, outgoing, and domineering. Bob was low-key, pleasant, and reluctantly submissive to Judy. As I separated them and heard their sides, she explained how she was sick of doing all the work while he sits around. "He was babied by his mother and a bunch of aunts who thought he was cute. He never learned what life is all about. He works in the family business and seems to do all right there, but when he comes home he just sits around and smiles. I'm ready to belt him one!"

Bob countered, "From the moment we got married Judy took over. She's run her whole family and she took me on as a new project. When I did anything, she told me I was too slow and she pushed me aside and did it herself. She wants me to mow the lawn, but she's timed me and told me she can do it in 20 minutes and it takes me an hour-and-a-half. When she announces that the cars need to be washed I think about when I might want to do them. While I'm sitting and thinking about it, I hear the water going and she's out there working with a vengeance. One day I went out to help and she aimed the hose right at me. As I stood there soaked, I decided never to offer again."

Here were two nice, well-meaning people, total opposites in temperament. She was a strong Choleric who wanted action now. He was an easygoing Phlegmatic who had learned that if he held off even five minutes she would do the work and he wouldn't have to stir. Yet in spite of their differences, both of them were willing to change.

We worked out a schedule of what duties he would do on Saturday morning. He asked things such as: "Would I have to wash the cars every Saturday?"

"Why do I have to do it on time?"

"What if the grass didn't grow much that week?"

Bob thought of all kinds of outs until I explained, "You have to prove to her that you are able to do something on time and consistently, without her having to ask you. You have to grow up and become responsible. You have to show her you have some initiative and can be a leader. You have made her become your mother and you are her lazy child. She looks down on you with contempt and has no interest in you as a man. Is that how you want it to be?"

He had difficulty connecting his avoidance of work with her indifference in bed, but he was willing to try.

As we set up the list of his duties, Judy had to promise to leave his jobs alone even if the grass grew over her head. She told me later that she has to go out on Saturday mornings because she can't stand watching him "mow slow." Once he got it through his head that she wasn't going to do his work, he became more responsible and has even picked up speed. He told me recently, "I hadn't realized my pattern in life was to appear willing but hold back long enough until others did the work. It went over with my mother and my aunts, and it seemed to work with Judy. I was really surprised when she yelled at me and said if I didn't get out of that chair, she was going to divorce me. That's when we came to you."

When *both sides* are willing, there is *real hope.* There can be change!

Isaiah 1:19 says, "If you are willing and obedient, you shall eat the good of the land" (NKJV). Are you willing? Are you willing to obey what God wants for your life, or are you going to resist until your partner shapes up? Are you willing to go all the way, looking for nothing in return? Remember, God holds *you* accountable for *your* actions, not the other person's reactions.

Memorize our favorite verse on this subject: "God is always at work in you to make you *willing* and able to obey his own purpose" (Philippians 2:13 TEV).

Is it in God's purpose that Christians have positive, happy, exemplary marriages? Certainly! And it is God's purpose for *your* marriage as well. Are you willing to do *more* than your part and stop trying to shape up your mate?

We received the following letter from a couple who had attended one of our marriage seminars.

Being the emotional Sanguine that I am, I was unable to thank you in person yesterday for our time together. Even though Ted and I had heard you speak before, I was deeply touched and, in a new way, burdened for my parents.

Ted and I have such a good, open relationship, but we both know that it is only because Christ means so much to both of us and because He is the head of our home. We too have experienced changed lives and homes, with the difference being that both of our first marriages did end in divorce. I totally left God out of my decision of whom I should marry, knowing full well that I was going against His will. I knew well the verse that says that we are not to be "unequally yoked together" with an unbeliever, but I really didn't believe that God meant what He said.

After seven years of marriage and two years of my husband being in and out of a mental hospital, I really didn't care anymore that our marriage had fallen apart. Ted also knows the pain of a home where Christ is not in control, as his ex-wife has been an alcoholic for over 20 years now. We have learned the hard way, and I guess that is why, when I am reminded of the contrast and the change Christ can make, I am brought to tears for those whom I love and who resist Him so.

My parents were on my mind so much this weekend as they celebrated their 32nd wedding anniversary on Saturday. My parents are both Christians, and for most of the time I was growing up Father was employed as a producer of Christian films. My parents were the image of what a Christian couple should be, but ours was not a Christian home. My mother lives in fear of the moment when she might say or do something that will upset my father and he would walk out for hours or sometimes all night. There is no communication whatsoever, and to this day my mother still asks me to give messages to my father for her with the hopes that he will respond in a positive way. This is still so vivid in my mind as they were just here for a visit and I was even asked to call my father to the table because he wouldn't come if my mother asked.

The games they play are so tragic, and that is why your ministry is so important and your testimony such a help to those who would never before let the Christian world know that they just might possibly have some problems. I am so glad that the majority of Christians I meet today are willing to be honest with God, with themselves, and with others for the first time.

In His love, Carol

Decide if *you* want to improve the situation—not gloss it over, run away from it, cover it up, or look the other way. Once you have made the decision to work on your problem, regardless of your partner's attitude, you are ready for step 2.

2. Examine yourself. Take an objective look and find your own errors.

The reason we start all our seminars with a quick examination of the four basic personalities is because we have found this to be the most effective tool for self-examination. We can see our strengths and weaknesses clearly, and because it's done on a group level, we don't feel threatened individually.

At this point, look back at your personality test scores and review your charts. Find three of your weaknesses that you know need to be changed, and set to work on them by daily asking God in prayer to help you overcome them. Remember, you *Sanguines* are quick to admit that you have some minor faults and to apologize for them, but underneath you think they are really trivial matters and you're not concerned enough or disciplined enough to act on them. Remember, change in you requires effort from *you*.

You *Cholerics* don't think you really have any faults. You have proven over the years that if everyone else would do what you tell them to do when you tell them to do it, everything would go just fine. You have great difficulty in believing that your perfect behavior and instructions could possibly be offensive to others—but they are! Watch when people react negatively to something you have done or said. This may well be an area or trait you should focus on.

You *Melancholies* get easily depressed when you look at all the things wrong with you. It's too much; there's no hope. But that's not true. You are most able of all personalities to accept your weaknesses and to systematically get to work on self-improvement. Choose only three areas; you know that you and the Lord can do it. Ask your partner to help you by encouraging you when there is evidence of effort and improvement.

You *Phlegmatics* admit that you have some flaws. You've managed to get along so far without having to do much about them. Other people have done your work, and you're so easy to get along with that you've never been pushed into change. Are you willing now to look at three areas of weakness (or at least one or two) and force yourself to do something about them? Stand up now, flex your muscles, and let's move!

If we were trying to handle our problems in a strictly human manner, we would now be at a point where we would heroically try to change ourselves in our own power. Secular seminars are telling us we are little gods; we can do all things ourselves.

There is much we can do for ourselves. We women can change our hairstyles, lose ten pounds, buy new clothes, and repaint the kitchen. You men can buy new cars, grow a mustache, or have an affair with your secretary. These are all changes, but they won't make you a different person. Internal, lasting changes come from above, not from without.

Many women we talk with put all their faith in some super weekend—a retreat to the mountains with some saintly speaker in hopes that the leader can heal them. When nothing dramatic happens, they get depressed and lose faith.

Fred and I tried to improve in our own strength, but we gave up. We couldn't understand how we could be so competent in the world and yet so weak with each other. We found the key to inner change in the Bible where Paul said, "I can do all things through Christ, who strengthens me" (Philippians 4:13 NKJV).

As Fred and I committed our lives to the Lord we were able to admit our failures and ask for help—two very humbling experiences. Fred had been brought up in a cult which said there is no sin in the world, and I had always been so religious that it was close to impossible for us to agree with Paul when he said, "Christ came into the world to save sinners, of whom I am chief." Could good little me possibly be bad?

Only when we were willing to admit our faults and our inability to overcome them in our own strength were we ready for step 3.

3. Confess your weaknesses as sin.

God tells us clearly, "If we confess our sins, He is faithful and just to forgive us our sins and to cleanse us from all unrighteousness." He then adds (in case we don't think we've really been unrighteous), "If we say that we have not sinned, we make Him a liar, and His word is not in us" (1 John 1:9,10 NKJV). Psalm 139:24 says, "See if there is any offensive way in me, and lead me in the way everlasting" (NIV).

Even though you are obviously a very good person, what is there about you that is offensive to others? Where do you need improvement? What habit have you been unable to break? What has just come to your mind? Confess this to the Lord and He will free you from this bondage. Don't hide it any longer—bring it out into the open before the Lord and He will give you forgiving peace.

"I acknowledged my sin to you, and my iniquity I have not hidden. I said, 'I will confess my transgressions to the LORD,' and You forgave the iniquity of my sin" (Psalm 32:5 NKJV).

How hard it is for many of us really good people to confess to the Lord that we are sinners! I first met Ann at a Christian Women's Club. She prayed with me that day to ask the Lord Jesus, into her life. Many wonderful changes took place in the next five years, and when I met her in an airport for a brief visit she told me proudly of her Christian activities and the ministry the Lord had given her with other women. As I asked her about her relationship with her husband she winced, and I knew I had hit a nerve. Later she wrote me:

Dear Florence,

I love you. Thank you for briefly visiting with me last Friday, harpooning into my heart much-needed truths.

I had planned to say very little about me during lunch but to listen to all about you and your exciting life and all the neat things you have to say.

But as you questioned me my feet turned to clay, my heart to stone, my brain to putty. I am only sorry that I could not have laid all that past history in front of you five years ago. However, at that time I could not even think about it, let alone talk about it. Anyway, I do recognize that your words of truth were divinely guided. I appreciate your gentleness and your ability to get the message across. I know that the Lord set it all up.

That night around 3 A.M. I awoke and knew that I had to confess the hatred and resentment I had for my husband and ask for cleansing and removal of that burden. I have known all along that this area needed shaping up, but I just kept putting it aside. It was my pet grudge. And all the time I was able to grow and grow and inspire others and have a terrific answered prayer record. Just that Friday morning before I met you, I had helped on a World Day of Prayer breakfast and had spent several spiritual hours shepherding, giving, praying, and all those neat things. And as long as I focused on others and not on myself, all was well.

Anyway, I did what I had to do. I did not feel elated and re-lieved afterward. Today I feel much different than I did Saturday. I know a healing is taking place. I was obedient, and that is where it is. I also feel no resentment and I am able to reach out to my husband and "treat him as I treat my Christian friends." That has been his request for some time.

Thank you for caring and shepherding.

In gratitude, Ann

It is possible for us to grow as Christians and yet not deal with uncleansed areas of our lives, but we will never have a clear conscience until we have pulled out the hidden sins and placed them before the Lord with a confessing heart. Perhaps you've left some sin in your life festering in a corner. Perhaps you've rationalized why it's not your fault at all. Perhaps you've shoved it into a closet but the stench keeps seeping out.

Don't try to keep your failures under wraps. Bring them out in the open and confess them to the Lord. He never gossips or tells tales. You can trust the truth with Him!

4. Ask God to remove any offensive traits.

Not only can you trust God not to violate any confidence you share with Him, but you can have confidence that He will rid you of any offensive ways. In 1 John 5:14,15 we find, "This is the confidence which we have before Him, that, if we ask anything according to His will, He hears us. And if we know that He hears us in whatever we ask, we know that we have the requests which we have asked from Him" (NASB).

When we are willing to ask in faith to be delivered of our offensive ways, we can have confidence that He hears and acts.

I struggled with this scriptural concept at first because I could always find people who were so much worse than I was—Fred, for a close example. I never smoked, drank, or robbed banks. What more could God want from me? Yet one day I found a convicting verse: "For all have sinned and come short of the glory of God" (Romans 3:23). Even Florence!

5. Forgive your partner silently and apologize orally.

Few of us enjoy forgiving others because it implies that what they did wasn't so bad, when it really was! If we really forgive we might also forget the evidence, and what if we need it for proof in the future? Our minds function on such a selfish level that we don't like to let go of the bad examples of other people. Not only do we not want to forgive, but we take pride in repeating the tales of others' grand mistakes because it shows we don't do any of these things ourselves. Obviously, if I have the discernment to see the error of your ways then I must be above suspicion myself.

I used to gather up Fred's faults with the fervor of a child picking berries. I had a whole shelf of overflowing baskets before the concept of forgiveness fell heavily upon me. To be spiritual I plucked out a few of Fred's faults and forgave them, but I didn't want to clear the whole shelf. Where would I go for future reference material?

God had to hit me over the head with my own bulging baskets before I was ready to forgive and willing to apologize. Even though I have learned this lesson and taught this lesson, it was some time before I was able to pick up a basket without starting to gather up some faults.

Why am I the only woman who married a man who doesn't come home at 5:30 for dinner? Why doesn't Fred pay our bills on the first day of the month automatically like every other husband? Why does he go into the office on Saturday to check on a few things and then stay all day and think he was only gone an hour?

You see how easy it is for me to find Fred's failures? They jump right up and cling to me like lint on a blue suit. Does this sound familiar to any of you? Have you been out berry-picking? Have you gathered in a bountiful harvest? Put it all in the trash today. Get rid of all bitterness, wrath, and anger. "Be kind to one another, tender-hearted, forgiving one another, just as God in Christ also forgave you" (Ephesians 4:32 NKJV).

One dear lady I met with learned the lesson of forgiveness and apologies too late to hold her marriage together, but she is willing to share her experience with others.

> *Dear Florence,*
>
> *I want to thank you for the invaluable advice I received at the Arizona Women's Retreat in Carefree last spring. You said if we had a strained relationship we should apologize to that person, tell him we are sorry for hurting him, and ask what we can do to help him feel better about us or the situation. Then be prepared for him to "dump" on us and let him spout what he will and tell him we understand—we will try to improve.*
>
> *I decided to try this approach on my ex-husband, who was very bitter. First I prayed about it (for about four months) until my heart was right. Since my ex lives in another state, I didn't know when I would have the opportunity to apologize, but God provided the time and means when He knew it was right!*
>
> *When I first approached him, my ex was suspicious, then astounded at my attitude! Nevertheless, his response was over-whelming to me because after eight years of sarcasm and bitterness he responded with tenderness and understanding.*
>
> *This result is going to mean not only a better relationship between us (not to mention taking away my guilt), but it will take the pressure off our two sons and all of our relatives and friends, who up until now have had to take sides. Humbling yourself can really break down barriers between people.*
>
> *Sharing this concept with others has been such a pleasure, and I urge you to continue to do so. May God bless you and continue to keep using you for His glory.*
>
> *Most sincerely, Betty*

6. Look at the good in your partner, not the weaknesses.

Often after I have listened to the terrible description of an obvious ogre of a husband I ask the angry woman, "How did an intelligent lady like you ever get attracted to such a loser? What did you see in him in the first place?"

Usually her response is, "Well, he used to be different. When I first met him he was handsome, witty, and generous."

"What caused all this to change?"

"Not everything changed. He's actually still good-looking if he'd ever smile. He can be funny at parties, though he's dull as dishwater at home. He's still generous with the kids, but he wouldn't give me a nickel."

It's always easy for an outsider to see that there are still many good qualities in this man, but she seems to bring out the worst in him. Is he really as bad as she perceives him to be? What is there positive about this person?

In Philippians 4:8 Paul directs our attention to a checklist of the good in others: "Finally, brethren, whatever is true, whatever is honorable, whatever is right, whatever is pure, whatever is lovely, whatever is of good repute, if there is any excellence and if anything be worthy of praise, let your mind dwell on these things" (NASB).

When you read this over, can you find something true, honorable, right, pure, lovely, or of good repute about your mate? Is there any excellence? Anything worthy of praise? Let your mind dwell and think on these things.

Right now, before you forget, list ten things or traits about your partner that attracted you in the first place. In doing so you will be obeying the Lord's word to you in Philippians 4:8: "Let your mind dwell on these things" (NASB).

1._____   6. _____

2._____   7. _____

3._____   8. _____

4._____   9. _____

5._____   10. _____

7. Don't keep digging up past problems.

Many marriages are doomed forever because of past mistakes. The partners are unforgiving and are constantly digging up what happened ten years ago. Whenever a disagreement arises they reach into their bag of tricks and find their two favorite words: *always* and *never. Always* goes with everything bad and *never* goes with everything good, such as:

"You are *always* late."

"You *never* say a kind word."

The past becomes so much a part of today that there is no hope for the future. Years from now we will still be trudging down this dreary trail because we've *always* had problems and things will *never* get better. When you look at these thoughts on paper, you can easily see that a constant review of the bad past precludes any improvement in the future. Yet there is hope once we realize the rut we're in and want to rise out of it. Paul says, "The one thing I do ... is to forget what is behind me and do my best to reach what is ahead" (Philippians 3:13 TEV).

I received a lengthy letter from a depressed lady, who spent pages listing things such as:

> Dick has *never* remembered my birthday.
> Dick has *never* brought the children presents.
> Dick has *never* disciplined them.
> Dick has *never* played games with them.

Dick has *never* taken their pictures.
Dick has *never* planned a vacation.

Sometimes she added *absolutely never* in case *never* wasn't strong enough.

From this letter there appeared to be no hope. She was going to kill herself. I no longer remember what I wrote, but in my reply I tried to encourage her to get rid of the past problems in order to live positively for the future. Months later she wrote:

> *Dear Florence and Fred,*
>
> *Thank you for your letter showing that you care. I am writing to tell you this time of my healing, my freedom from depression! I asked God to forgive my long-held resentments and anger. (I had watered them constantly with the tears of my depression and they had grown and grown!) I asked Him to take away the memories of the wrongs (the things I wrote to you about), and to fill my mind with creative new thoughts of ways to live and act. He did! He has! For the first time in my life I've accepted His forgiveness.*
>
> *Words cannot express the joy I feel to be free of the tears and heaviness and dread of working through another day on earth. I'm sure you know about the prison that depression is. Perhaps I'd still be there except for the love and concern you showed to me. (God made our paths to cross.)*
>
> *This is a message of rejoicing—that the hurts and the past are forgotten and I have a new chance!*
>
> *Thank you from the bottom of my heart.*
>
> *Love, Helen*

As Christian believers we have the power to lay our past problems to rest when we are willing. "If anyone is in Christ, he is a new creation; old things have passed away; behold, all things have become new" (2 Corinthians 5:17 NKJV).

8. Believe that God can help you and THANK Him ahead of time for what He is going to do in your life.

Do you really believe that God *knows* you? Do you believe that He *knows* the hairs on your head? Do you believe that not a sparrow falls without His *knowing?* The Bible assures us that God *knows* His own. He is our Father and He *knows* His children. A father wants the best for his family and will give his children all he has.

"When you pray and ask for something, believe that you have received it, and everything will be given you" (Mark 11:24 TEV).

Sometimes we ask for things that are wrong and wonder why we don't receive them, but our Father God knows our needs and He knows our future. If our children ask permission to go to a party where drugs are available, we do them no favor by allowing them to go. So it is with our heavenly Father. He knows what's best for us.

Those of us who are parents are always thrilled when our children appreciate us, when they say thanks. Several times during Marita's teen years when she fussed because we wouldn't let her do a certain thing, she returned later to say, "Thank you for saying no." In the same way our Father loves to hear thanks from His children even when we are not enthused over our circumstances. We're here for a reason, and only our Father can weave together our past, our present, and our future.

"In everything give thanks, for this is the will of God in Christ Jesus concerning you" (1 Thessalonians 5:18).

What's your problem today? Are you ready to take action?

> Will you DECIDE to improve the situation?
> Will you EXAMINE yourself and not your mate?
> Are you big enough to CONFESS your weaknesses as sin?
> Do you care enough to ASK God to rid you of your faults?
> Can you really FORGIVE your partner and apologize?
> Are you willing to LOOK at the good in your mate?

THE CURE FOR MARRIAGE PROBLEMS

Do you want to FORGET the past and stop reviewing the failures?

Do you BELIEVE that God can help you? Will you THANK Him ahead of time for what He's going to do in your life?

Simple steps to a wonderful solution!

7

ॐ

AM I GROWING UP OR
JUST GROWING OLD?

As a little girl I enjoyed playing "grown-ups." I would parade around in my mother's old dresses and pretend I was a lady. I remember how thrilled I was when a neighbor gave me a pair of her old green silk shoes. As I scuffed along, dragging those high heels behind me, I dreamed of the future, when I would surely be a sophisticated lady with green silk shoes that fit. I assumed that as one got older one grew up, and it was not until I became a believing Christian that I knew the difference.

At the age of 38 I asked the Lord to show me areas of weakness in my life. I didn't expect much of a list, but I had been told that this was a proper prayer for a new Christian to make. I soon began to realize, although I thought I was grown up, that I was still somewhat of a child. While I had a mature exterior, I was plotting for my own way inside. I got angry when people didn't agree with my authoritative statements. I knew how to turn every situation to my own advantage, and I was a master at dropping the blame for failure on others. I occasionally slammed the dishwasher shut to show I was made for better things than housework. While I was a charmer in public, I was often a child at home.

I asked the Lord to correct this area of my life and help me to grow up. The first step in overcoming any problem is recognizing that there is one. I saw for the first time that I had a problem, and as I sought solutions the Lord gave me the following lesson.

What Is Maturity?

According to the dictionary, maturity is "a growing up, a completeness, a ripening, a full development." We all feel that we've grown up and that each one of us has completed something. A few of us may be overripe and some are too fully developed. A better way to check our maturity is to ask, "Have we learned to *accept responsibility* and *adjust to our situations?*"

When God directed our family in 1968 to leave Connecticut, where we had lived for 13 years, to move into the desert of California, I was brokenhearted. I was very new in my Christian faith and I had not experienced God's firm direction and constant care for me. All I could see was the leaving of a secure situation for a frightening future. I didn't know enough about the Bible to realize that when God wanted to teach people lessons, He often sent them to deserts. As I sat sadly in San Bernardino studying God's Word, I found Paul's verse on maturity in Philippians 4:11: "*I have learned in whatever state I am, to be content*" (NKJV).

Did this mean that I should be content in the State of California? Yes. Could I leave lush, green Connecticut with its assets and be happy in the desert of California with its uncertainties? Paul said that he had to learn to be content. It didn't come easily. I determined to learn to be content in California. That agreement with

God was my first step in growing up. I must learn in whatever state I am—even the state of California—to be content.

Where Do We Start?

How can we begin this process of growing up? Paul tells us that our first job is to look at ourselves, to sit back objectively and see if we ever outgrew our childhood. In Galatians 6:4 he says clearly, "Each one should judge his own conduct" (TEV).

"But, Paul, it's so easy for me to see what's wrong with others. I have such talent in this direction."

And it was true. After 15 years of living with Fred, I had a list of his immature manifestations that would have convicted him in any court. I even had professional proof: My obstetrician once told me after he had a meeting with Fred that my marriage problems stemmed from Fred's immaturity. How happy I would have been to tell Fred he was behaving like a child! However, Paul did not say I should judge Fred, but myself.

"You mean, dear Paul, there might be something wrong with me?"

In 1 Corinthians 11:28 Paul answered, "Everyone should examine himself" (TEV).

"Not Fred?"

In 2 Corinthians 13:5 Paul repeated, "Put yourselves to the test and judge yourselves" (TEV).

As I conversed with Paul he seemed to say, "Florence, when you get to heaven, God is not going to give you a reward for how well you remade Fred, but for how freely you let God remake you."

"You mean I'm part of the problem?"

"Yea, verily, even you."

What Is Our Aim?

What is our goal in the Christian life? If it's not to shape up others, what is it? Paul instructs us to "grow up in Christ."

Since our own human control keeps us self-centered, we only grow up when we "grow up *in Christ.*" Paul speaks to us on this subject when he writes in Ephesians 4:13-16, "We shall become *mature* people, reaching to the very height of Christ's full stature. Then we shall *no longer be children.* . . . *We must grow up in every way to Christ, who is the head.* . . . The whole body *grows and builds itself up* through love." We can never grow up in Christ until we study His life and read God's Word to learn what He wants us to know. Paul spoke to baby believers like us when he said, "I had to feed you milk, not solid food, because you were not ready for it" (1 Corinthians 3:2 TEV). Let each one of us eat God's Word so that we might *grow up in Christ.*

How Can We Check Our Maturity?

When we look in a mirror, we can see how we are dressed. If we use a three-way mirror, we often see more of us than we wish to see. We may find that from the back our hair doesn't look as good as the front view promised. You men may notice a bald spot appearing which will take some artful combing to disguise. We can only make improvements on ourselves after we have assessed the negatives, so let us try this approach in checking our maturity.

Do We Blame Others?

How easy it is when things go wrong to blame other people!

"If only I had a different husband, I would be happy."

"If only I had more money, I could put up with him."

"If it weren't for those kids, I might amount to something."

"If my mother had only loved me, I would know how to love my children."

"If I had had a decent boss, I wouldn't have been fired."

"If only my husband didn't drink, we could have a good marriage."

If only the other people were perfect, I would be all right! If we were surrounded by delightful people who thought exactly as we did and were excited by our every suggestion, life would be much more pleasant. Unfortunately, this utopia will never come true, and we must grow up to accept the personalities around us *as they are.*

I'll never forget the morning as I came out to breakfast, young Freddie, who was nine at the time, walked in the door from the patio. I said, "Well, Freddie, how are things going with you this morning?" He sighed, "Pretty good so far—I haven't run into any people yet."

How much easier life would be if we didn't run into any people! It is those other people with those other ideas that really get us upset. In any problem we must ask ourselves, "What part of this situation is my fault?" As long as we put the blame on others, we will never grow up.

Our Freddie first heard this lesson on maturity when he was five years old, and I was amazed at how quickly he got the point when I overheard this dialogue on the patio:

Freddie: "Who broke the wheels off my truck?"

Kevin: "Kenny did it."

John: "Kenny's not even here."

Freddie: "Don't you know that putting the blame on others is a sign of immaturity?"

How important it is to teach our children to grow up, to accept responsibility for their own behavior and not put the blame on others! Yet it is virtually an impossible task for immature parents to bring up mature children. Where do our children learn the fundamentals of marriage? Their opinion of the marital relationship grows on the foundation that we establish in their young lives by what they see in us!

As Fred and I became aware of our manifold immaturities, we determined to grow up and bring our children along with us. We stopped blaming others for our problems and made the children own up to their mistakes. When we asked them a question, they had only two choices—yes or no. They were not allowed to skirt the issue with "Those kids down the street were over" or "I think the dog did it." They had to own up, accept the blame, and say "I'm sorry. It was my fault."

One night Fred and I came home late and found the following note taped on our mirror from our 12-year-old Marita:

Gee, Dad

I'm really sorry. Please pray with me that I will not be tempted to disobey the rules.

Love, Marita

While we were grateful for this spiritual confession, what was missing? What was it that she had done? My Sanguine nature wanted to wake her up and ask her, but Fred said, "The morning will be soon enough to find out." I could hardly wait until morning, when she told us she had ridden her minibike way up into the hills where the signs said, "No trespassing during fire season." She knew she was wrong and she had accepted the blame before we even knew what she had done.

In recent years I overheard Marita reviewing this principle with Freddie: "The sooner you learn to confess your fault to them *before* they catch you, the better off you'll be." And then she sighed, "I have learned this from bitter experience."

We have all learned together what it means to grow up and not put the blame for our failures on others.

Do We Blame Our Situation?

"It's this house that has me down."
"It's this town that's depressing."
"It's my husband's hours that ruin our fun."

"It's those cheap clothes that make me ugly."

How easy it is to blame our situation for our daily discontents! When we bought our very first home in Connecticut, I knew it would make me happy. It was a spacious six-room ranch house on one of the loveliest streets in town. However, within three years it grew smaller, and I decided I could never be content until I had more room—much more room. I called in an architect and made plans to double the size of our home. I knew that when this sprawling 12-room house was complete I would really be happy. I loved the new part of the house, as each detail had been done under my daily direction. But then the old part looked drab. I started on a program of interior decoration that I would be working on yet if God had not become weary of my seeking happiness through home improvements. He picked me up and moved me into a tiny bungalow in California, added three people to my family, and said, "Now the eight of you rejoice in me in these five rooms!" And we did.

At first I said, "Lord, what am I doing in this little old house with the plaster falling in, with the ancient plumbing that doesn't work, and with a hot plate on the porch for a kitchen?"

And He said to me, "You're going to sit in this little spot until you learn that it's not your surroundings that make you happy." It took two years for us to learn this priceless lesson, but it was all worth it. As I looked at four girls in layers in one bedroom and two boys stacked in the next, I asked myself how I got into this. I know now that this sardine experience had its rewards. No longer could a child say, "This is *my* room, *my* dresser, *my* desk"; everything was *everybody's*. What a humbling and necessary experience this was to get us ready for Christian service!

When I first joined the Women's Club in San Bernardino, I met an unhappy lady who told me she was miserable because her husband had been transferred here to this desert city and that she had to live in this dull town she didn't like.

"We won't be here long," she assured me, "and when we leave here, I'll be happy."

I suggested that she try to think positively about San Bernardino, as I was trying to do, but she said there was no point in wasting energy to like the city, as she would be leaving soon anyway. Twelve years later she was still there and still miserable, waiting for that great moving day in the future when she could be happy. Ironically, she came up to me a few months ago and said, "Guess what, Florence. My husband has decided to retire in San Bernardino!"

Our friend Lynn was sent to a town she did not like, and she vowed that she would not put up any curtains as long as her husband made her stay there. She explained to me, "If I put up curtains, he might think I was adjusting to my situation." They lived unhappily in the sight of all the neighbors for two years, until he ran off and married a woman with drapes!

One lady told me she had never been happy since she got married because her husband was in the bread business, where he had to work on Sundays. She had been waiting for 12 years for him to change jobs and have Sundays off so she could enjoy life "like normal people." He had risen to an executive position and loved his job, but she tried to persuade him to change so she could be happy.

A man once told me his wife was never content. "I've tried to please her in every way I can, but she's never happy. First it was the stove. It was an old-fashioned one and didn't have a self-cleaning oven. Everyone needs a self-cleaning oven. After listening to her gripe for months, I went out and bought her a new avocado stove with every possible feature. I had it sent home and I knew this stove would make her happy. I walked in that night expecting her to be thrilled with me, but do you know what she said? 'Why did you buy green? The white refrigerator looks terrible next to that avocado stove. We'll have to get a new refrigerator.' I didn't want to prolong the agony, so I got her a new refrigerator with ice cubes in the door, and I was hopeful this would be the end. But it wasn't. Do you know what happened next? When we removed the old refrigerator, the floor tiles cracked and now she wants a new kitchen floor. She also mentioned that the cabinets look shoddy and that the curtains are in shreds. I can't stand it any longer. I know she'll never be happy!"

When Marita went off to college she took everything from our house that wasn't nailed down. Her car was so full she couldn't shut the windows as she and her friend Peggy pulled out on a Sunday afternoon. They were going off to a Christian college specifically to take a course taught by our family friend, Dr. Henry Brandt. At 7:45 the next morning Marita called to say she was through with college and was coming home. I replied, "That has to be the shortest college career on record."

She explained that Dr. Brandt was not coming this term and so she was not going to stay.

"Don't they teach any other courses at that school?" I asked.

"I knew you'd be no help," she fumed.

"This will be a great opportunity for you to put the maturity lesson into practice," I said. "So find some other class and make the best of your situation."

At the end of the week Marita came home for a visit and brought me a note from Peggy.

"We want to show our parents that even though the class wasn't our favorite choice, we will make the best of it anyway."

Do We Blame Our Lacks?

"If only I had been brought up on the right side of the tracks."
"If only I had gone to college."
"If only I hadn't gotten married so young."
"If only my mother had given me piano lessons."
"If only I had been trained for something."

Is it *lack of training* that is keeping us down? We had a contractor friend who had a mountain of money but had never progressed an inch in the social graces. He was unhappy that he had not made headway in the country-club circles, but he would excuse it all by saying, "It's just my background. I never got no education. I worked up the hard way. I'm a self-made man." Then he would belch loudly and wipe his mouth off on his sleeve. Many of us use our lack of training as an excuse for our social failures, but anyone who cares enough to make an effort can learn from observation how to be inoffensive and acceptable.

Those of us who are truly believing Christians know that God will make up for our lacks by giving us the power to do what He wants us to do. When God called Jeremiah to be a prophet, Jeremiah answered, "Ah, Lord God! Behold, I cannot speak, for I am a youth" (Jeremiah 1:6 NKJV). He did not feel he had the qualifications to do God's work. He was too young, too inexperienced; however, the Lord answered him, "Do not say, 'I am a youth,' for you shall go to all to whom I send you, and whatever I command you, you shall speak" (verse 7 NKJV). God is patient with us, but He also has expectations of us. He is direct. When He gives us a job to do, we should do it on the authority that He knows better than we do what our abilities can become.

When God called Moses to deliver the children of Israel to the Promised Land, Moses answered, "Who am I, that I should go unto Pharaoh, and that I should bring forth the children of Israel out of Egypt?" (Exodus 3:11). Who am I? Why pick on me? I'm just a poor shepherd sitting out here in the wilderness playing with the sheep for 40 years. Surely You can find someone more qualified than I am. "O my Lord, I am not eloquent.... I am slow of speech and of a slow tongue" (Exodus 4:10). I am not even trained as a speaker. I wouldn't know what to say, so You can't use me. Because Melancholy Moses was so insecure, he was reluctant to do what God told him to do, and finally God gave up and sent Sanguine brother Aaron along as a mouthpiece.

Many of us refuse to do what God wants us to do because we don't think we have the proper training! Fred and I began teaching Bible studies before we had studied the Bible. We knew that this was what God wanted us to do. If we had waited until we felt sufficiently trained, we would not have started yet. God knew what He was doing with us. In having to teach we had to study, and the majority of our Christian growth has come from the preparation we have had to do to keep ahead of a class. When God calls us to do a job, we should never answer that we are not prepared; we should just get to work. He will give us the power of performance!

Some of us feel that it is a *lack of money* that holds us down. Gideon replied to God's request, "O my Lord, wherewith shall I save Israel? Behold, my family is poor in Manasseh, and I am the least in my father's house" (Judges 6:15). With no finances behind him at all, Gideon was turned into a wise prophet by God's commanding power. Many times I have had sweet Christians tell me they cannot have friends in for fellowship because they do not have good china or matching napkins, because their house is too small, or because their talent is too slight. But these are only excuses for our unwillingness to do as God has asked us. "Open your homes to each other without complaining" (1 Peter 4:9 TEV). I would enjoy a peanut butter sandwich if someone else prepared it and handed it to me.

One of our most successful dinner parties was the night we arranged to have the Good Humor Ice Cream truck come to our driveway at 8 o'clock. As the bell clanged, all the surprised guests filed out to choose whatever flavors they wished and to stand in the street and eat ice cream for dessert. We don't need to have a large income or great culinary skills to entertain; we can invite Christian friends to our homes and have fellowship while eating ice cream outside.

The world tells us we need money to be happy, but as God told Gideon, "Surely I will be with you." Should not His presence be assurance enough?

Do We Make Excuses and Rationalize?

One woman confessed to me that she was an expert on excuses. She realized that as soon as her husband asked her to do something, she would start constructing creative excuses. When he would come home at night, she would explain in detail why this chore had been impossible to do. She said she analyzed the time she spent each day dreaming up reasons for her failures and found that she could have accomplished the tasks in less time than it took her to make up the excuses. She was so good at excuses that she never accomplished a thing. How many of us would rather make excuses than do the job?

How many of us make excuses when we are caught? "My speedometer must be broken, officer—I had no idea I was doing 80." It's difficult to bring up mature children when they observe our shifty behavior.

My favorite excuse in the Bible comes when Moses returns from the hills of Mount Sinai and finds his people dancing around the golden calf. He had enjoyed a mountaintop experience, but it is all over when he comes down and sees the party (Exodus 32:22-24 NKJV). In fury (we Christians would term it righteous indignation) Moses asks Sanguine Aaron what's going on, and he answers, "Do not let the anger of my lord wax hot." What a dignified way to say, "Cool it, Moses—don't get yourself all upset!"

"You know the people, that they are set on evil." It's not my fault, brother, it's those people you left me with. If you had given me a decent group, I could have become a great leader. "For they said to me, 'Make us gods that shall go before us.'" It was all their idea. They wanted some gods they could see.

"As for this Moses, the man who brought us up out of the land of Egypt, we do not know what has become of him." While the cat's away the mice will play. You see, Moses, if we had known you were really coming back, things would have been different. But we thought you were gone for good. Out of sight, out of mind.

"And I said to them, 'Whoever has any gold, let them break it off.'" I really didn't think they'd donate any of their own gold, but was I ever amazed!

"So they gave it to me, and I cast it into the fire, and this calf came out." I don't really know how it happened, Moses. I surely didn't intend to make any idols. It just turned out that way. "This calf came out."

Does this story sound familiar? Have your children ever told such tales?

"I didn't know when I threw the stone that it would curve toward the window."

"I only said they could have one piece, Mother. I didn't ever dream they'd eat the whole cake."

"I didn't mean to go to that party, but that's where the boy driving the car ended up."

Have we as adults ever told others something like this?

"I really don't know how it happened."

"I never dreamed it would turn out this way."

"I was only trying to help her out."

"Most people would be glad to know their faults."

"If you'd been in my shoes, you would have done the same thing."

Why do we make excuses for our unbecoming behavior? Why do we cover up our failures? By putting the blame on others, we protect ourselves. We never have to accept the fact that the problem might be *me*.

Abraham Lincoln said, "I am responsible to the American people, to the Christian world, to history, and on my final account, to God." He was mature. He accepted the overwhelming responsibility that history gave him and was willing to shoulder the blame for his mistakes. Why can't we be mature enough to say, "It was my fault; I'm truly sorry"? That takes a big person, the kind of person that God can be pleased with in eternity.

Why do we rationalize away our faults instead of facing them?

"Everyone in my family is fat, so that's why I don't bother with diets."

"I know I could never remember names, so I don't try."

"I inherited my mother's stubborn disposition."

"That's just the way I am and you might as well get used to it."

We use statements like these to obliterate the possibility that we have not yet grown up and to cover the fact that the fault might be ours.

Do We Hold Grudges?

"I'll never forget what she did to me."

"I can remember it as if it were yesterday."

"I have those words etched deeply into my heart."

"I may forgive what you've done, but I'll never forget it."

A young lady came to me with a tale of hostility toward her husband. As she poured out all his misdeeds, they seemed so trivial that I asked her when her feelings of hatred had started. She replied quickly, "I was mad at him before we even got married."

He had written her a letter instructing her to find a car for their honeymoon trip. She had answered that it was his responsibility to provide transportation, and besides, his family had three cars while hers had only one. He made it clear: "If you want to marry me, you had better find a car!" She found a car, but she vowed she would never forget his injustice.

She looked up at me with bitterness lining her face and said, "In case you don't believe me, I'll show you the letter he wrote." She reached into her handbag and pulled out a worn and tattered envelope that had moved from bag to bag for ten years. As she handed it to me she said, "I always carry it with me so I won't forget." I always assumed this lady was the only one carrying a letter of proof, but one day when I used this example in speaking, a middle-aged woman came up, opened her bag, and pulled out a torn and worn letter she had been carrying around for years. "I didn't realize that I kept my hurt and anger handy to remind me of what my husband had done to hurt me. There, take it. I don't want to look at it ever again."

Probably none of us has a letter in our handbag like these women carried, but we may have one in our heads. How can God work in a heart hardened with hatred? How can we ever know joy when we are busy recording indelibly our partner's mistakes?

One of the first Bible verses that spoke directly to me was 1 Corinthians 13:5: "Love does not keep a record of wrongs" (TEV). At that point in my life I was unhappy with my husband. Every night as I did the dishes I would review my list of the wrongs he had done to me. As the list grew throughout the years, I had to concentrate harder to keep the facts fresh in my mind. I thought there would be some great day of judgment when we would all be called before the throne to recite our grievances, and I wanted to make sure my list was longer and better than Fred's and that I would be able to give it faster. As God spoke to me through that verse, I realized that I did not love Fred. I confessed this startling truth to the Lord and asked that He take away my records of wrongs and cause me to fall in love with my husband. God not only answered my prayer, but He has continued over the years to build upon the foundation He established when I became willing. Today Fred and I are so closely bonded that we cannot imagine life without the other. Truly, God still works miracles! Have you ever said, "I forgave him, but I won't forget it"? Love doesn't keep a record of wrongs. In God's reasoning, as long as we are harboring ill will, we haven't forgiven.

Paul tells us we should be "forgiving one another, just as God in Christ also forgave you" (Ephesians 4:32 NKJV). Our Lord Jesus Himself said, "For if you forgive men their trespasses, your heavenly Father will also forgive you" (Matthew 6:14). These phrases are so familiar to us, and yet we often slip into the childish error of an unforgiving spirit, which quenches any chance for happiness.

Do We Wallow in Self-Pity?

"How come they're all going to Disneyland without me?"

"How come the MacDougalls inherited all that money when we're the ones who really need it?"

"How come Joe got promoted and I'm still sitting at this stupid little desk?"

"No one has ever really loved me."

"If only I had a big house like Hazel, I could be happy."

"Poor little me."

As children we express our displeasure with life by tears or tantrums. When we grow up we are proud that we have such self-control that we keep all those negative emotions hidden. We do not cry when our friends plan a shopping trip without us—we are just deeply hurt. We do not slam down the receiver when our neighbor tells us she bought a new Lincoln; we just instruct our husband to start working overtime.

How easily we slip into the sin of self-pity instead of accepting the fact that God's plan for our life may not include a new Lincoln!

A lovely young woman of 23 came to me recently with severe depression. "I'm not going to do any housework until I have a better house," she stated. I assumed that she was sitting in some pit until her husband told me how hard he had worked to buy her a nice home, how he had quit college to make more money for her, how he had paneled the garage into a playroom, and how he did most of the housework while she sat around in self-pity. I asked them both to come to a local marriage seminar, where I taught this lesson on maturity. Later she wrote me this note:

> Dear Florence,
>
> I just want to say thank you for all the help and the love you have given me. Thank you so very much for allowing Jesus to speak through you to me and for being such a good listener.
>
> I know the Lord has given me some new insights through you and Fred, and He has given me the strength I need to stand up and get moving again. I pray that "in whatsoever state I am, therewith to be content."
>
> I have been trying too long to do things by myself and only calling on Jesus when things started getting difficult. I have given the whole show back to Him now, and I'm going to follow His leading in my life day by day.
>
> I am also going to start doing things for Brad and Laura instead of always thinking what is best for me. Somehow in the past few months I have become a little too selfish, doing most things only when I felt like it. It sure takes a lot of extra energy to think of me all the time. It's a lot nicer to think about Jesus and the person He is helping me to become.
>
> Florence, please pray for me that I will keep my eyes on Jesus and not myself. Please pray that I will learn to be content in whatever state I am. And please pray that I will not be lazy, but work on my weak areas and follow God's leading.
>
> I love you,
> Jan

Do We Spend Time in Judging?

"If you knew what I knew about Mabel, you wouldn't let her into your house!"

"When I see Horace passing communion I get sick to my stomach."

"If they only knew what their son was doing behind their backs, they'd never be able to face the church."

"When I see how often they go to Hawaii and how little they've pledged to missions, I wonder if they're really Christians at all."

I grew up believing that if you didn't drink, smoke, swear, or sew on Sundays you were a good Christian. Using these negatives, I built standards by which to judge others. It was not until I began studying the Bible in a meaningful way that I found out that the Christian life is not a list of don'ts. I was also relieved to find that I am not responsible for anyone else's spirituality. The Lord Himself said in Matthew 7:1,2, "Judge not, that you be not judged. For with what judgment you judge, you shall be judged" (NKJV).

As mature adults, it is not our job to decide whether other people's behavior is acceptable to God. Gratefully, God has arranged it so that we are to examine only ourselves, not others. Yet how we love to watch the world and decide who is and who is not a Christian!

Where do you stand today?

Are you still blaming others for your troubles in life?

Or are you ready to look at yourself and see what part of your problems could be your fault?

Do you still give excuses for why things went wrong?

Or do you say, "It was my fault; I'm sorry"?

Do you feel:

Nobody understands me.
They never give me the breaks.
The odds are always against me.
The whole universe is conspiring against poor little me.

We all grow old, but not all of us grow up!

8

HOW CAN I CHECK MY MATURITY?

$\mathbf{T}$here's an old saying: "Too soon old and too late smart." It's true that our physical bodies are getting older every day and that we never do know everything we'd like to know. But what about our emotions? Is it possible to be grown up on the outside, mature in our minds, and yet emotionally a child?

One of the biggest problems counselors have is assuming that they are dealing with a mature, responsible adult, only to find that the person doesn't follow through on instructions and needs to be handled as a first-grader: "If you're a good girl I'll put a gold star on your chart."

Check Yes or No to the questions on the maturity index that follows.

Maturity Index

	Yes	No
1. Do you tend to blame other people when things go wrong?	___	___
2. Do you make excuses for your failures? (I had a headache. It was raining. I shouldn't have even tried to do it.)	___	___
3. Do you prefer to ignore difficulties and hope they'll go away on their own?	___	___
4. Do you sometimes blame your poor background for why you've never fulfilled your potential?	___	___
5. Do you tell a little white lie if it will get you off the hook?	___	___
6. Do people sometimes say, "When are you ever going to grow up?"	___	___
7. Do you avoid responsibility if possible? (Let someone else do it?)	___	___
8. Do you find it difficult to adjust to new situations?	___	___
9. Do you wonder if you'll ever get all of your life together at one time?	___	___
10. Do you often think—or tell others—next year will be different, better, a success?	___	___
11. Are you usually able to talk your way out of most anything?	___	___
12. Do you feel you never get the breaks you deserve?	___	___
13. When you're caught at something you shouldn't have done, is your first thought to lie or make excuses?	___	___
14. Do you feel if you had a bigger or better house you'd be happy?	___	___
15. Do you sometimes instruct a child answering the phone, "Tell them I'm not home"?	___	___

As you checked off this list you probably noticed that all of these questions focused on taking responsibility for your own life and not blaming people or circumstances for your failures. If you checked No to every question and you were telling the truth (immature people tend to lie), you are probably a mature person who has made the best you could out of your circumstances and who can adjust to changes without falling apart or getting hysterical. The more Yes answers you checked the less mature you probably are, and if you have all 15 answers in the Yes column you quite likely have never grown up emotionally, even if you appear to be an adult.

If you are really immature, you may have already gone back to reread the questions, rationalizing that you were too hard on yourself. Changing some of your answers doesn't change the truth. If you came close to answering all questions Yes, you can see that for some reason you have stayed a little child inside when others around you were growing up.

Children are appealing, with wide-eyed innocent smiles, lack of worry and tension, and freedom from restraints and time pressures. All these qualities are engaging to other people who are under tremendous stress. In the same way, immature people are attractive at first, and they can always find friends who will babysit them for a while. But when one person has to do all the work and bear all the responsibility, the relationship wears thin. If you know in your heart that you make excuses and avoid responsibility, then you need to find out why. Why do you run from responsibility? Why do you rationalize failures? Why do you blame other people? Why do you have difficulty in maintaining meaningful relationships?

Perhaps looking at someone else's case history would help you see yourself more honestly.

~>☙❧<~

"My husband is like a little boy driving around in a big man's body!" Nicole, a strikingly attractive woman, told Fred. "He hasn't had a steady job in the 20 years we've been married, and I don't have much hope that he's about to change." Nicole's husband, Tom, was standing across the room, and as she pointed him out to Fred, he saw a tall man, movie-star handsome, with a group of women standing around him, hanging on his every word.

"See?" Nicole said. "He's always got women around him. They love him! I used to love him but I'm sick of supporting him. He's like another child."

We made arrangements to meet later after the personality seminar was over. "Watch out for him!" Nicole worried. "He'll con you just the way he's done all the other counselors."

When we got together we found Tom to be a delight. He had twinkling eyes, an adorable smile, and a quick sense of humor. We could see why he attracted women wherever he went. As we sat down he winked at Florence. "I'm really not as bad as she says I am," he declared. "She always gets to the counselors first and turns them against me."

"I just tell them the truth," Nicole stated coldly.

"How many counselors have you been to?" we asked.

They both gave answers simultaneously. She said "Five," while he sighed, "A whole bunch."

"What have you learned from the counseling?" Fred asked.

"They tell him to get a steady job and stop playing around," Nicole replied.

"But they all like me. One even told Nicole [here Tom chuckled] that if she had a husband this good-looking she'd be glad to support him," Tom smiled and winked again, pleased with himself.

"I wouldn't mind so much if he were at least faithful, but he's got some new girlfriend every week," Nicole said. "He's hardly ever home."

"It's no fun to come home," Tom said.

Does this conversation sound familiar? Can you see the pattern? Can you guess their personalities?

In working with this couple we found a typical Sanguine/Phlegmatic immature man married to a Melancholy/Choleric controlling woman. She had come from an alcoholic family with an abusive father and had assumed the role of little mother when she was very young.

Tom had been pampered by his mother, who tried to keep him a baby forever to make up for her lack of love from her husband. She had told him he was "God's gift to women" and had once said, "With your looks you'll never have to go to work. You'll always find some woman to support you."

Doesn't this sound like a marriage made in heaven? Tom needs a woman to take care of him and Nicole needs someone to take care of. But somehow it didn't work out right. Nicole got more and more depressed, and Tom pulled further away because she was no longer any fun.

When Fred asked what the five counselors had said, Tom and Nicole answered together. The first one told the couple there was sin in their lives and they should go to church more. The second one took Nicole's side and told Tom not to come back until he had a steady job.

"The next two he conned," Nicole reported in disgust. "Tom agreed with everything they said, but he didn't change a bit. I was made to look like an ogre."

Tom flashed his winning smile.

The last counselor told them they were the healthiest couple he'd seen in a long time. Then he reviewed some of the really bad cases he was working with and sent them on their way with the words, "Thank God for what you have and stop looking for trouble."

"He let us know we were wasting his time on minor issues," Nicole said with a sigh, "but I don't think our marriage is a minor issue."

"It's sure the biggest problem I've got," added Tom.

We all could give this couple advice. Tom needs to get a job and stop fooling around, and Nicole needs to be warm and loving so he'll want to come home. In spite of their different memories of the various counselors, each counselor had suggested "behavior modification," but none had helped them to see where their problem had come from in the first place. Until people see why they are reacting a certain way, it is almost impossible for them to shift gears and change their ways.

When Tom went over the Maturity Index he could see he was still a child. This shocked him because he considered himself to be a macho hero. He began to see why he couldn't maintain a mature relationship: He just played childish games with people, and only the unstable and emotionally needy stayed around. Mature and secure people saw through him and left. He had never looked at the fact that most of his friends were, in his term, "basket cases" who were so much worse than he was that he felt like their counselor.

Tom had an office and he did some consulting on personnel problems at local factories, so he thought he worked, but he had few calls and often didn't bill those he serviced. Much of his time in the office was spent in "counseling" distraught women he had met at his last account. Barely enough money came in to pay the rent and utilities.

It took us several reviews of this situation to get him to see he was not really working; instead he was playing. As he conned others, he had also conned himself into thinking he was a personnel consultant who was hoping next year would be better.

"I really hate to think of myself as a child," Tom reflected, "but I guess that's what I am." For the first time Tom took a clear look at himself. He saw that his mother had needed him to need her and had happily supported him financially and emotionally with unrealistic and overstated compliments. He had married his mother all over again and was hurt when Nicole no longer succumbed to his charm.

The necessary changes didn't come overnight, but at least Tom and Nicole had found the sources of their individual faulty behavior patterns. They were willing to work on themselves, instead of always seeing the faults in each other. They found a Christian male counselor who didn't fall prey to Tom's charms and who understood women. They went to him with their personality scores and with the results of the Maturity Index in hand.

If you scored poorly on emotional maturity, you can find out where your problems began by looking over the following list and prayerfully reflecting on the possibilities.

Roots of Adult Immaturity

Place a check beside the statements that apply to you.

1. _____ You were the youngest child and everyone thought you were adorable.

2. _____ You had a parent who needed you to need him or her.

3. _____ You had a parent whose own immature behavior made him or her keep you as a child.

4. _____ You were never taught responsibility.

5. _____ When you were told to do things no one ever checked up on you.

6. _____ You were never taught to manage money.

7. _____ You never learned experientially that all actions bring about consequences.

8. _____ One parent slipped you money when the other wasn't around.

9. _____ You could always con at least one parent and get what you wanted.

10. _____ One parent taught you not to cross the other one.

11. _____ You learned to cover up, or lie, if it would keep you out of trouble.

12. _____ One parent doted on you and the other didn't seem to want you around.

13. _____ The opposite-sex parent made you his or her little confidant.

14 _____ There was some sexual touching that you hadn't considered to be all that bad.

15. _____ You took showers or baths with the opposite-sex parent frequently as a child.

16 _____ You were the "happiness pill" for one parent.

17. _____ You learned that if you cried you could get almost anything you wanted.

18. _____ One parent fixed up your problems in school and took your side against the teacher.

19. _____ If you started a job and didn't like it, you learned it was all right to quit.

20. _____ You found you could play one parent against the other to your own benefit.

21. _____ You never liked facing the big world out there without a parent beside you.

22. _____ Your personality is a combination of Sanguine/Phlegmatic: "Let's have fun and not worry about the consequences."

23. _____ You expected that you'd get married and live happily ever after.

Now that you are aware of your areas of immaturity and have figured out where they come from, you are halfway there.

Scripture tells us to grow up in Christ, who is our Head, and no longer be children. When we don't grow up in Christ we continue to make the same mistakes over and over again. We have unfruitful and short-lived relationships, and we never reach our potential.

How do we grow up? First we become aware of our needs. Then we study Paul's description of a mature Christian in the book of Ephesians. We begin to use these standards as measuring sticks for our lives. We start writing to the Lord about our weaknesses, elaborating on one weakness each day until we run out of them. We stop ourselves each time we make excuses, rationalize, or blame others.

We start taking responsibility for our own mistakes. We see what part of our faulty behavior stems from our parents' treatment of us, and we realize they probably did the best they could at the time. We resolve now to take responsibility for our own actions and decisions and not blame our parents. We make a choice to forgive them for what they did. We check to see if we are doing the same things to our children. If we are, we work at changing and we apologize for the hurts we have put upon them. We find someone who will keep us accountable and stop us lovingly each time we lie or blame others. And we check ourselves constantly to see if we're making progress.

Now that you have examined your personality strengths and weaknesses, and measured your maturity, it's time to look at your home situation. Do you have an immature mate who refuses to consider himself or herself as part of the home problem? Perhaps you need to ask yourself if it's time to sit down together and review these maturity questions. Discuss each one openly, without accusations. Determine to grow up together.

9

WERE ADAM AND EVE MATURE?

Each Saturday the *Los Angeles Times* prints summaries of all the leading soap operas for the ardent watchers who may have had to perform some productive task on Tuesday and missed a meaningful episode.

Today, in glancing over these scintillating synopses, I learned that "Frank collapsed from heart trouble after kidnapping Carl. Devon denied to Ellen that she's carrying on with Sean, then was almost caught in the sack with him by Tom. Edna told Kelly about Hank and considered a Caribbean love trip with him. Ellen got nervous thinking that Anne would remember spotting Ellen and Paul kissing. Chuck sent Donna on another jealousy trip over Tara. Meanwhile Rachel and Mac remarried. Cecile left Philip waiting at the altar with egg on his face. Lloyd died and Miranda warmly greeted Taylor. Miranda also breathed heavily in Philip's presence.

Larry and Clarice warned Buzz to steer clear of Blaine even though Blaine denied she's seeing Buzz on the sly. Willis reconciled with Mac after burying Janice. Dee suspected Melinda and Brad of hanky-panky. Grant told Lisa to mind her own business and not butt in about Joyce. And Marlena was green with jealousy when Don worked with curvaceous PTA members."

Are these "Young and Restless" people really in "Another World" or are they just symptoms of a selfish society that will never grow up? How many of us get into sad situations because we are confused, immature people trying to act out our roles on a grown-up stage?

Is life one big soap opera? If so, where did it all begin?

≈§⌘§≈

Let's tune in to "The Garden of Eden" on Channel 7 of the Creation Network and watch today's episode: "Were Adam and Eve Mature?"—a question that has been burning in the hearts and minds of the viewing public for years.

As we push the button we find an empty screen, and the deep-voiced announcer says, "Let there be light!" And there is light! The light is followed by the sound of rushing waters, and soon a division splits the firmament into heaven and earth. As we watch, oceans surround the dry land and grass begins to grow. Fruit trees burst forth and stars start to shine. As the moon fades from view, a brilliant sun lights up the screen and we see birds in the sky and little bunnies and Bambies frolicking on the turf. And the deep voice says, "Let us make man in our image, after our likeness"—and Adam appears.

We all know the plot, we all know the rest of the story, but have we ever looked at Adam and Eve as the first real people instead of as little plastic actors in a lush tropical setting?

Have we ever asked ourselves how good people like Adam and Eve got into trouble? They didn't mean to go wrong, so how did it all happen?

When we look into Genesis chapters 2 and 3 (NKJV) we read:

> The LORD God planted a garden eastward in Eden, and there He put the man whom He had formed. And out of the ground the LORD God made every tree grow that is pleasant to the sight and good for food. . . . Now a river went out of Eden to water the garden. . . . And the gold of that land is good. Bdellium and the onyx stone are there. . . . Then the LORD God took the man and put him in the garden of Eden to tend and keep it (2:8-15).

Adam was put into a perfect setting. He had trees that produced food and shrubs that were pretty to look at. God ran a river through the garden to water the land so Adam didn't even have to install a sprinkler system. God gave Adam gold and precious stones so he would be lacking nothing, and then he placed him in this perfect setting to keep things even.

How many of you would be thrilled if you could only get up to even? Do you sometimes wish that God had done your landscaping? Would your cares really be over if you had a rich vein of gold running through your backyard?

Yes, Adam had a perfect setting. He couldn't blame his circumstances for his problems. He couldn't blame any other people because there weren't any other people. But wait: "The LORD God said, 'It is not good that man should be alone; I will make him a helper comparable to him'" (Genesis 2:18).

You men may feel that this act was God's first mistake, for if He had left Adam alone with the birds, the bees, and the bunnies he wouldn't have gotten himself into such trouble.

You women may not like the fact that God made us to be help-mates for our men, but that's what God says, and He means business. We have to ask ourselves, "Am I really a help to Fred, or would he be better off without me?" One man said to me one day, "She's more trouble than she's worth." How about you? How about Eve?

"The LORD God caused a deep sleep to fall on Adam, and he slept; and He took one of his ribs, and closed up the flesh in its place. Then the rib which the LORD God had taken from man He made into a woman, and He brought her to the man. And Adam said, 'This is now bone of my bones and flesh of my flesh; she shall be called Woman, because she was taken out of Man'" (2:21-23).

Then God gave His first bit of marriage advice: "Therefore a man shall leave his father and mother and be joined to his wife; and they shall become one flesh" (2:24).

Here we have two perfect people in a perfect setting, just as Fred and I had planned to be. They had no problems—just a pleasant atmosphere, plenty of free food, no children, no housework, and no rules except one: "Of the tree of the knowledge of good and evil you shall not eat, for in the day that you eat of it you shall surely die" (2:17).

Later, when the serpent asked Eve what God had said, she tried to repeat it: "Of the fruit of the tree which is in the midst of the garden, God has said, 'You shall not eat of it, nor shall you touch it, lest you die'" (3:3).

To encourage you men who think your wife is the only one who can't ever repeat anything exactly as she heard it, look at what Eve said. She added "nor shall you touch it" and watered down the threat to "lest you die."

How did this well-intentioned woman get into trouble? To make this story apply more easily to our own lives, I have divided it into sections and titled it:

The Six Steps Into Trouble

1. Doubt

"The serpent said unto the woman, 'You will not surely die' " (Genesis 3:4).

When the devil wants to lead us astray, he sends an attractive item to cast doubt on God's Word. "You won't really die." "God didn't mean that line for you." "His Word is for old people in the old days." "You're free to do your own thing."

2. Temptation

The minute you begin to *doubt* that God's Word really applies to you today, *temptation* is ready to grab you.

"For God knows that in the day you eat of it your eyes will be opened, and you will be like God, knowing good and evil" (3:5).

The serpent told Eve that God was trying to fool her, trying to hold down her potential, trying to keep her unfulfilled. If you eat the fruit you'll be as smart as God. Try it; you'll like it.

3. Action

"When the woman saw that the tree was good for food, that it was pleasant to the eyes, and a tree desirable to make one wise, she took of its fruit and ate" (Genesis 3:6).

When *doubt* and *temptation* get together they lead us quickly into action which becomes a sin. When Eve was convinced that God didn't mean what He had said, and that the fruit would make her wise, she took it and ate it. She used her own free will and disobeyed God's clear command that she knew so well. Sanguine Eve was out looking for fun when she found the serpent. When he told her she could be even better, she quickly did what he said.

4. Guilt

What happens when we ignore God's clear warnings and follow *temptation* into *sin?* We instantly feel guilty. God has equipped us with a guilty conscience to help us know when we are in violation of His expectations. When we step off to the tune of our own drummer, guilt stops us in our tracks and we quickly try to involve someone else to dilute our own pressure.

"She also gave to her husband with her, and he ate" (Genesis 3:6).

Phlegmatic Adam did what his fun-loving wife told him to do. He didn't think about it or pray about it—he just ate it.

5. Cover-Up

What happens after we *doubt* God's Word, are easily *tempted*, enter into *sin*, and feel *guilty*? We're so afraid we'll get caught that we hide from authority and try to cover up the evidence. That's what Adam and Eve did too.

"And they heard the voice of the LORD God walking in the garden in the cool of the day, and Adam and his wife hid themselves from the presence of the LORD God among the trees of the garden. Then the LORD God called to Adam and said to him, 'Where are you?' So he said, 'I heard Your voice in the garden, and I was afraid because I was naked; and I hid myself'" (3:8-10).

When Freddie was little and knew he had done something wrong, he would run to his bed and put his head under the pillow, assuming that if he hid this way I wouldn't find him. In recent years many politicians have doubted that the law was for them, have been tempted by the allure of power and money, have sinned and felt guilty, and have been caught in their own nets of cover-up.

6. Blame

When we hide and are afraid of getting caught, we plan how to ditch the blame on someone else. Does that sound familiar? We have already learned that mature people don't put the blame on someone else. And now to the great question, "Were Adam and Eve mature?" God asked them a simple question: "Did you eat of the tree?" A mature person has only two possible responses to such a question: yes or no! But what did Adam reply?

Adam replied, "The woman." It was not my fault, God, it was that woman. She led me astray. I never would have done it on my own. You know me, God; I'm an obedient, law-abiding citizen. It was that woman "whom You gave to be with me." On second thought, God, it's really Your fault because You're the One who created her in the first place. I didn't ask for her. *You* decided I shouldn't be alone. If You had just left me alone with the chipmunks I wouldn't be in the trouble I'm in today.

"She gave me of the tree." That woman whom You gave me handed me the fruit and I guess I had my mind on other things, because "I ate."

What an excuse from Adam! He first blamed Eve and then he blamed God, the only two persons available. Now what about Eve? Was she any more mature?

"And the LORD God said to the woman, 'What is this you have done?' And the woman said, 'The serpent deceived me, and I ate'" (Genesis 3:13).

There was no one else around. Eve was not ready to accept the responsibility, so she blamed the serpent: "He deceived me."

Have you ever said, "I know I didn't need a new vacuum cleaner, but the salesman was so adorable and he was working his way through college. I guess he just deceived me."

How easy it is for good people to get into trouble! We mean well, but we *doubt* that God's Word applies to us today. *Temptation* comes attractively packaged and *sin* is so appealing. Our *guilt* is followed by our *cover-up,* and when we're caught we *blame someone else.* But ultimately we *are punished.*

God cursed the serpent and threw Adam and Eve out of the Garden of Eden. From then on women have known sorrow, pain, and heartbreak, and men have had to work hard to support their families.

One day when our son Fred was ten, he was scrubbing the foyer floor for me when he sighed, "If it hadn't been for Adam and Eve getting in all that trouble I wouldn't be in the fix I'm in today."

Even the first man and woman in perfect circumstances made immature choices. What about you?

How does a well-intentioned Eve get into trouble today?

Karen came to me with a problem. She was at the stage of *guilt* and *cover-up* when she told me this story:

Karen got into trouble because she loved to sing—at least that's where she felt it all started. Karen was a good Christian lady. Her husband was the head deacon in their church, and they taught a Bible study in their home. She always did the right things and never intended to go astray; she only intended to go to choir rehearsal. Surely one couldn't go wrong by singing hymns in a choir loft. Or could one?

On Karen's first night at rehearsal she sat next to a tall, handsome man who was the church finance chairman. In between anthems he leaned over and whispered, "I love your perfume." A pleasant, flattering, and innocuous statement, to be sure. Or was it?

The next week Karen could hardly wait to go to choir rehearsal. She sprayed herself from head to toe with a new perfume that guaranteed romance, and off she went early to get the same seat. She wasn't disappointed, for he came early and placed himself quickly beside her. He said his name was Tom and he took a big sniff of her perfume. "You smell even better tonight," he commented.

That did it, Karen told me. She became a perfume collector and increased her love for singing. Her husband never commented on how she smelled and wouldn't have noticed her perfume if she had been sitting in the bottle on top of his dresser.

But Tom cared. Within a month Karen lost ten pounds, had her hair restyled, bought all new makeup, and even glued on false eyelashes. When someone cared, Karen was willing to change.

One night the choir went out for coffee, and Tom and Karen happened to end up together. They discussed how their mates hated music and how much they had in common. After that they always went out for coffee and reviewed their love for music.

One morning Tom called Karen and said he just happened to be in her neighborhood. She lived at the end of a long road on the edge of a cliff and no one just happened to be in that neighborhood, but she invited him over. He came to visit often, and soon she began to travel with him on business trips, saying she was going to visit friends and leaving ticket stubs around to provide evidence of her supposed trips.

Here was a good girl with a good husband in a dull marriage. She never set out to get in trouble, but an attractive man sniffed her perfume and she fell apart. She knew the commandment "Thou shalt not commit adultery," but she soon *doubted* that God meant those words for her today. *Temptation* came quickly, and *sin* was hot on its heels. *Guilt* fell heavily on a woman who had set out only to sing, not to sin, and she was involved in elaborate *cover-ups* for her runarounds when she came to me. She already planned to *blame* her husband for his indifference and Tom for his aggression if she ever got caught.

How easy it is for a good person to get into trouble, and how quickly we place the blame for our problems on someone else!

10

TWO PEOPLE FOR LIFE

I collect articles on marriage as others might collect stamps or seashells. As I stand in the supermarket line I read the covers and buy those articles whose titles sound intriguing. By weaving these together I have the world's view on marriage. Way back in 1971 a very perceptive Morton Hunt dared to say in *Family Circle,* "One is justified in wondering whether something is terribly wrong with modern marriage." This was our first hint of public trouble, and it led to *Woman's Day* asking, "What Do You Want from Marriage?" with the obvious answer, "Happiness, of course, but what does that mean?"

As we all began to ask ourselves what happiness really was and to wonder if we had enough of it, *Woman's Day* listed "The Real Reasons Behind Marriage Failure" and concluded that there were two reasons: unhappy husbands and unhappy wives. As with most secular articles, these were full of bad case histories with no tangible solutions. Lee Truman asked for Copley News Service, "Will Marriage and Family Life Survive in Our Modern World?" Somehow to be modern we must search for our rights, and if we don't find them we take off for greener pastures. Dr. Truman gave a brief case history about Sarah, a decent girl, and Bob, who did honestly love her, who "never went out at night, hardly ever drank a beer, was a good guy, but just didn't make her happy. Happy—that is what marriage is for—to make you happy. 'Bob just doesn't try to make me happy.'"

That's what marriage is all about—having someone to make me happy. I deserve to be entertained and pampered, and if I don't get what I want, I'll leave. How appealing these thoughts are for the liberated mind! Soon marriage articles began sprouting up like weeds after a spring shower, and for you Melancholies who like numbers there appeared many appropriate articles:

Five Ways to Save Your Marriage
by Gary Alexander

Ten Guidelines for a Happy Marriage
by Mildred Tengbom

24 Ways to Make Your Marriage More Exciting
by Dr. Frank Caprio

Dr. Caprio suggested kissing your wife in public. "She may fuss but she'll be delighted." Bring her presents, buy records of the songs you courted her by, and "consult with her about your financial affairs." When you take her out make her think she's with Cary Grant. "Open doors; light her cigarettes." Who knows what might happen to your marriage if you followed the good doctor's advice?

Spotted amongst the trivia were a few constructive thoughts. *Lady's Circle* showed "How to Build a Happy Marriage." Dr. Rebecca Liswood said, "A happy marriage is possible only when a husband and wife are emotionally mature. . . . Neither Jane nor

Pete, escaping into marriage, had a single thought of what they could do for each other; they thought only of what the other could do for them." Isn't that the norm? Isn't my mate supposed to please me?

An article I found in *Vogue* magazine got right down to a personal question: *Could your marriage use help?* Author Claudia Dreifus gave ten questions to ask yourself to determine if you need marital therapy. Number 3 on the list says you need help "if either of you is involved in a destructive infidelity." And then she said to my amazement, "Most marriage therapists are quick to say that an affair is not, in itself, necessarily a sign of an endangered relationship." How can I be sure I'm enjoying an affair that is not destructive? Will lights flash when I'm about to go too far and say "Danger Ahead"? Will a sign appear that states "You Need Help"? I was dumbfounded at this secular advice that only a "destructive infidelity" was a source of concern. Any infidelity, even an illegitimate longing, is a sign of an endangered relationship.

Dr. Joyce Brothers in *Good Housekeeping* warns in "When Your Husband's Affection Cools" that "marriage is not just spiritual communion and passionate embraces; marriage is also 3-meals-a-day and remembering to carry out the trash." That kind of life sounds so dull that we may want to try for a new mate. It all seems so natural, as Betty Rollin exposed for *Look:* "The American Way of Marriage: Remarriage":

"I take thee ... and thee ... and thee ... "—and why not? If at first you don't succeed, try, try again.

Harriet Van Horne questioned in an article in *McCall's:* "Are We the Last Married Generation?" And we've been answering that query with adjustable living arrangements ever since.

The *San Bernardino Sun* one day suggested: "Do-It-Yourself Kits for Divorce Given Backing by Lawyer." Why not? We can buy kits for creative stitchery and changing spark plugs. In the article, lawyer Nathaniel Colley said, "The forms can be completed within just a few minutes by any legal secretary worth her salt. The court proceeding consists of the lawyer mumbling a few words about the truth of the allegations." The kit can save as much as $350 and "the process is exceedingly simple, fleeting quick, and failure-proof." That's what we want in this busy life: whatever is exceedingly simple so we won't have to think, fleetingly quick so we won't waste any time, and failure-proof so any dummy can do it.

In case you want to make a real study of terminal marriages and get college credits at the same time, a later article in the same newspaper announced: "Course on Divorce Set at U.C. Riverside." Come find out how to do it yourself!

To show how many potential students the course might attract, *Parade* magazine stated, "About 40 percent of all marriages among women in their 20's will end in divorce."

When 40 percent of anything is available, new businesses spring up overnight. A *Newsweek* article I read a while ago told of "cut-rate divorce."

Moses Aspan found a cheap way to get divorced, and soon his friends wanted help. He started Divorce Associates, which "sells $99 divorce kits—Master Charge and VISA cards accepted—helping couples beat the high cost of saying 'I don't.'" One clinic in Los Angeles sells divorces for $40, seven days a week, and makes house calls. "Getting a divorce from a clinic is like driving into McDonald's for a quick hamburger."

Once divorce is accepted, we have to make it look like the right thing to do. *Newsweek* gave a series of case histories of people learning to adjust to a new life. One author is pictured typing his manuscript and holding his two children on his lap, while his ex-wife is shown smiling as she shapes pottery in some secluded spot.

If you follow the advice given in these articles on the ease and glory of divorce, then find yourself alone, you needn't be alone for long, as the personal columns will find you a mate. In a San Francisco paper under "Personals" I found these amazing thoughts:

> Single? Select your next date or mate from our Television Videotape library of Bay Area singles. Counseling for singles available. Video Introduction and Counseling Service.

> Big French man—6' tall, 170 lbs., wants woman, any size, race, 18–30 years old for lasting relationship. Call Joseph 886-_____, leave message.

> Woman companion who enjoys walking, eating, and receiving foot-rubs wanted by attractive Caus. man 31. Henry, 881-_____.

You need never be alone again!

As our national introspection surges on, quizzes on marriage abound in the magazines. One asks, "How Healthy Is Your Marriage?" and provides 35 questions for your annual marital checkup. "If you never ask the questions, you'll never know the answers."

Another article asks, "Did You Marry the Right Man?" I didn't answer this because I felt it was a little late to find out whether marrying Fred was a big mistake!

Parade says, "Test Yourself: Are You the Perfect Wife?" This one I did take, and I am!

The media offers alternative lifestyles for those of you who don't feel led to get divorced but are bored with your present partner. A newspaper article in the "Living" section tells of "Swingers: They'd Rather Switch Than Fight!" The article assures us that wife-swappers are probably healthier than the average couple, that stag movies are informative, and that "yesterday's pornography is today's text."

If you happen to be like I am and have no idea how one would start to "swing," you can learn in an academic setting at Golden West College in Huntington Beach, California. The *Los Angeles*

Times regales us with a sprightly article: "A Popular Lecture: Class Gives a Mixed Reaction to Swinging."

Shearlean Duke tells of visiting the class, taught by Bob and Geri McGinley, "a happily married couple who also happen to operate one of the largest swing clubs in America." The eager students learn that "swinging is a social sexual act—one of the fastest-growing recreations in the country." As with any game, there are some rules, although few authorities will be checking your adherence to them. The McGinleys suggest inviting 20 couples (thus effectively eliminating those of us with modest homes) for cocktails, dinner, socializing, and sex. (I assume it works best in that order.) They insist that swinging improves all marriages, and they compare recreational sex with a game of tennis. Imagine learning all these exciting possibilities in life and getting college credits besides! It sure beats laboring over Latin.

Creative Confusion?

When we look at the provocative presentations of the world, the promotions of alternative lifestyles and loose living, we could become utterly confused. Should we start—

> swinging
> switching
> swapping
> stretching
> sampling
> slugging
> or
> splitting?

Is there any solid advice anymore? Is there any constant code to judge our current conduct? Do people want any godly guidelines, or has promiscuity produced a new heaven and a new earth?

It does not take a team of researchers to come up with the conclusion that the "new morality" has dropped disaster upon the American family. Some social scientists say it is only a matter of time before the traditional family fades into the sunset. Doomsday proponents compare us with the Roman Empire before its fall and Germany before the rise of Hitler. Wedding ceremonies are often turned to nightmares by the hostile appearance of mother and stepdad seated next to father and stepmother, all of whom hate each other. Should we all give up and run off to Tahiti to find ourselves? Is there anywhere to turn for help?

Even a person who never goes to church will admit that the Bible has been around a long time. Most people would agree that it says good things and is probably true, but few have any idea that it speaks to modern people today, and few know how to find out what it teaches even if they wanted to seek.

When Fred and I first wrote this material as an adult Sunday school course, we were not Bible scholars and we had not even read one book on marriage, yet our home had been changed by applying scriptural truths to our lives. We wanted to share the excitement of Christian principles with others, and so we began to study. Armed with several Bibles, a concordance, and a topical Bible, we set out on a search to show others the standards of Scripture in practical terms.

The first advice on marriage in the Bible is given in Genesis 2:24, where God says, "Therefore a man shall leave his father and mother and be joined to his wife, and they shall become one flesh" (NKJV). When we marry we are to set up a new unit of living; we are to leave our parents and start a separate entity. If we are not economically or emotionally ready to leave home, there is little hope for a mature marriage. God gives us sound advice, and when we ignore it we open ourselves for heartache.

In Mark 10:9 we learn that man must not separate what God has joined together. When we take this direction seriously, we do not leap into marriage with the idea, "If it doesn't work I can always get divorced." How many distraught men and women have we talked with who thought divorce would be a simple alternative! I have never yet met a person who had a good divorce.

God knew what He was doing when He told us to marry for life. When we enter into any activity with a single-minded purpose, we don't look for alternative routes.

Hebrews 13:4 instructs us that marriage should be honored by all, and that a husband and wife must be faithful to each other. God doesn't give loose options. He tells us that marriage is an honorable estate, a binding relationship, and that we are to be faithful. If we follow this scriptural principle, we won't start looking for diversions. The Bible doesn't say, "Be faithful for the first year," "Be faithful unless society says to swing," "Only wives have to be faithful," or "Be faithful most of the time, unless you're out of town or your wife is sick."

In 1 Timothy 3:2,12 Paul tells us that a Christian leader should have only one wife and be able to manage his children and his family well. Each one of us believers is a Christian leader in some sphere of life—at work, at school, at the club. In many places we go, we may be the only true believer in the group. As people begin to identify us as Christians, how important it is that we manage our children well!

Fred tells this story:

> A pastor we once knew was so preoccupied with his congregation that he overlooked his family. One day his son shared with me how he didn't ever want to be a Christian because the church kept his father away from him. Later I suggested to the pastor that I had some helpful information from his son to give him when he had a few spare minutes. Unfortunately, he

never had those "few spare minutes" to hear what his son was feeling. The son, feeling neglected, soon after started getting into trouble to attract attention. The father, busy with good works, never had the time to deal with his own problems, and the son was arrested for selling drugs to a federal agent. The pastor's wife left him, the second son began to drink heavily, and his daughter ran away from home. His Christian ministry was over. Here was a well-meaning man too involved to have time for his family.

All Bible principles are there for practical reasons, and if we accept them and apply them we will save ourselves much grief.

Proverbs 18:22 encourages us men with the simple statement, "whoso findeth a wife findeth a good thing." Men, do you have a good thing? Women, when you think about it, are you a good thing? I've had some husbands say to me, "Frankly, I'd be better off without her; she's more trouble than she's worth."

Paul reminds us of the unifying force in marriage when he says in 1 Corinthians 11:11,12 TEV, "In our life in the Lord," meaning in our Christian life as believers, "woman is not independent of man," but is to put her husband's needs first and not be leading a totally separate life.

"Nor is man independent of woman." The man is to put his wife and family first and not spend all his time apart from home. Men and women need each other. They were not designed by God to be alone, but to be interdependent and supportive.

"For as woman was made for man [Eve was formed from Adam's rib], in the same way man is born of woman; and it is God who brings all things into existence." Women are chosen by God to give birth, yet neither man nor woman is superior in God's sight. He made us equal.

Many unchurched people get their total opinion of Christianity from legalistic and unloving believers. They assume that the

Christian life means giving up everything fun and retreating to a monastic existence. They are sure the Bible proclaims, "Frigidity is next to godliness."

Yet God created sex and He approves of intimate relations within marriage. In 1 Corinthians 7:3-5 Paul instructs us that "the husband should give to his wife her conjugal rights, and likewise the wife to her husband" (RSV). It is our loving duty. Does that sound like a God who wants us to be so sex-starved at home that we are ripe for roaming?

"Each should satisfy the other's needs" (verse 3 TEV). This phrase is preventive medicine. If each one of us satisfied the other's needs within marriage, we would have no reason to stray. What needs does your partner have that you are not meeting? So often when we talk with women whose husbands are unfaithful I ask, "What is that woman providing for him that you were unwilling to do?" Upon a little prodding she usually responds:

"She looks up at him like he's really worth something."

"He says she enjoys sex and I only tolerate it."

"She's willing to try new things."

"She's not overweight like me."

"He claims she listens to what he has to say and hangs onto his every word."

Be brave enough to ask your partner what needs he or she has that you are not meeting. Remember that the Bible says, "Each should satisfy the other's needs."

"A wife is not the master of her own body, but the husband is; in the same way a husband is not the master of his own body, but his wife is" (verse 4 TEV). We are not to be selfish and deprive our mates of the physical pleasures of marriage. We are not the sole owners of our bodies; we give them to our partners when we marry them.

"Do not deny yourselves to each other, unless you first agree ...
in order to spend your time in prayer" (verse 5 TEV).

Did you know that the Bible made any such statement? God
does not want us making excuses on why we can't get together. I recently saw a nightgown hanging in a store, and across the bosom it
said, "not tonight, I have a headache." How many deprived men give
their wives a real headache after years of colorful excuses and a
decade of dull nights!

Yet there is one legitimate reason for abstinence—a time of
fasting and prayer (verse 5). We've talked to a lot of men with frigid
wives, but I've never had one tell me it was because she fasted and
prayed too much!

Our husbands are to be our number-one friend in life. We are
to put them first, care for them, and please them. This principle
does not mean that we sit home like doormats waiting to be
stepped on. It does not mean that we don't have an original thought
of our own. It means that we put our husbands first—before our
children, before our parents, before our friends, and before our activities. No one has ever thought of me as meek and mild, and yet I
put Fred first. Men, for us to put you first and make our lives re-
volve around you, you've got to have some wit, some knowledge,
some personality, some manners, and some style. How can we put
you in your rightful position if you're dull, drab, dreary, selfish, con-
ceited, and arrogant? Help us out, please!

What Men Should Be

Men, when you marry you are responsible to support your
wife, to care for her, and to maintain the home. Are you keeping up
with your bills or have you so overextended yourselves that she
must work night and day to pay the rent? Have you mowed the lawn
or is the grass so high that your backyard looks like a wild
meadow?

While you men are to be our heads, do not misread this as meaning tyrants or dictators. You should use honest will in dealing with us and provide inspirational leadership. You are to be our guides, our reference material, and our spiritual leaders. You are to be our priests, providers, and protectors.

George Gilder in "The Suicide of the Sexes" (in *Harper's*) tells how men must fulfill these roles in life. He maintains that when men "are no longer compelled by the institution of marriage to assume responsibilities, they are robbed of the self-esteem that comes to the protector, the teacher, and the provider. They become only itinerant studs, a career that may look alluring for the moment, but after 35, what?"

While many wives are comfortable letting their husbands carry total responsibility for their families, many men are likewise comfortable in having total authority. After all, it's surely easier to make decisions alone than to consider someone else's viewpoint and carefully weigh all the pros and cons. But we are convinced that Scripture teaches otherwise. Why? Come along and we'll lead you through the scriptural journey that revealed the answers to us.

Let's begin at the beginning, in Genesis: "Therefore a man shall leave his father and mother and be joined to his wife, and they shall become one flesh" (2:24 NKJV). This truth is such an important part of Scripture that it is repeated no fewer than five times, once in the Old Testament and four times in the New (Genesis 2:24; Matthew 19:5,6; Mark 10:7,8; 1 Corinthians 6:16; and Ephesians 5:31). We are not aware of any other single passage that is repeated more than this one. In addition, there are at least two other passages that directly relate to this concept of the two becoming one (see John 17:22 and Galatians 3:28).

What happens when two of anything become one? What happens when two companies merge and become one corporation? What happened when 13 colonies became one nation? What happens when a husband and wife join their two bodies? They become *one*. And remember that Jesus said, "I and my Father are one" (John 10:30; see also John 10:38; 17:22). Think of two round circles of paint, one blue and one yellow, on a piece of wax paper. As you lift the sides of the wax paper the two circles run *into* each other. How many circles are there now? Just one! And what color is the circle? It's green! The two have become one. The individual properties of the two paints are still present, but they have become one new paint.

Two become one. This is God's order for the husband-wife relationship. This is unity: the one mind, one body, one heart, and one soul that the Bible speaks about.

Now think about this: When two equal parts merge together, which one is dominant? When the thirteen colonies merged, which one was in charge? When two similar circles of paint merge into one, which one is dominant? When a husband and wife merge their lives in the sight of God, which one is in charge? The answer in each case must be the same: No one entity or person is in charge. The separate parts become equally subject to a higher authority.

Let's look at this question from another perspective. Are these two parts, husband and wife, the same? No. Men and women have bodies that differ and emotions that differ, and in the family, a nuclear part of the body of Christ, they have functions that differ. These functions are a most important part of understanding this whole question. We will discuss this facet of the scriptural concept in a moment. But first let's look at another question: Are the husband and wife equal in the sight of God? Again we must turn to Scripture.

> So God created man [that is, mankind] in His own image; in the image of God He created him; male and female He created them (Genesis 1:27 NKJV).

> From the beginning of the creation God made them male and female (Mark 10:6; see also Matthew 19:4 NASB).

> In the Lord, neither is woman independent of man, nor is man independent of woman. For as the woman originates from the man, so also the man has his birth through the woman; and all things originate from God (1 Corinthians 11:11,12 NASB).

> The wife does not have authority over her own body, but the husband does; and likewise also the husband does not have authority over his own body, but the wife does (1 Corinthians 7:4 NASB).

> There is neither Jew nor Greek, there is neither slave nor free, there is neither male nor female; for you are all one in Christ Jesus (Galatians 3:28 NKJV).

> You husbands...grant her honor as a fellow heir of the grace of life, so that your prayers may not be hindered (1 Peter 3:7 NASB).

What does it mean to be a fellow heir? The Greek word used here is *sunkleronomos*, which according to *Vine's Expository Dictionary* refers to a co-inheritor. Can one equal inheritor have authority over another equal inheritor? The answer must be no, or else they would no longer be equals. Scripture clearly shows us that man and woman, male and female, husband and wife *are equal*. But if they are equal, what does Ephesians 5:23 mean when it clearly states, "The husband is the head of the wife"?

To understand any biblical principle we must search the whole body of Scripture to see that there is harmony. "God is not the author of confusion but of peace" (1 Corinthians 14:33). His wisdom is "first pure, then peaceable, gentle, and easy to be entreated, full of mercy and good fruits" (James 3:17). We must be careful that we do not base a position on a single verse if it is not consistent with the whole body of truth, the whole counsel of God. This is how misconstructions are most apt to occur.

That the husband is the head of the wife is without question. Scripture makes this a certainty. The position that he is the authority over the wife, however, is not consistent with the body of Scripture we have examined. Therefore, if the husband is not the *authority* over the wife, if he is not her *lord*, then saying that she must obey him, that he has the right of lordship over her, is inconsistent and must be deemed faulty. Proponents of this faulty position generally refer to Titus 2:5, which advises older women to teach younger women "to be discreet, chaste, keepers at home, good, obedient to their own husbands." The use of the word *obedient* in the King James Version is generally considered to be an inferior rendering. Virtually all scholarly translations prefer the word "subject." Also, because this passage speaks of the older women's responsibility to teach the younger women, it therefore portrays what is to be the *wife's* condition, not the *husband's* position. This is an important differentiation.

Another facet of this principle, that the wife must be subject to her husband, that she must be submitted to him, is also not subject to question. This is clearly stated in Ephesians 5:22-25 and affirmed in Colossians 3:18,19 and 1 Peter 3:1-7.

Who Does God Instruct First?

When you look at these three passages of Scripture related to wives being subject to their husbands you may notice an interesting and curious fact. In each case this instruction is given first to wives, then to husbands! Why this consistency? Is there a significance? Scripture itself does not answer these questions. We can only ponder this certainty and draw our own conclusions, realizing that nothing is in Scripture by chance. Every word, every "jot and tittle," is by design and is placed in the original manuscripts exactly as God intended.

Why do you think God chose to instruct wives first and then husbands? I (Fred) have thought about this question many times and posed it to both men and women. One answer I have heard (and one that I tend to agree with) is that God knows the different natures of men and women, and He knows women tend to be more readily responsive, more in tune, to matters of the Spirit than men do. When a husband and wife are struggling and the idea to go to someone for help or counseling comes up, who initiates it? Counselors and pastors will consistently tell you it's invariably the wife! And who do you think is usually the first one to quit, saying something like "I don't need this." Invariably it's the husband! When a husband and wife go to someone for help, the husband's attitude is often: *There's nothing the matter with me. If she would only shape up and be what I want her to be, we wouldn't have any problems!* Be honest—does this sound familiar to you?

Men, what's wrong with us? We're just as interested as our wives in having peace and harmony in our homes, aren't we? Then why do so many of us allow our wives to take the first step toward achieving it? Are you starting to understand why God gave His instructions about the marriage relationship to women first?

Perhaps another reason He addresses women first is that we men tend to have a pride barrier. As a rule we are very reluctant to discuss with anyone those issues that get too close to our emotions and feelings. We are rarely able to discuss these things with the person who is closest to us, the person who should be our best friend: our wife. Men seldom discuss their deep feelings with each other.

This was demonstrated for me many years ago. I had been visiting a new church, and on the fourth Sunday I had been there an acquaintance invited me to visit his men's Bible study class after the service. I had been enjoying the church service, the music, and the preaching; so I accepted with joy. We went to a small room where six or seven other men joined us. After several minutes of relatively inane banter and introductions they began a seemingly inconsequential discussion of the weekly lesson. All of this had been very pleasant, though not personally penetrating. Then came the time for prayer and requests. I was stunned that this group of men who had been meeting together for months knew nothing about each other. The few prayer requests appeared to be very impersonal and remote from what must have been going on in their lives. I wondered to myself, *Don't these men have any problems at all? Am I the only one who is struggling with any issues in my life?* Needless to say, even though I continued to worship at that church when I was in town, I felt no desire to return to the men's class.

It was not until several years later, when I found myself ministering to the man who had invited me to the class and his wife, that I learned of the very severe and deep issues in both their lives. They were struggling with problems they had had when I attended that class, and they are still working through them today. But no one would have guessed that he or any of the other men had any problems that Sunday morning. So many of us men put on our plastic smiles and head for church on Sunday morning, giving every evidence that we have life fully under control. Because most of us tend to wear this unreal facade, anyone would be reluctant to share his hurts lest he be considered unmanly or unusual. Our pride barrier keeps us from opening up and sharing our deepest needs and feelings.

But our Father in heaven knows each of us well. He knows that we men are often slow to respond to Him. He knows that we are hesitant to seek help, that we find it easier to focus on our wives as the imperfect one, the one who needs help, the one who needs to change. He knows about this pride issue. And I think He knows that our wives are more apt to set the tone for healthy change in the home. *I think He knows that in reality most of our wives are actually the spiritual leaders in our homes, and in many respects our wives are actually the heads of our homes!* It ought not to be so. I think that is why He gave the instructions in the three Scriptures cited to wives first.

What Does Submission Mean?

We have already seen that God created a man and his wife to be one flesh, and we have seen that He created them as spiritual equals. We have also seen that Jesus can be the only authority in the home. And we've identified the Scriptures in which God tells wives first, and then their husbands, that the wife is to be submitted, or subject, to her husband. Now let's look at what this submission really means.

The answer lies clearly and simply in an often-overlooked verse in Ephesians: "Submitting yourselves one to another in the fear [reverence] of God" (5:21). When studying this verse it helps if we read this entire passage, verses 21-28, clearly tying in verse 21 to the whole text. It describes how and why the wife must submit to her husband (verses 22-24) and how the husband must treat and regard his wife (verses 25 and 28). Verses 21, 22 and 25 summarize the thought:

> Submitting to another in the fear of God. Wives, submit to your own husbands, as to the Lord (verses 21, 22 NKJV).

> Husbands, love your wives, just as Christ also loved the church and gave Himself for it (verse 25 NKJV).

When we husbands understand that we are to love our wives the same way Christ loved the church, we get a clearer understanding of what that kind of love means in the relationship. Christ gave Himself for the church. He voluntarily surrendered His will in obedience to God. He submitted Himself, His very life. "So ought men to love their wives" (verse 28). Our Lord Jesus demonstrated to us the nature of what our love for our wives should be. It is to be *giving*, and to give also means to submit, to surrender our will. This is completely in harmony with verse 21, in which both husbands and wives are directed to submit to each other.

Who, then, is to submit? Scripture clearly teaches us that I am to be submitted to Florence and she to me. Likewise, you are to be completely submitted to your wife and she to you.

One of the best definitions I have ever seen of the word *submission* is "voluntary selflessness." This means I always endeavor to put my wife's needs, desires, and wishes ahead of my own. It also means that I try at all times to treat her like a queen, like a beautiful, precious flower. How do you think Florence feels when she knows I am always putting her interests ahead of my own, that I am always doing my very best to take care of her, nurture her, provide for her, and protect her? How do you think she reacts when she knows that, aside from my love for the Lord, my love for her is always preeminent in my mind and motivation? Frankly, a woman finds it hard to resist a man who treats her that way!

Of course, I would like it very much if she were to understand Scripture the very same way and treat me as that handsome hunk of a man she adores and respects, looks up to and trusts, and brags about to her friends. I would like it if she always tried to put a priority on my needs and desires. Isn't that what "voluntary selflessness" means? Isn't that what submission means? Can you imagine how life would be if we both made that our goal and each of us diligently strove to make that a reality in our marriage? Now, finally, in our forty-fourth year of marriage, this is exactly the way we relate to each other. Florence knows I am completely submitted to her, that I am voluntarily selfless. She is also fully submitted to me and my needs and desires. We have put God's instructions into practice, and it should not be a surprise to anybody that it works! God's laws always do.

God's law of mutual submission will work in your home too. I am reminded of John 13:17: "Now that you know this truth, how happy you will be if you put it into practice!" (TEV). I am happy and I am fulfilled as a man and a husband. My only regret is that I didn't know and understand this principle many years earlier. Had I been aware of its significance we might have enjoyed our current marriage relationship many years sooner. But back then I had a lot of emotional trash and baggage to get rid of before I could earn my wife's love and respect. We had some rebuilding that had to be done before she felt she could trust her emotions to me, before her fear of my anger was gone. We husbands can never *command* respect. It's like that clever investment company's commercial that insists they make money the old-fashioned way: They *earn* it!

One word of caution: *This instruction for mutual submission is not conditional.* It does not mean you are only to do it for your wife if she does it for you. Jesus' examples to us were never conditional. He always did those things that were pleasing to His Father in heaven, no matter how others responded. Do you want to be the leader of your household? Do you want to be the head of your wife? Then by definition you must take the initiative and put this truth into practice. Let her see that you are a Christian husband who is worthy of her respect and her trust; then she will want to follow you.

So What Exactly Does Headship Mean?

We have seen that *headship* cannot mean *lordship* because the husband is not and cannot be the authority over the wife. We have also seen that the popular chain-of-command interpretation cannot be valid because the wife is not under the husband's authority; she is spiritually equal. Yet Ephesians 5:23 clearly states that "the husband is the head of the wife, even as Christ is the head of the church," and 1 Corinthian 11:3 says, "The head of every man is Christ, and the head of the woman is the man, and the head of Christ is God."

Let us begin this study by trying to understand the significance of God as the head of Christ. Does this mean that God has authority over Christ? We already understand that the Father, the Son, and the Holy Spirit are one. These are the three parts of the one Godhead. The Lord Himself clearly states "that they all may be one, as thou, Father, are in me, and I in thee . . . that they may be one, even as we are one" (John 17:21,22). And in John 10:30, 38 Jesus states, "I and my Father are one. . . . The Father is in me, and I in him."

Are you struggling with this concept? Philip, one of Jesus' own disciples, also had difficulty understanding it. Jesus said to him, "Have I been so long with you, and yet you have not come to know Me, Philip? He who has seen Me has seen the Father; how do you say, 'Show us the Father'? Do you not believe that I am in the Father, and the Father is in Me? . . . Believe Me that I am in the Father, and the Father in Me"(John 14:9-11 NASB).

One of my most interesting studies in understanding this scriptural principle was in searching out all the different functions I could find for the three parts of the Godhead: the Father, Son, and Holy Spirit. I became interested in this study from 1 Corinthians 12:4-6.

> Now there are varieties of gifts, but the same Spirit. And there are varieties of ministries, and the same Lord. And there are varieties of effects, but the same God (NASB).

These verses showed me that each part of the Godhead had clearly defined and distinct functions. The Holy Spirit gives the gifts; the Lord Jesus gives the ministries where the gifts are to be exercised; and the Father determines the effects of the gifts. It is interesting to me that as I searched through both the Old and New Testaments I found no duplication in the functions of the Trinity except one. Both the Son and the Spirit are our intercessors before the Father! In their perfect oneness the three parts of the Godhead have specific roles in the kingdom of heaven, yet in their unique oneness they function in perfect harmony without overlapping or question of authority. So it is to be in the relationship between husband and wife.

The Scriptures frequently use figures of speech to illustrate a truth, just as the Lord used many parables to teach the disciples. The word *head* is one of those figures of speech, also known as a *metaphor* (a word or phrase used in place of another to suggest a likeness between them). When I realized this, suddenly the meaning of that word *headship* became clear for me. It is a *function of responsibility* rather than a *position of authority*, as it is often described. "For just as we have many members in one body and all the members do not have the same function, so we, who are many, are one body in Christ, and individually members one of another" (Romans 12:4,5 NASB).

When we read that "The husband is the *head* of the wife" we need to understand that *head* is used as a metaphor, a figure of speech, to suggest the relationship of the husband with the rest of the body. We can readily see that the husband is an integral part of the body: He is the head, the top, the summit, the leader. But nowhere is it unequivocally stated that he is the ruler or the authority! Even in the analogy used in Scripture the head is not the ruler of the body. All parts of the body are placed in the body just as God wills, and each has its own purpose or function, as described clearly in these verses:

> For the body is not one member, but many. If the foot should say, "Because I am not a hand, I am not a part of the body," it is not for this reason any the less a part of the body. And if the ear should say, "Because I am not an eye, I am not a part of the body," it is not for this reason any the less a part of the body. If the whole body were an eye, where would the hearing be? If the whole were hearing, where would the sense of

smell be? But now God has placed the members, each one of them, in the body, just as He desired ... that there should be no division in the body, but that the members should have the same care for one another (1 Corinthians. 12:14-18,25 NASB).

The husband and the wife are equally important members of the body, but they have functions that differ. They are not the *same*, but they are *equal*. They exist in harmony, working out the purposes or functions God has ascribed to them. With this as our understanding we see that all truths of Scripture are in harmony and in agreement.

Now we can understand the verse that says, "The wife does not have authority over her own body, but the husband does; and likewise also the husband does not have authority over his own body, but the wife does" (1 Corinthians 7:4 NASB).

Can there be any question now about who is the authority in the home? It must always be *the Lord Jesus Christ* and none other. The husband and wife must function as equal parts of their unity. Neither should try to exercise power or authority over the other. Anything else is in contradistinction to the will of God as given in Scripture and precludes the full blessings that God would bestow on the family. Yes, the husband is to be the spiritual leader, the head of the wife; that is his function. But is he to be the authority? No, God has not given him that position.

If you or your wife have subscribed to the interpretation that the husband is the *authority* over the wife and therefore she must *blindly obey him*, I would urge you not to simply accept what I have presented here. Instead I strongly encourage you to do your own study and research on this subject, reviewing the verses that have been used in this chapter. Several good Greek word-study dictionaries are available to assist you in understanding and grasping the mind of God on this very important issue. As you do your study, pray and ask the Lord to reveal His truth to you. Ask Him to inscribe on your heart His purpose for you and your home. If you ask He will answer, and the Holy Spirit will "guide you into all truth" (John 16:13). You will no longer be in bondage, thinking you must make all the decisions in your family alone, without the benefit of your wife's insight, counsel, and guidance.

We penalize ourselves when we don't avail ourselves of our wives' wisdom. "Where there is no counsel, the people fall; but in the multitude of counselors there is safety. . . . The way of a fool is right in his own eyes, but he who heeds counsel is wise" (Proverbs 11:14; 12:15 NKJV). How much grief I could have spared myself in the past if I had listened to my wife's counsel or heeded her concerns! Now, at last, I have learned.

Including Our Wives in Family Decision-Making

God created our wives to be our helpers, to be an important part of our team. He gave them understanding and perception that we husbands often don't have. They can see things we don't see, and therefore they need to be a part of the decision-making process in everything that affects the family.

Obviously there are certain minor decisions that affect no one else that we can make ourselves. (I am presuming that for these relatively minor decisions you are already seeking the mind of Christ through daily prayer with Him and that He is therefore directing your path.) For example, I do not ask my wife what I should wear each day. That decision I make myself. On the other hand, if we are going someplace special and I know my appearance will be important to her, I might ask her what she would like me to wear. Sometimes she likes our outfits to coordinate. Is this infringing upon my freedom? No, I don't feel it is because my ultimate desire is to please my wife in every way I can! I am simply putting her needs and desires ahead of my own. "Do nothing from selfishness . . . but let each of you regard the other as more important than yourself" (paraphrase of Philippians 2:3 NASB). Likewise, my wife makes those decisions that only affect her. I do not question her about these decisions, and I do not help her unless she asks. And I am the leader in doing this. *By my actions*, not by my words, I set the tone in our relationship for mutual submission, voluntary selflessness. Like an officer in battle, I am leading the charge and not telling the troops to go on ahead of me. My wife finds it both easy and comfortable to follow this kind of leadership.

How do we make the major decisions, those that affect us jointly or affect our family as a whole? We look first to God for our answers. The Scriptures speak again and again about the importance of unity among the body. The family, being a microunit of the body of Christ, falls within this framework. "Now I plead with you, brethren, by the name of our Lord Jesus Christ, that you all speak the same thing, *and that there be no divisions among you, but that you be perfectly joined together in the same mind and in the same judgment*" (1 Corinthians. 1:10 NKJV). "*Be of one mind,* live in peace; and the God of love and peace will be with you" (2 Corinthians 13:11 NKJV). "For He Himself is our peace, who has made both one, and has broken down the middle wall of division between us" (Ephesians 2:14 NKJV). "Finally, *all of you be of one mind*, having compassion for one another" (1 Peter 3:8 NKJV).

These are only a few of the many verses that urge oneness and accord, and they apply to the husband and wife as well as to all Christians. They show us how God expects us to make our decisions: We are to be like-minded, in agreement.

First, we analyze together all aspects of the issue we are considering. Second, we count the costs so we can determine, to the best of our ability, that we can complete the project and that it will not cause undue stress or strain upon us. Third, together we weigh all the factors involved in reaching our decision to see if we are in agreement. If we are of one mind, we can proceed. If we are not in accord, we pause until we do have unity of mind. If we do not, we simple shelve or discard the question. It is far better to make no decision than to make one that is going to cause grief or pain later.

If you are considering a decision that involves a substantial commitment, such as a major purchase, private school for the children, a job change that would mean uprooting the family, or anything that might make a significant impact upon the family or one of its members, there is an important fourth step: PRAY! Ask the Lord either to confirm your decision or to remove the peace, or the accord, you initially had about it if it is not His will for you. If you ask Him, He will do it.

There is an important value in decisions made in accord with one another. If, in the light of experience, we see that we made a poor decision, we both hold ourselves equally accountable. There is no finger-pointing. There is no "I told you so" and no second-guessing of the other person. We made the decision together. We agreed on it, and now we rise or fall together on whatever the outcome may be. It does not affect our respect or our trust of each other. We made the decision in unison, we were in complete agreement, and we remain harmoniously bound to each other! If there are lessons for us to learn, we learn together. "Two are better than one, because they have a good reward for their labor. For if they fall, one will lift up his companion. But woe to him who is alone when he falls; for he has no one to help him up" (Ecclesiastes 4:9,10 NKJV).

A Word About the Functions of Husbands

We have already discussed how the statement that the husband is the head of the wife refers scripturally to a function of responsibility rather than to a position of authority. Briefly, let us see how Scripture portrays some of those functions of the husband.

Protector. Christ provided all the spiritual weapons we need to protect ourselves, the church, and our families against the spiritual attacks of the enemy (Ephesians 6:10-18). We are to be the spiritual leader, the head. We should also be first in scriptural knowledge, understanding, and wisdom. One of the tragedies of modern life is that in many homes the wife is spiritually far ahead of the husband. On average, women spend far more time in Bible study and prayer than men do.

We are also to protect our wives emotionally as well as physically. What man would not willingly and without hesitation lay down his own life to save the lives of his wife and children? Most of us would do it instinctively, without a thought, in a moment of danger. But how about protecting them emotionally? Generally we men are created to be stronger emotionally. We don't tend to fall apart as easily or have a low point each month as many women are apt to do. God created us to see things, particularly stressful things, from a different perspective. We are to be the calming influence in the home, the shield that fends off stressful issues from our wives. But what if we are the ones causing the stress and the strain? That gives us something to think about, doesn't it?

Provider. Looking to Jesus for our example once again, we see in Ephesians 5:29 that He nourished and cherished His church and that we husbands are to regard our wives in the same way. We are to provide for their material needs, their natural needs, and their emotional needs. We are to be the bulwark they can lean on. Looking further, we see that "we are to grow up in all aspects into Him, who is the head, even Christ, from whom the whole body, being fitted and held together by that which every joint supplies, according to the proper working of each individual part" (Ephesians 4:15,16 NASB). As we "grow up in all aspects into Him," we become an integral part of the supply system, and all the parts work together in harmony. This is an awesome responsibility the Father places on each of us husbands. Are we fulfilling this role He has established for us?

Presenter. Jesus desired to "present to Himself the church in all her glory, having no spot or wrinkle or any such thing; but that she should be holy and blameless" (Ephesians 5:27 NASB). This Scripture gives us additional insight as to how we are to regard and love our wives. Husbands are to become so Christlike that through the process and the journey of the marital union with us our wives will become spotless and "wrinkle-free." We are to create such an atmosphere in the marriage that they will be seen by the Lord as holy and blameless. This does not imply that the wife has no responsibility of her own to reach for these objectives. She surely does. The verse is only speaking of our responsibility as husbands before the Lord. (Similarly, you might recall that the wife's instruction to be subject to her husband only speaks of her responsibility. It speaks nothing of any authority of the husband.)

How can we mere mortals accomplish such a seemingly impossible task? On our own, we cannot. But with the power of the risen Christ freely flowing through our lives, our minds, and our bodies, we can make surprising strides in that direction. This responsibility places upon us another awesome challenge to become so "at one" with Him that we become like Him. This means continuing our spiritual growth and maturity. Where are you today spiritually compared to where you were five years ago? Have you made the progress you should have? Where will you be five years from now? Determine today what your own spiritual future will be.

Partner. In Ephesians 5 we see the repetition of the important truth from Genesis that "A man ... shall cleave to his wife; and the two shall become one flesh" (verse 31 NASB). As the two of you actually become one in flesh, in mind, in spirit, in objectives, in decisions—as you become one in the Lord—you are truly equal partners. However, since the husband is the *head,* we husbands have the additional awesome responsibility to see that this equal partnership becomes a reality. It is only by our leadership, which means by our example, that this can happen. Only then will we be fulfilled as men and our wives be fulfilled as women, for we will be functioning as God intended.

It has taken many years and many mistakes, but at last Florence and I are functioning as equal partners. We each have very definite and assigned roles and functions. I know I am to protect her in every way I can. I know I am to provide for her needs and desires as much as I can. I know I am to grow up in Christ so I may provide for her a stress-free environment where she can grow as well, holy and blameless. I know I am to make her feel that she is a fellow heir with me, my equal partner. And one more thing I have learned: *These are my responsibilities as her husband.* Therefore I am never to look over her shoulder and see how well she is doing on *her* part! That is one responsibility God has never given me.

Is the husband the head of the wife? Scripture says yes, he is. Is the husband the authority over the wife? Scripture never says he is. But we do have an immense responsibility to love our wives in the same way Christ loved the church. He loved the church so much that He died for it!

Isn't it time we men wake up and retake the ground we have lost as spiritual, emotional, and physical leaders in our families?

11

HOW TO BE A
PLEASING WIFE

Today's Christian woman is utterly confused. The world is telling her to swing and switch. The books are warning her to look out for number one. Magazine covers show the typical woman as stripped to the waist. Newspapers do features on women who left the diapers for instant success on the Board of Directors for General Motors. Television glorifies infidelity as it shows the normal woman having a midday rendezvous in a suite at the Century Plaza—no more tawdry times in a cheap motel.

In contrast to the Playboy Bunny image, worldly feminists say that we should no longer be sex objects. We should wear flat shoes and a hat like Bella Abzug, and march a lot. We should demand our rights, carry big signs, and look on abortions as we do going to the dentist.

Then we go to a church and too often we see women who are blank-faced with no makeup and so serious as to be depressing. They look as if they were in the running for "Evangelical Frump of the Year Award."

But this will change, for the bulletin announces a new class to be held in the church basement starting next Thursday. Its title, "Sex and Spirituality," promises to make the plain provocative and the sad seductive. One imagines returning six months hence and hearing of a congregation full of transformed nymphs who report that they are now wearing at home lace negligees trimmed with black marabou to match their Bibles.

What's a Christian woman to do? It's all too confusing! As with every other personal problem, we have to get back to the Bible and find out what it really says, for while the world's standards fluctuate, the Bible is the same yesterday, today, and tomorrow.

Where do we start? Proverbs 31:30 says, "Charm is deceitful and beauty is vain, but a woman who fears the Lord, she shall be praised" (NKJV).

Love the Lord

It is impossible to love our husbands until we love the Lord. When we can communicate on a personal level with the Lord, we can hope to be in tune with our husbands. *Redbook* magazine, in one of its many surveys, proclaimed on the cover, "Religious Women Make Better Lovers." While they couldn't put their finger on the reason, they had to conclude that those women surveyed who had a "strong faith" were more happily married. When we start each day talking quietly with the Lord, we're less apt to scream at our husbands. When we keep our eyes looking up instead of around, we're not going to keep a record of wrongs. When we're able to see our husband's inner self, we're not so concerned with physique. When we do all things heartily as unto the Lord (Colossians 3:23), we consider housework an investment in marriage.

Fred shared these principles at a Marriage Seminar in Massachusetts and received this letter from a happy homemaker who had seen changes in her husband when she changed herself.

Dear Fred and Florence,

It's been over three weeks since you were here. I have to tell you that this has been the best week of our marriage, even though Wayne wasn't there. Our home has been so quiet and tranquil it's almost unbelievable.

Doing dishes seems to be one of my downfalls, so whenever Wayne volunteered to do the dishes if I dried them I thought I'd drop. I'll tell you, each one of those dishes was caressed dry. It was really neat!

The other day I was really sick and the baby was awful so I called Wayne at work to cry, so home he came dashing. He sent me to bed, played with the baby, and cleaned the house. Could not believe it! Praise the Lord!

I've really seen the results of "Thank you, God" for the bad things. Every morning at exactly 5:09 Faith would wake up, ready to start her day. The first morning after you had shared your experiences with us, I tried it and it worked. She didn't ruffle my feathers a bit. By the morning after you had left, Faith was sleeping until 7:00 A.M.

What a beautiful Christmas and New Year our family is going to have! Every new day is such a wonderful unique experience.

Thank you again.

Love and prayers,

Jane

When we can say "Thank You, Lord" on faith, our attitude and then our actions will change.

Have a Submissive Attitude

The word "submission" has been so abused that no one wants to hear it mentioned. One pastor's wife informed us ahead of time that we were not to use the word "submission" at all in her church. Some feel that it means being a doormat, lying down on the floor to be stepped on. Some feel that it means suffering in silence for the glory of the Lord. Some feel that it means giving in to male superiority and worshiping chauvinism.

Submission is voluntary selflessness, the absence of self-assertion, a willingness to yield versus resistance and rebellion. When we look at the word in its true significance we see why the Lord tells us all to be submissive.

Submit yourselves to God (James 4:7). Start first by yielding to God.

Submit yourselves one to another (Ephesians 5:21). Ideally, when the Lord is working in all of our lives, both husband and wife will want to please each other. The godly man does not want to trample down his wife but lift her up. The spiritual woman wants to honor her husband and admire him. Unfortunately, this verse is often used as an excuse for women not to be submissive until the husband has reformed. Few men are inspired to become spiritual giants when they see their wives holding the axe like Jack in *Jack in the Beanstalk,* ready to cut them down to size.

Submit yourselves to your husbands (Ephesians 5:22). Be willing to please your husband, to put his needs before your own. Do not resist his suggestions and incite rebellion among the troops. Before I understood this principle I pretended to be submissive but was actually rebellious underneath. I rallied the children around good-fun mother and let them know that even though we obeyed Father when he was watching, we could live it up once he left town. Little did I realize what a terrible example of rebellion I was setting for my family!

Peter compares us with little sheep who have lost their way and need to be brought under control by the Shepherd and Keeper of our souls. "In the same way you wives must submit yourselves to your husbands, so that if any of them do not believe God's Word, your conduct will win them over to believe" (1 Peter 3:1,2 TEV).

There is little hope for us to have happy husbands when we are belligerent and domineering. When we preach liberation and are trying to find ourselves, it is impossible to have our men want to be the kind of sweet Christians that we are. Yet when we aim to please, our husbands see a spirit in us that is hard to resist. We can win them over by our conduct. We won't have to say a word.

My friend Molly, a tiny dynamo of a woman who teaches marriage classes in a large suburban church, has anything but a doormat personality. She outtalks and outmoves me and she has been a success at everything she's touched. She overwhelmed her husband for years until she found God's principle of submission and realized that she could adapt her life to please David without becoming a zombie. Her testimony of how she turned from being a business executive to being the wife of a happy husband is both hilarious and heartwarming. By sharing her own personal experiences and the principle of submission she has seen life-changing miracles among the hundreds of women she teaches each week. "When women remove their rebellious spirits and start putting their husbands first in their lives, their whole marriage becomes exciting."

One lady in Molly's class had a husband who had been having affairs for years. The lady had preached to him, evangelized him, and shamed him—all to no avail. When she began to love him without lectures and submit to him without sermons, he began to respond. As she prayed more, he strayed less. One day while he was on a fishing trip, his boat capsized and he was rescued by a Christian Women's Club village missionary, who then led him to the Lord. Only God could have arranged such a divine appointment!

When we stop talking and start loving, we give God a chance.

Aim for a Quiet and a Gentle Spirit.

Although the world tells us to be assertive, the Word tells us to be gentle.

> Your beauty should consist of your true inner self, the ageless beauty of a gentle and quiet spirit, which is of the greatest value in God's sight (1 Peter 3:4 TEV).

The Phillips paraphrase says it this way:

> Your beauty should not be dependent on an elaborate coiffure, or on the wearing of jewelry or fine clothes, but on the inner personality—the unfading loveliness of a calm and gentle spirit, a thing very precious in the eyes of God.

How many of us could truly say that we have this inner personality?

There was never much "inner" about my personality; I wanted it all to show. But as I studied the Bible I saw the necessity of a gentle spirit for the first time. I was not to be bossy and controlling but loving and gentle. I was not to be the loud life-of-the-party but the quiet supporter of my husband. Fred once said to me, "When you talk all the time you don't learn anything, for you already know what you're saying."

As I have aimed for quiet dignity I have come closer to the goal. As I meet socially I try to listen more than I talk. This is extremely difficult for me because I always have a story that is apt to top any being told. To keep a loving check on me, Fred will come up to me at a party and say, "What is your new friend's name?" Now when I see him coming I quickly ask questions so I'll have an instant biography upon request!

You may not be as talkative as I, and you may feel you are already quiet, but do you have a truly gentle spirit underneath? I've seen many bitter, silent women who manipulated their men with iron glances.

The Lord says, "Take my yoke upon you and learn from me, for I am gentle and humble in heart."

Why are religious women better lovers? Because they *love the Lord,* have *submissive attitudes* toward their husbands, and are aiming for *quiet, gentle spirits* that are of great value in the sight of God and man.

Quiet doesn't mean we don't talk, but that what we do say is to be given with a gentle spirit. Our aim as women is to create peace, not agitate toward war.

How easy it is to shout orders, yet sometimes how difficult to be in obedience to the Lord! God wants us to have attitudes of true self-lessness (Philippians 2:3,5), a desire to do what would please our partners. "Do nothing from selfishness ... but with humility of mind, let each of you regard one another [_____] [enter spouse's name in space] as more important than himself [_____] [myself]. Have this attitude in yourselves which was also in Christ Jesus." As many women I talk with scheme and manipulate to avoid doing the thing their husband most wants to do. Many men postpone repairing the dishwasher until the motor has burned out. So often we work to avoid fulfilling our partner's needs because we're not going to let anyone else tell us what to do.

One man told me, "When I walk in the door at night she throws down the gauntlet and we're off to war." Can't we care enough to say the words that lead to love and not to war?

"I'm so glad you're home!"

"You always look good even at the end of a hard day."

"I've got dinner all ready and it's one of your favorites."

Instead of—

"You didn't fix that leaky hose and there's water gushing all over the basement."

"You're late as usual. I sometimes wonder why you come home at all."

"I'm leaving immediately and you can feed the kids whatever you can find."

One day Fred came home late and tired. Instead of commenting on his tardiness, I fixed him a cool drink, took it to our room, where he had collapsed in a chair, and knelt before him holding up the tray. He was so amazed and thrilled at this action that he's never forgotten my one servile moment. While my knees may not often bend, our hearts should be seeking peace in our home.

Improve Your Looks

Not all of us are natural beauty queens, but we should do the best we can with what we have. Fred says that if you could see the real me, you would know that I have done more than could be expected with the raw material available. While God looks on our hearts, humans see us on the surface, and we should make the view as pleasant as possible.

One very chubby lady told me she didn't think it was important how she looked, because if her husband were really spiritual he would see the beauty underneath. I wasn't sure the Lord Himself could have gotten through that 250 pounds to the beauty underneath!

I've taught my daughters, "If you walk out the door looking any less than acceptable, go back and change." One day my daughter Lauren called me up and said, "Mother, I want to tell you there's something you taught me that stuck." Now that's encouraging because sometimes we spend 20 years in training and we're not sure they heard a word we said! "I just thought you would like to know that I started out the door this morning in cut-off jeans and an old T-shirt, with no makeup and my hair kind of straight. I was just going to run to the store for something but as I walked out the door I remembered your words, so I went back and changed. I want Randy to be proud of me."

We Christian women need to be examples in our community; we ought to shine and let others see both our inner and our outer beauty.

12

❧

HOW TO BE A
LOVING HUSBAND

Men: Now you realize that God has personally appointed you to be the spiritual head of your household.

What an overwhelming thought—a divine appointment! But are you ready for it? Do you have to wear a white robe and a tinsel halo? Move the family to a monastery? Mumble a mantra?

No, you just have to know more about the Bible than your wife, and put what you know into practice. For a few of you this may be easy—your wife doesn't know Abraham from Ananias—but for many of you whose wives are consistently involved in Bible studies and regularly worship in church and have an active and effective daily prayer life, becoming the spiritual leader of your home may require time and a concerted effort on your part.

Let's look over one verse and take it apart in a logical, masculine way. We'll choose 1 Peter 3:7, a man's verse written by a real man who had a wife who died young, leaving him to live with his mother-in-law. Peter was not a celibate recluse, but a man who spoke from experience. Let's see what Peter has to say to the man of today.

> Likewise, ye husbands, dwell with them according to knowledge, giving honor unto the wife as unto the weaker vessel, and as being heirs together of the grace of life, that your prayers be not hindered.

The first word is *likewise*. For those of you who remember high-school grammar, likewise is a conjunction, a word that connects two parts together, a joining link for different thoughts. You don't have to be a Bible scholar to realize that little "likewise" is holding two ideas together. Something has gone before likewise, and whatever we are going to be told, someone else has already heard it. Who has been previously instructed? The wives. How do you know? Because the verse says, *Likewise, you husbands.* The women have been instructed already! Isn't that good of God to tell them first?

Do you know why? Men often tell me it's because the women need it more; they're not so bright; it takes them longer to catch on. But I have found that women are more aware of their problems and more receptive to spiritual truth. While men are ordained of God to be the spiritual leaders, they sometimes have the mistaken idea that to be spiritual is to be weak. But of course that concept is not true at all; it takes a real man to discipline his life and to apply scriptural truth to himself and his family. Becoming a better man is not easy.

When I study a verse I divide it into sections and take it a bit at a time.

Likewise (our conjunction)
ye husbands (the specific subject)

dwell with them (dwell with whom?)

You men are to *live with your wives*—in the same house.

Several years ago I would have taken this thought for granted, but today I hear such twisted tales of tawdry life that I feel this point must be made clear.

Mary tells me her husband can't stand the children. They interfere with his music, so he lives in a garret with his guitar and comes home on weekends.

Judy wonders about her husband, who goes off to "sensitivity sessions" and comes home in a daze.

Beth is bewildered by her husband, who joined a swingers class given for credit at the local university and who stays out all night for the lab work.

Cindy is upset that her husband takes his sensuous secretary on frequent business trips while she's at home keeping the store.

No matter what hedonistic headlines tell you it's okay if you stray, remember that God's Word, the only stable psychology manual available, says don't stray—stay. If you cared enough to marry her, live with her.

According to Knowledge

What knowledge? Knowledge about marriage. If any one of you men were starting a new job on Monday on a new subject, you wouldn't dream of walking in cold, with no knowledge of the requirements. You would study as much as possible to pick up pointers on your new position.

Several years ago I conducted a business seminar for the administrative personnel of a metal company in Indiana. Although I was confident on my subject matter of personality types in business, I knew nothing about wire wheels. The president of the company sent me policy statements and background information to read ahead of time, and the day before I spoke I toured the factory for three hours observing the progress of the wheel from its inception on the blueprints to its departure on the docks. I had no idea how much there was to learn about wheels. By the time I met with the executives the next day, I was able to speak with them according to knowledge.

It makes practical sense to be intelligent about business, and to want to succeed. But how about marriage? How much time did you spend in preparation for marriage? I myself read two copies of *Bride's* magazine and walked down the aisle. The week before the wedding my mother asked:

"Do you know what it's all about?"

"Yes," I said, hopefully.

"Thank goodness," she replied in relief.

With no more thought than that, I married Fred. I had spent six months getting ready for the wedding but no time training myself for the role of a wife. It's a miracle that any of us have harmonious relationships when we spend so little time learning how to live with each other according to knowledge!

Once Fred and I decided to revive our gasping marriage, we began to study God's Word and find out what it said and how it applied to us.

Honor to Your Wife

To give honor means to treat your wife with respect, be courteous, and use good manners. I've met many men who were gallant gentlemen at work and offensive oafs at home.

Fred and I were recently invited to a couple's home for dinner. When we arrived the husband greeted us with "That poor dummy hasn't got anything ready yet." Before we got inside the door, he had communicated to us that he is married to some dull incompetent who is probably not going to be able to get this dinner on the table at all. Now that's a discouraging word to hear when you arrive hungry and hopeful.

As we sat down in the living room he said, "She's never very good when she's under pressure." As we began to observe their relationship, we could see why the poor thing was under pressure. He was standing over her, nagging her every inch of the way, pointing out what she was doing wrong, and not helping her at all. "Why don't you hurry up? They're sitting there waiting! Why don't you put the bread on the table? What's wrong with you, anyway? The peas are boiling. You know I hate peas when they boil. You've got the butter too near the burner and it's melting. Why can't you ever do anything right?"

Fred and I were embarrassed and wished we'd never come. McDonald's would have been marvelous compared to this chronicle of criticism. When we did sit down at the table, he pointed out her errors. "You forgot the water again. You didn't make enough gravy. Don't we have a decent knife in the house?" The table had been attractively set and the dinner was well-prepared, but the conversation was strained.

What did this young man think he communicated to Fred and me? That he had a real case on his hands and that anybody who had to put up with this stupid woman would have to be a hero. I'm sure that's what he intended to tell us, but what did he in fact communicate? By the time we left, how did we feel about him? I got in the car and said, "How she lives with him for ten minutes is beyond me!" So many men feel that by downgrading and insulting their wives they are impressing others with how tolerant and competent they are in comparison with the poor dumb thing they have had to live with all these years.

Men, when you try to convince others of your competence by cutting down your wife, what are you really saying? "I am an insecure man who hopes to cover up my inferiority complex by browbeating my wife into abject submission so you'll be impressed with my strength." We want to flee from that type of a rude, insensitive brute who has to build his ego at the expense of others!

Honor and Courtesy to Your Children's Mother

It's important for you men to train your children to give honor unto your wives as well. It's been proven in many statistical studies that what children see in living color in the home is what they learn. You can preach and teach, but they learn from what you *do*.

Paula was sharing with me that her husband, Hal, who gets out of work at 5:00, does not come home for dinner until 9:00 at night, after the children have gone to bed and everything is all cleaned up and quiet. When I asked her why, she said, "Because his father never came home until 9:00." Before they were married Hal told her how much he hated his father because he never came home to spend any time with the family. When he was growing up he vowed that when he got to be a father he would do better. But in reality, when he got to be a father, he reacted the very same way to pressure that his father had, and he stayed away. What are you doing in your home that your child will carry into his marriage? Whatever you allow your son to do to your wife now he will in turn do to his wife in the future. It's critically important to train your sons and daughters to treat your wife with respect and honor.

Sometimes I visit a home where a child is openly insulting his mother and calling her names, but the husband listens to the whole thing and does nothing. The wife may call, "Say something to him!" and he'll grumble, "They're your kids, you take care of them."

When Freddie was about ten years old he yelled some nasty comment to me. Fred reached over to him, grabbed him by the shoulders, picked him up off the ground, and shook him hard. "Don't you ever let me hear you say one bad word to my wife again!" And he plunked him down. Young Freddie got the message quickly and clearly. He was never to say anything like that to me again! And he didn't. If you have a Choleric son you may have to grab him often and shake him harder, but he will soon get the idea that you do not tolerate any disrespect for your wife. Give honor to your wife and make sure that your children do also. Today our son Fred is a gracious and mature young man who always treats his mother with the greatest respect.

As to the Weaker Vessel

Some of you may be thinking, "If you knew my wife you'd see she's not the weaker vessel." There are some very strong women, yet we have found that women generally become only as controlling as their husbands allow them to be. Obviously, if you abdicate your responsibilities as a father and leave child-raising to her, she will take over. If you ignore yardwork and house repairs, she will be forced to assume your role. If you leave church attendance in her hands, she'll become the spiritual leader. We met one couple at a seminar in Arizona who fit this picture. He was a successful Phlegmatic businessman with a Choleric wife. He worked hard at the office and tuned out at night. When Joe came up to Fred, he said, "I am the weaker vessel. I let Carolyn run everything. It's the easy way. I bring home the money and she makes all the decisions. I see that this is wrong, but how can I change?"

Fred answered, "When you go home, call the family together and apologize to your sons. Say, 'I'm sorry! I have given you the wrong impression of what a man should be. I have been weak. I have allowed your mother to run everything. I have learned that I am to be the leader of this family, and I am going to start. Please be patient and help me.'" When we returned to Phoenix a few months later, we met again. Carolyn came running over. "You wouldn't believe what's happened in our household. Joe came home, had a meeting with all of us, told his sons he was sorry he hadn't been a stronger father and husband, and promised to make up for lost time. When he was through, our boys came up to him and said, 'Dad, we never thought we'd see the day when you would stand up and be a man.'" They had all been waiting for this kind of leadership, and yet Joe had never realized his family role.

As Joe studied the Scriptures and worked to become the head of the household, Carolyn and the boys supported his efforts. Joe started a Bible study in their home, his sons respect him, and Carolyn is relieved of the pressures she used to bear alone. Joe is still a success at business, but now he's also a success as a husband and father.

God promises that we will be equal recipients of the gifts He has for us, whether we are men or women. He loves us all and will prepare a place in heaven for each believer who loves the Lord Jesus Christ.

Unhindered Prayers

Why is it that you men should dwell with your wife according to spiritual knowledge of marriage, give honor to her, and be her loving leader? You do this so that "your prayers be not hindered." Conversely, if you don't follow the instructions in this verse you cannot expect to have a very effective prayer life. Fred takes this admonition seriously and spends at least an hour a day in written prayer and Bible Study.

Let's take a quick review of 1 Peter 3:7:

Likewise—the connector between words to the women and to the men.
Ye husbands—listen, it's for you!
Dwell with them—live with your own wife, not somewhere else. This might be amplified to say live with her emotionally, as part of her life and of the home. Too many husbands "dwell" there but do not "participate" there.

How?

According to knowledge—spiritual understanding of your role in marriage.
Giving honor unto the wife—treating her with respect and courtesy, esteeming her as worthy of honor.
As unto the weaker vessel—knowing that she needs your leadership. God designed men to be the leader and the protector.
As being heirs together of the grace of life—equal in God's sight.

Why?

That your prayers be not hindered—to experience answered prayer.

Any other formula is outside the will of God. "Let not that man think he will receive anything of God."

Men, see how simple it is to take apart one verse and apply it to your life? Why not be brave and share some Scripture in this simple way with your family!

Leave and Cleave

The first marriage advice in the Bible was given in Genesis 2:24: "Therefore shall a man leave his father and his mother, and shall cleave unto his wife, and they shall be one flesh." This verse can be stripped down to two rhyming words—LEAVE and CLEAVE. God used His great wisdom when He told us that we should not live with our in-laws. When we are mature enough to accept the responsibility of marriage, we should leave our father and start a new life. This advice seems so obvious, and yet many couples today have left home physically but are still bound to Mother emotionally. Or else they have never learned to set the rightful boundaries for their own life together; they allow Father or Mother to control their every move and decision.

Alicia cried, "All holidays are terrible. We have to go to his mother's first or she has a fit. Then she takes so long with dinner that we never get to my family at all. Why isn't he man enough to stand up to her sometime and say no?"

Peggy explains, "We got married before Dave was out of college and we had to accept money from his parents. Since they were paying we had to live in the house of their choice and buy what they liked, and we've never changed. I feel like Big Mother is still watching over me."

Martin said, "Mama never approved of my wife. She told me right from the start, 'That girl's not good enough for you—she's trash.' I bucked her for a few years and then she began to point out flaws in Mitzi and I listened. Nothing Mitzi did was as good as Mother did it. One day Mother said, 'Why don't you move back home and let me give you the treatment you deserve?' I left Mitzi for Mama and I'm so ashamed!"

From Helen: "He can't even take an hour off to take me to the doctor, and he's missed all the children's graduations, but if his mother calls he drops everything and runs."

JoAnne sobs, "I just found out that his will is made out to his mother. He says she'll dole it out as I need it and manage my life much better than I could. I can't believe it!"

At lunch with Darla: "When I think back over my four marriages I can see that my parents quietly and persistently broke each one up. I guess since they were never happy they wanted to make sure I wasn't either."

Conversing with Christine: "I don't even know if we have any insurance. When I ask him, he says not to worry—his father knows where the papers are. What kind of marriage is that?"

Bewildered Bob: "Her family has loads of money and she doesn't dare cross them up or she'll lose her inheritance. We have to take our vacations with them and live next door. They really control our lives. I'm about ready to give her back to them and have a fresh thought of my own."

Do any of these statements sound familiar? Are you letting some parent rule in your home? The Bible tells us that we must honor our mother and father but that when we marry we are to leave their authority and establish a new home. We are to *leave* and *cleave*. In any disputes our allegiance must be to our partner. It is up to the husband to see that his home is not torn up by interfering in-laws on either side.

When You're Old Enough to Leave

When you're old enough to leave, *leave*. And then *cleave*: latch onto one another, cling tightly, merge together, become one. Many of the secular articles on marriage tell us not to get dependent on one another or become too close. Then why get married at all? God tells us to unite and become as one.

One couple came to us with cleaving problems. Toby had a house from a former marriage and they lived in that. Dan rented his house and kept the money. Once she was short of cash and he lent her $500 with interest from his funds. When Toby missed the date on one payment, Dan added a late charge. She got an insurance settlement and he took it all to cover a stock margin call. She tried to charge him interest and he got furious. Their marriage was not a merger but two feuding corporations!

The Lowells had each been widowed and they decided to marry, but not to move. He lived in one house with his daughter, who didn't like the new wife, so she stayed in her home with two sons. They alternated nights from one place to the other, and no one ever knew where either one was supposed to be. You may think this sounds like a one-in-a-thousand extreme, but even though the Lowells did this physically, many couples are doing this emotionally.

This charade was not what God had in mind when He said to *leave* and *cleave*. Now that Fred and I understand our different personalities, we realize that my strengths fill in his weaknesses and his strengths fill in my weaknesses. Now we truly are as one.

Love

What advice does God give especially for men? He says to love your wives: "Husbands, *love* your wives, just as Christ also loved the church and gave Himself up for her" (Ephesians 5:25 NASB). "So husbands ought also to *love* their own wives as their own bodies. He who *loves* his own wife loves himself" (Ephesians 5:28 NASB). "Husbands, *love* your wives, and do not be embittered against them" (Colossians 3:19 NASB).

Women want so much to be loved. They want their man to put his arms around them, to comfort, to speak kindly, to care. "If we know you love us, we can put up with other discomforts, but if we're not sure, we'll ask for the moon to test you."

Men, where is your relationship with your wife right now? Is she really in love with you or do her eyes keep roving to the side? Have you done anything to turn her off? Have you pushed her aside with disinterest? Open up for a little friendly advice.

Don't Neglect

Men can't understand that a wife can be sitting in an expensive home on a new chair pouring tea from a silver pot and still feel neglected. "But she's got everything she could ever want!" you say. What's her side of the story?

"His business is his life. He doesn't even know I'm around."

"He bought me a new car and said, 'I hope that will make you happy.'"

"His secretary knows him better than I do, and no wonder— they spend every waking minute together."

"As soon as he gets home he goes to the garage and sticks his head under a hood. When I complain, he tells me to take a course in auto mechanics!"

"There's some sporting event on every weekend to take up his time. If I want to speak to him, I have to wait for a commercial."

"Every night he watches TV. I told him I was sick of television, so he bought a set with a bigger screen so I'd like it better."

I (Fred) wish I didn't relate so well to that last example, but unfortunately I did something quite similar during a time of grief. Our first son, my namesake, was dying. He was having convulsions and screaming much of the time. I couldn't bear to look at my son who should have been perfect and see him in such agony. I was in the restaurant business in the daytime, and to give myself an excuse not to come home, I opened up a bistro for the evenings. I leased an old New England red barn, gutted the inside, paneled the walls in light wood, made a hardwood dance floor and bandstand, built a kitchen and restrooms. We didn't have a bar but we did serve beer, peanuts in the shells, and hamburgers. I hired a banjo band and we all wore red-and-white striped vests and 20's boater straw hats.

I named my place "Good Time Charlie's" and I was Charlie. I could put the pain away and have fun. We all sang along with the band and we all seemed happy. For me, as with many others, I could blank out my problems and deny the reality if I didn't have to see the evidence.

But where was Florence? I had totally forgotten that she might be deep in grief also. I had so successfully covered mine that I was unaware that she was mired in hers. It wasn't long before she began to complain about being alone every single night. I wasn't unhappy. I was out singing, thinking I was having fun. Why, I wondered, couldn't she rise above her circumstances too?

159

Finally I decided to do something to pacify her complaining and loneliness. I went to a friend from our Rotary Club who had a radio and TV store. As a surprise for Florence, I had them deliver to our house the biggest and best stereo-TV and radio console they had. It consumed most of the limited profits we were earning from "Good Time Charlie's." I was willing to do anything to try to placate her.

I thought, "There, that ought to make her happy!"

She was! She was as thrilled and excited as any child with a new toy. Her joy and her appreciation lasted, just as you might have expected, for only two weeks. Then she started playing the same old tune again. I had no understanding. What she needed was an emotionally understanding and attentive husband. She did not need a bigger TV console to stare at every night alone.

Gratefully, it didn't take all 44 years of marriage to learn that when Florence wants to talk, I drop whatever I am doing and listen. I have learned to put her needs ahead of my own. And it's been worth it!

Florence adds, "No matter how heavenly a house or how heavy a wallet, we women feel neglected when you don't put us first. We want to *know*—not *guess*—that you love us and put our interests before business, cars, TV, or sports."

Don't Correct

Before we were married, Fred thought my colorful stories were cute, but the minute I became Mrs. Littauer he felt obligated to correct any errors in my conversation. We sounded something like this:

FLORENCE	FRED
"Let me tell you about our trip"	"not again"
"We left on Tuesday at noon"	"Wednesday at 10:05"
"and headed south"	"southeast"

"for a couple of hours"	"48 minutes"
"We stopped at this adorable restaurant	"El Torito"
"with these little Spaniards"	"Mexicans"
"draped with towels"	"serapes"

Not only did I feel I was speaking in an echo chamber, but the constant corrections decreased my credibility with the crowds. We were like a stereo set playing two different songs. After a while I learned to flee from Fred at the first opportunity and find people who would appreciate my humor and not get hung up on details.

Later, when Fred and I began to communicate, I explained how little it mattered to the listener whether we drove for two hours or 48 minutes and how annoying it was for others to hear the two of us in tandem. We discussed this issue and I agreed to stay closer to the facts while Fred pledged not to correct me short of an inflammatory statement apt to cause war.

Don't Direct

Some men give a constant lecture course to the little woman. Harry gives his wife instructions on how to cook in such a demeaning manner that one would think if he left the kitchen she would pour ketchup on the strawberry ice cream.

Mel is a purveyor of the obvious in the car: "That's a traffic light. It's green now. You can go on green. That car has its signals on. He's going to turn left. Go to the right of him. Here's where I work. Stop the car just in front of that white one and let me out there. I hope you can get home without me."

Paul barks out orders to his wife: "Call Joe and tell him I'll pick him up at eight. No, not eight tonight—eight in the morning!" He then goes off with a sigh of disgust.

No woman becomes more attentive when she feels neglected, corrected, or directed. Let her know she's *first* with you. Allow her stories to fall as they may and don't tell her how to perform unless

161

she asks you. Even then proceed with caution. She may only be asking for an affirmation, not a dictation.

Approve

Disapproval is probably the most cutting thing a man can give.

"Greg thinks I never do anything right."

"Pat never says a kind word."

"He's always telling me how much better his mother does. This makes me more nervous than I already am."

"His constant criticism and judgment of my every move is driving me crazy."

"No matter how much I do right, he only notices the negatives."

"If he'd only be tender and touch me, but he looks at me like I've got the plague."

So many women are desperate for a word of approval! They see magazine articles that show the average "Now Woman" leading the board meeting of General Motors while all the men are looking up in admiration. One man is, of course, glancing down at her legs to see what she's wearing. Her dress-for-success ensemble is custom-tailored, her briefcase is gold-tooled leather, and her silver pen is held high in her bejeweled hand.

The average woman is doing great things today. How does your wife feel? Is she so secure in your love and approval that she is content and fulfilled, or have you said nary an uplifting word to her in years? Don't take her for granted or Grant may take her from you.

An article in *U.S. News & World Report*, "Why So Many Wives Are Running Away," tells us, "In ever-growing numbers, unhappy wives across the U.S. are on the run—from husbands, children, and household responsibilities. . . . Wives are told by women's groups that they should be tired of being confined at home, of being sex objects. . . . She is typically a middle-income woman who married at 18 or 19 and started to have children soon thereafter.

She runs away when she is about 35 and feels the children are old enough to take care of themselves. . . . We must remember that these runaway wives are caring, loving, hardworking, solid people. When we find them, they're generally living alone. This type of woman is not bent on divorce."

Why are women running away? What might make your wife want to skip town? Are you negative, critical, demanding, unenthusiastic, dull, boring, uncomplimentary? Or do you let your wife know how much you appreciate what she does? Do you approve of her looks and personality? Do you encourage her when she's weighted down and uplift her spirits when she's had a hard day? Do you listen to her problems and work with her toward solutions?

No woman wants to quit and run away, but many do it. Why not analyze your behavior and take out flight insurance on your wife before it's too late?

Admire

A wife who is genuinely admired by her husband will seldom run off to seek approval elsewhere. Notice your wife's clothes, her hairstyle, and her makeup, and encourage her.

"When he tells me I look good, I want to look better."

"His compliments keep me taking care of myself."

"He never noticed what I wore so I don't bother to dress up anymore."

A bright Sally Sanguine came up to me one day just before I went in to speak to the husbands. She said, "Tell those men that if they're too dumb to compliment their wives, at least be smart enough not to compliment other women in their presence." She then dumped this story on me. "At Christmas we were going to the office party for my husband's business. I bought a new red velvet dress, had my hair done up in an elegant style, and got sparkly eye shadow. When I walked out of the bedroom to leave, I could hardly wait for his reaction. I should have waited. He glanced at me and said, 'You're late.' I stood in shock as he threw my coat over my shoulders and walked to the car. Neither of us said a word. We got to the party and walked in the door, and he spotted my friend Jean. His whole personality changed. 'Jean, my love, how gorgeous you look! Your dress fits like a glove and your hair is soft. Wow! I can't take my eyes off you.' "

You can imagine Sally's reaction—she was furious. "Why don't they notice a thing *we* wear and then fall all over a stray woman who doesn't even look that good?" Why, men, why?

One levelheaded lady said, "I wish husbands would explain what they like about a woman they comment on so we wives could try to achieve these 'neat' qualities so we'd be more attractive to them."

Admire what's admirable and we'll work to improve. Ignore how we look and we'll quit trying.

During the low period of our marriage, I felt unloved and insignificant. Fred only noticed what was wrong with me, and mentally I ran away. I went out to find myself years before most women knew they were lost. I got jobs that always put me on center stage, where people had to look up and notice me. If I got enough compliments during the day I could stand Fred at night. Gratefully, all that is changed now, and Fred makes me feel that I'm the most important part of his life. When I know I am a person of significance for Fred, I don't need to hear words of praise from other men.

Some of you may be thinking, "If you could only see my wife you'd agree there's nothing there to admire." All the more reason to hunt, for she must really need to be uplifted. There is always something in the worst of us to be praised, and the less lovely a person is the more he or she needs encouragement.

Marita and I play a game as we're traveling. We observe people and find something complimentary about each person we see. If we have the opportunity, we verbalize our feelings and watch the face of a drab lady light up as we find something about her to praise.

One woman in a plain print dress loomed up before us in an airport and Marita whispered, "I'll give this one to you, Mother—I can't find anything good to say." Always loving a challenge, I looked her over and said as she pushed into line, "Aren't those adorable buttons on your dress!"

She stopped short, stared up, and said, "Are you talking to me?" I assured her that I had noticed her silver heart-shaped buttons and found them unique. Her whole personality changed as she explained how her friend had brought these buttons home from Germany and she had made the dress to go with the buttons. "But you're the first person who ever noticed them."

My comment made her day. There's something good to be said for everyone—even if it's only the buttons she's wearing. We've all got buttons!

Administer

Harry Truman had a sign on his desk that read "The buck stops here." Each wife needs to know that there is one step beyond her, a higher court, a final authority, a place where the buck stops. You husbands are to be that place; the Bible says you are to administer the problems and be the manager of the family.

For Phlegmatic husbands this leadership seems difficult. It is so much easier to let her handle the finances, check the children at school, and make all the major decisions. This easygoing attitude eliminates friction and allows you to sit back, relax, and tell her how she could have done it better.

Indecision is a basic decision to never make another decision. By not offering clear opinions, you avoid specific responsibilities and escape from ever being to blame for family mistakes.

This passive attitude may keep you from getting an ulcer, but it is an abdication of your scriptural position as the head of the household. When a man lets his wife assume authority, one of two things usually happens as the years go on. Either—

he feels henpecked and wants to leave.

or

she looks down at him in disgust and wants to throw him out.

Jackie was the organist and choir director in a local church. She was a strong, husky, domineering Choleric who took charge of everything she touched. Jason was no dummy (he had a Ph.D. in chemistry), but his Phlegmatic nature allowed her to run his entire life. The roles were reversed and he felt increasingly insignificant. As an elder in the church, he presented a steady balance on the board, but everyone knew that his ideas were firmly dictated by Jackie.

One day while on a business trip to New York he went through a revolving door which hit a tiny lady and sent her sprawling across the lobby floor. Jason ran over, picked her up, and laid her gently on a nearby couch. She looked up and said admiringly, "You're such a strong man."

"That did it," he told me later. "I hadn't felt like a man in so many years that I couldn't resist."

Jackie screamed, threw things, and called him an idiot, but Jason calmly packed up and left for New York, never to return again.

Herb came from a wealthy family, and he gave Helen everything she wanted. They got his-and-her Cadillacs each year and had both summer and winter homes. Herb never wanted to rock the boat, so he let Helen make every decision for their family of five. He thought their marriage was peaceful, though unexciting, and he never got hurt by her sharp comments on his insignificance in life. One day when the last child was off to college, Herb came home and found all his possessions on the front porch of his rambling home. The locks had been changed and there was no way to get inside.

Herb came to us for help, and when I reached Helen she said, "I've taken all the responsibility for this family for years. Now they're all gone, so why do I need him? He couldn't make a decision if his life depended on it. He's been like a sixth child, and I'm sick of babysitting."

When a man does not assume his God-appointed role as administrator of the family, his avoidance will ultimately lead to trouble.

Here are some suggestions which women have shared with me:

Have family meetings to discuss overall goals.

Maintain unity in disciplining the children.

Keep the family aware of your business and its pressures.

Assume financial responsibility and let everyone know what's available for household expenses. Be realistic.

Plan a family budget.

Don't make your wife have to beg for money.

Don't make foolish purchases on a whim.

Don't charge unnecessary things or allow the family to do so.

Pay the bills on time. Don't procrastinate.

Keep up the maintenance on your home and be prompt with repairs.

Be reliable. When you say you'll take the family out on Friday afternoon, remember to show up.

Keep the cars in repair. One lady told us, "My car is a death trap and I know he's trying to kill me."

Have your will and insurance up-to-date, and be sure your wife knows where they are.

See that the yardwork is done. The wife of an evangelist lamented, "We bought a house with perfect landscaping and within a year it was a shambles. The neighbors hate us. How can we be any kind of witness to them?"

Ask your family what help they need that you are not providing.

Being a leader takes time, self-discipline, and effort, but what good is it if you gain the world and lose your own family?

Admonish

To admonish means to reprove gently and kindly. Even if you were a perfect man trying to organize a perfect family, there could be times when your wife got so far out of hand that you would need to pull her back in line. How do you handle this touchy task?

The quickest way is to yell at her immediately in front of the kids and show them all who's boss.

You could wait until she's about to do the same thing again and remind her firmly how badly she botched this before.

You could hover over her as often as possible and watch for impending doom.

All of these ideas are guaranteed to make her fall somewhere between discouraged and defiant. So how do you tell her that something has to be done differently?

Fred has finally mastered the art of admonishing. When he needs to change one of my behavior patterns, he takes me out to lunch and tells me how great I am. What a wonderful thought!

Problem: There was a time we had a Bible study in our home each Tuesday evening. Fred wanted dinner early on Tuesdays so we could be cleaned up before the guests arrived. I never seemed to remember when it was Tuesday. Fred came home ready to eat and I wasn't even there. When I arrived, we threw something together quickly, wolfed it down, cleaned up in a hurry, and welcomed our friends "with the peace of the Lord in our hearts."

What could Fred do about me? He could scream at me when I walked in oblivious and late. He could sulk and get depressed. He could go out for dinner on Tuesdays—there's a good thought! He could tell the people the mess is my fault. Or he could do what he did.

Fred took me out for lunch, and while I was so grateful for this oasis in a busy day, he began to compliment me.

"You accomplish more in a given day than any woman I know."

"How you write, speak, teach, travel, and run a home is beyond me."

"Because of how well you do and how much you have on your mind, I hate to add one pressure to your life."

"However, do you think it is possible to have some simple supper on the table by 5:30 on Tuesdays?"

When Fred approached the problem this way, I wanted to be part of the solution. When he let me know it was too much to ask, I wanted to show him I could do it. We worked it out. He would let me know it was Tuesday—that's the biggest help right there—and I got home on time. He was happy with some light meal and he helped me clean up. We even had time to sit down, pray together, and review our lesson before the doorbell started to ring. Tuesdays became a time of joy and fulfillment rather than excess stress. Fred had taken the time to lovingly and caringly help me plan. His strengths filled in my weaknesses.

Men, the best of us women will make mistakes, but with a positive approach from you we will try to improve.

Admit

Some men feel that to admit they've made a mistake is a sign of weakness. Some men will drive 40 miles into the wilderness before admitting that they should have turned right in Tucumcari when their wife said so.

Admitting we're wrong is not a sign of weakness, but of strength. It takes a real man to say he's sorry. Fred and I were married 15 years before he ever said he was sorry for anything, and the first time he verbalized this thought I was overcome. I couldn't believe that perfect Fred could admit he was wrong.

When he said "I'm sorry," I heard "I love you."

In a teenage group we took a survey of the words they most wanted to hear from their fathers. The majority reported:

"I love you" and "I'm sorry."

Your family knows you're not perfect, so why try to keep up an act and have them see through it? Humble yourself when you're wrong and say those favorite of words— "I'm sorry."

13

How to Have a Romantic Wife

"**H**ow come the women at the office think I'm hot stuff and my wife couldn't care less?"

How often we are asked this question by some attractive man whose wife is turned off!

Is it possible that you treat the women at the office better than you treat your wife?

Do you walk in each day with a cheerful greeting and make them all glad you've arrived?

Do you notice which woman had her hair done and who has a new dress?

Do you jump up to open doors for the attractive women and adjust their air vents so they won't be chilled?

Do you fix the pencil sharpener the first time the secretary asks and not even tell her she was stupid to break it?

Do you buy funny little gifts and cards to brighten up their spirits?

Do you praise their good deeds to keep them moving and overlook their faults so they won't get discouraged?

If you tried some of these tricks on your wife she might think you were hot stuff too. Many men are full of compliments in the office and complaints at home but wonder why their wife is not so adoring as the women at work.

The media makes us think that a male's appeal lies mainly in his manly physique, seductive glances, designer shirts, and costly cologne. While these attributes may enhance the chase, it takes more than a front to keep romance in a marriage. If your wife has been insulted or ignored, she is not likely to be impressed by a quick flash of Aramis or muscles that were toned up by a body-building course.

Several years ago when Masters and Johnson first came out with their now-discredited exposé on the massive numbers of unfulfilled marriages, they made the sexual side of wedlock sound like a staged production that had to be done according to certain rules to be effective at all. They told us we weren't enjoying life because we hadn't studied the proper techniques. Self-help books and articles sprouted like weeds on every shelf, and the country began to find new methods for "doin' what comes naturally." *Cosmopolitan* printed outlines on how to do things that we didn't even know we wanted to do, and the rush was on.

We began to examine the physical prowess of our mates, and they all fell short. Stripped down, none of us looked a bit like a femme fatale or a Hollywood hunk, and were we ever disappointed! Just being married to the corner druggist or the local schoolmarm wasn't enough—we deserved daily euphoria, a trip to heaven. We became demanding and then discouraged. We assumed that everyone but us was contentedly married to a centerfold. We felt cheated as we got diminishing returns on our investments.

Many men opened their eyes to new possibilities they hadn't really considered before. Why not try out a new number, since this one's not up to the norm? I deserve the best. Some got rid of the steady little woman for a new vision that promised paradise, only to find when she moved in that she became a rerun of the old flick.

From the book *Divorced in America* we find these words: "Once, people suffered sexual shortcomings in their partners, and, while these shortcomings might be difficult to live with, they were nonetheless generally deemed endurable. If love was there to begin with, making love posed no great problem. Sex itself had not yet become a highly compartmentalized activity like high-jumping; medals were not yet handed out for performance: people did not as yet feel so clearly deprived, as they would later, if on the sexual side their lives fell somewhat short of The Arabian Nights....

"Instead of deepened and enriched relationships, instead of shedding guilt and developing inwardly, we have today the Bedroom Olympics, with the accompanying tyranny of performance, unreal expectations and misplaced salvationism....

"Perhaps nowhere is more asked of sex than in marriage, yet perhaps no other institution is less set up to deal with the modern sexual imagination. The ideal of the modern sexual imagination is variety and multiplicity. But in marriage—theoretically, at least—one person must serve where multitudes are forbidden. One's wife must be not only a good mother, cook and housekeeper, but a terrific sex partner. One's husband must not only be a good father, provider and companion, but give full satisfaction at night. Old dogs are under the constant obligation to learn new tricks."

When are we going to settle down and be lovable old dogs content with the bones at hand?

Has all this emphasis on performance improved American marriages? Obviously not. Instead, families are floundering and affairs are abounding.

In the last few years we have spent much of our time trying to piece together the remnants of broken hearts and bandage up the bodies felled by unrealistic expectations.

Imagine our amazement when we found out that even Masters and Johnson have admitted that the sexual revolution has not lived up to its promise. In an article from the Gannett News Service about their book *The Pleasure Bond* we read:

> "The cure for an unhappy sex life doesn't begin in the bedroom," say Drs. William H. Masters and Virginia E. Johnson. Rather, they say, it's rooted in a warm, loving relationship and in the couple's ability to communicate love and affection to each other in their everyday life.

> "The best way to maintain an effective sex life is to maintain a strong ability to communicate honest affection."

> "The best foundation for a good sex life," Dr. Johnson said, "is simply knowing your partner is for you in every respect. That they're on your side. Willing to put out for you. That they're not just giving to get. And that you can communicate openly, honestly, without fear." The pair obviously didn't follow their own advice because later they got divorced.

In each of these preceding statements we see the word "communicate" as a prerequisite to romance, and yet seldom do men ever connect the two! A recent survey said that the average couple spends 12 minutes a week in eye-to-eye communication. If this is true, no wonder some of you are better acquainted with your secretaries than your wives!

When your wife tries to share some constructive thought with you, how do you respond? Do you accept her word and pledge to work on it as a mature person would? Or do you give a defensive, overreactive comment that will teach her never to speak to you about problems again?

SHE: I wish you'd dress up more often.

HE: Okay, if that will make you happy. I'll wear a tux to dinner every night.

SHE: You really didn't behave at the party last night.

HE: All right, I'll take care of that. We'll never go to another party as long as we live.

Answers such as these convince a wife that you will never have any meaningful communication with her and that every attempt will be met by stinging sarcasm or an immature overreaction.

Many women I talk with say they gave up trying to engage in an exchange of ideas years ago and have been playing a role ever since, a false part that hides the anger, resentment, and rebellion underneath.

I played Florence Goodwife for years. Fred constantly proved me wrong or went overboard on his responses, so I learned to pretend to agree with him while bottling up my real feelings inside. My doctor once said to me, "You're playing a role in life, aren't you? On the surface you seem to be the perfect wife, but I can see the tensions underneath."

I shared with him how Fred was impossible to talk with and I had learned to say yes and to shut up. Years later, when I took a personality test to go on staff at Campus Crusade, the psychologist told me, "Your results show you have a very rebellious spirit."

In a strong and defiant tone I said to the psychologist, "I do not have a rebellious spirit!" I had played the role so well that Fred did not recognize my problem either, and he defended me. "She definitely does not have a rebellious spirit."

The psychologist shrugged his shoulders and admitted that he could possibly be wrong, but he wasn't. As I began to think about his statement, I realized how much anger I had churning inside me and how I had suppressed any independent opinion because I knew that Fred would prove me wrong. I had learned to live with Fred in peace by never uttering a controversial word. I had existed in external submission but inner rebellion.

No wonder going to bed with Fred was no thrill. No wonder I was glad when he was exhausted. No wonder I stayed up till midnight folding laundry.

When a woman can't have open communication verbally, she won't want to have it sexually. She may go through the paces, but you'll know it's all an act. At this point many men with damaged egos hunt for a new conquest who will satisfy them instead of searching their own marriage to find the heart of the problem.

What do you try when your love life dies? Do you anoint yourself with musk oil and buy her a bottle of vitamin E?

Listen to the nightly soap opera that we once created. You may think you've heard this song before.

5:30   As we tune in to "As the World Sinks," we find that Fred has had a bad day at the office. HE comes home tired thinking that HE has to work while Florence just stays home and does nothing. Fred arrives home and almost runs over the children's bikes lying in the driveway.

HE: (WHY CAN'T THESE KIDS PUT THEIR THINGS AWAY IN PROPER ORDER! I'VE SURE TOLD THEM ENOUGH. I'LL TRY ONE MORE TIME!)

Meanwhile, we learn that ...

Florence has had a bad day at home. SHE feels sorry that SHE has to carpool twice on Fridays, and even had to take Freddie to the emergency room for stitches today when SHE had planned to be at the missionary luncheon. SHE has just returned with ten bags of groceries that SHE had to carry in by herself, and SHE is struggling to get dinner while the children scream.

5:31   Fred blows the horn loud and long.

SHE: (OH, NO. THE OGRE'S HOME ALREADY.)

Lauren, Marita, and Freddie all run out fearfully to the driveway.

HE: "CAN'T YOU KIDS EVER LEARN ANYTHING?"

SHE: (HE HATES THE CHILDREN.)

Fred storms in and trips over the bags of groceries.

HE: "WHY'S ALL THIS STUFF ON THE FLOOR? WHAT HAVE YOU BEEN DOING ALL DAY?"

SHE: (FRED THINKS I DO NOTHING BUT WATCH SOAP OPERAS AND EAT CHOCOLATES. MAYBE I OUGHT TO TRY THAT SOMETIME.)

Fred defends his nasty disposition.

HE: "I'VE HAD A ROTTEN DAY."

SHE: (HE THINKS *THIS* WAS A PICNIC!)

Fred looks in the pot on the stove and slams down the cover.

HE: "WHY ARE YOU MAKING STEW? THAT'S WHAT I HAD FOR LUNCH."

SHE: (YOU'RE LUCKY YOU HAD *TIME* FOR LUNCH!)

HE: "KEEP THE KIDS OUT OF THE LIVING ROOM. I NEED A LITTLE PEACE AND QUIET."

Florence salutes.

SHE: "YES, YOUR HIGHNESS." (HE NEEDS A LITTLE PEACE AND QUIET! WHAT ABOUT ME?)

Fred passes by the bedroom.

HE: "HOW COME THE BED'S NOT MADE? DID YOU JUST GET UP?"

SHE: (JUST GET UP? HE SHOULD FOLLOW ME AROUND ALL DAY AND SEE WHAT I DO. HE THINKS I'M LAZY, WHILE I'M KILLING MYSELF FOR HIM.)

Fred tries to relax and keeps sending the children out of the room.

Florence storms around getting dinner, slamming pots and hoping the kids will bother him.

SHE: "DINNER'S ON THE TABLE."

HE: "IT'S ABOUT TIME. I'M STARVING."

SHE: (IF HE'D LIFT A FINGER TO HELP, IT WOULDN'T TAKE SO LONG. HE THINKS I'M SLOW.)

HE: "YOU FORGOT THE NAPKINS AGAIN."

SHE: (HE COULD JUST GET UP AND GET THEM IF HE REALLY CARED ABOUT ME. HE THINKS I CAN'T REMEMBER ANYTHING.)

HE: "DON'T YOU KIDS HAVE ANY MANNERS?"

SHE: (HE'S PICKING ON THEM AGAIN. HE THINKS I'M A BAD MOTHER.)

HE: "MY *MOTHER* MAKES GREAT STEW."

SHE: (SO GO TO YOUR MOTHER. SHE HAS NOTHING TO DO ALL DAY BUT COOK.)

HE: "ICE CREAM AGAIN! COULDN'T WE HAVE CHOCOLATE CAKE ONCE IN A WHILE?"

SHE: (I SHOULD HAVE SUCH TIME TO BAKE!)

HE: "WATCH OUT FOR YOUR MILK, MARITA! THERE IT GOES! CAN'T YOU WATCH WHAT YOU'RE DOING?"

SHE: (HE COULD HAVE GRABBED IT—HE HATES THE CHILDREN.)

HE: "I'VE GOT SOME IMPORTANT PHONE CALLS TO MAKE AND THEN I'M GOING TO TURN ON THE TV. ANYTHING WOULD BE RELAXING AFTER THIS KIND OF MEAL."

SHE: (HE HATES US ALL.)

Lauren requests help with her homework.

HE: "ASK YOUR MOTHER. I HAVE TO THINK ALL DAY."

SHE: (DOES HE THINK IT TAKES NO BRAINS TO RUN THIS PLACE?)

Fred locks himself in the study and later he lies in the recliner and watches TV. Florence does the dishes, helps with the homework, gets the children to bed, and washes the kitchen floor. Fred alternates between laughing and snoring. Florence reviews the day in her mind.

SHE: (HE'S AN OGRE. NOTHING PLEASES HIM. HE HATES THE CHILDREN, HE THINKS I'M LAZY, A BAD COOK, SLOW, FORGETFUL, STUPID. HE THINKS I'M A FAILURE COMPARED TO HIS MOTHER. HE NEVER LISTENS TO ME. HE HATES US ALL. WHY DON'T I RUN AWAY WHERE SOMEONE WILL APPRECIATE ME?)

Fred watches the conclusion of *Charlie's Angels,* rises romantically from his chair, grabs Florence (who is passing by with an armload of laundry), and whispers in her ear.

HE: "COME ON, LOVER, LET'S GET TO BED."

Florence kicks him and screams.

SHE: "TAKE YOUR HANDS OFF ME, YOU BRUTE!"

Does this scene sound familiar? Are you standing by while your wife is sinking? Going down for the third time?

Let's write a new script which will get your world turning again in the right direction.

REMEMBER: TO HAVE A PLEASING WIFE, YOU MUST FIRST BE A LOVING HUSBAND.

Fred was not a loving husband. Although he always looked handsome, provided well for the family, and was highly respected in the community, I knew he didn't put me first in his life. I felt he didn't care what I thought because he had all the answers, and he never felt I accomplished enough even though I knew I ran circles around all my friends. I used to say to myself, "He ought to be married to *her* for a while and he'd appreciate me."

I was not a pleasing wife. I tried at first, but when I found that he criticized my very best efforts and proved me wrong in any situation, I gave up. I can't please him anyway, so why try?

Our world was sinking. What happened? Fred decided that change in the home starts with Fred.

All through our marriage Fred had worked on the premise that if only Florence would shape up, he could be happy. He had instructed me, prodded me, corrected me, directed me. His training program had been unloving and unwanted, and it had been established for his personal gain and contentment.

My feelings or desires were never considered, and I could hardly wait to get out of the house each day to spend time with my friends who liked me. I felt I had made sacrificial efforts in the past, but I had failed to please Fred and I had given up.

Within one year both Fred and I had, at separate times, committed our lives to the Lord Jesus. We were both desperately unhappy and we were looking for any change that would improve our lives. As I began to study the Bible, I changed many of my attitudes about my children, myself, and my friends; but because I had been so hurt by Fred for so long, I worked at being cold and hard with him, even though my heart was softening toward others.

As Fred plunged into his new Christian life, he prayed and asked God to show him where he was wrong. I'm sure he didn't expect much of an answer, but he kept getting the message, "You've been a difficult and critical husband. Stop trying to make Florence into a perfect wife and start making yourself into a loving husband."

Since we didn't communicate in those days any deeper than "Pass the salt," neither one of us told the other of our dedication to the Lord. I kept my Christianity in the closet, but Fred put his into action.

The first change I noticed was with the toys in the driveway. Every night Fred would blow his horn loudly to let us know he was home, and if we didn't all race out and move the bikes, I was afraid he would run over them. I knew I should pick them up before he arrived, but I got sadistic pleasure out of seeing him seethe over a barricade of bikes. I would scream "The Ogre's home!" and we would all plunge out the front door. I'd let them know I didn't care *where* they put their toys—it was only their fussy father who was fuming.

One day Fred drove home and parked in the street. He quietly picked up all the toys and put them away. Unaccustomed to such a peaceful arrival, we all stood in silence. No one made a comment. From then on each night he parked in the street and I pretended I didn't notice the change.

Once I was convinced that he wasn't going to scream about the toys anymore, I began to pick them up.

Fred had been trained when he worked for Stouffer's Restaurants to notice everything wrong in any room, and he had a natural talent for negative observation. His entrance into the house each evening was accompanied by a curt commentary on constructive changes I should make. His field was food, and so every lid was lifted and each tidbit tasted. Because he had trained me for so many years, I was a gourmet cook, but there was never a dish that didn't deserve some improvement.

Imagine my surprise when Fred walked in one night with a smile on his face and told me he liked my new dress, he thought the house looked great, and he could tell from the aroma alone that the Stroganoff would be superb! I stood there shocked and waited for him to trip on a truck. Instead, he picked it up and asked, "Is there anything I can do to help you with dinner?"

"Aha, I'll test him," I thought. "I'll give him a big list." He quickly set the table, gathered the children, washed their hands, settled them at the table, dished up the dinner, and asked us how our day had been. We were too amazed to talk. During dinner he didn't notice that Lauren avoided her carrots, he quietly mopped up Marita's milk, and he let Freddie go to the bathroom twice. He complimented me on the meal, disciplined no one, and gave no instructions on how we could have done anything better.

I pretended I didn't notice the change.

Each night I would give him a list of things to do to test him. He did them all cheerfully. After a while I began my dinner preparations earlier, and I set the table ahead of time and had the children clean. When he asked how he could help, I said, "It's all done, just sit and relax."

He was right back where he had started from. He was relaxing while I was serving dinner. But what was the difference? He was sitting with my approval. Once I was convinced he would help me, I didn't need his help.

One night Fred said, "We haven't had enough time to converse with each other. Let's set aside the hour after dinner and go to our room alone."

"You mean before you do your phoning?" I asked.

The first night I talked nonstop for over an hour, the second night an hour, the third night 30 minutes, and by the fourth night I didn't have much to say. It was amazing how my feelings changed. Once I knew Fred would listen, I no longer had a compulsion to converse.

Men, do you see a pattern here?

> When you criticize us, we get worse.
> When you compliment us, we get better.
> When you try to change us, we won't budge.
> When you accept us as we are, we try to improve.
> When you don't help us, we're mad because you're sitting.
> When you're willing to assist, we insist that you sit down.
> When you pick on the children, we think you hate us.
> When you are positive and encouraging, we know you love us.
> When you are too busy to listen, we nag and ramble.
> When you set aside time to converse, we condense our comments.

We're really so easy to please when you love us. You can turn our whole lives around when you let us know we come first.

As Fred continued to show me unconditional love for the first time in our marriage, I was doubtful that his changes could last. One day I decided to test him. I called his office and said, "Fred, I need you at home immediately."

"I'll be right there," he replied and hung up.

"I quickly dialed back to tell him I was just kidding, but he had already left. I spent a dreadful ten minutes trying to work up an emergency, but I couldn't come up with one. I ran out to the car as he drove up and confessed that there was no problem. I was just testing him. I expected either a blowup or a lecture, but instead he said, "I don't blame you."

I knew that Fred had changed, but I pretended I didn't notice.

One day Fred took my Ford to be fixed and left me his Lincoln. As I got in his car, I saw a 3×5 card taped to the dashboard. On it was printed PRAISE FLO.

For the first time my heart began to melt. I realized that it had been so hard for him to find something good to say about me that he had needed to put up a reminder. I sat in the car and cried.

For one year I resisted Fred's new charm, I tested his new sincerity, and I pretended not to notice his changes. I was cold and unresponsive. I was not going to forgive or forget years of emotional neglect so easily.

But Fred was willing to love me unconditionally, expecting nothing in return, and eventually I realized that the change in his life was real.

I knelt down beside my bed and asked God to cause me to fall in love with my husband. When I was willing, He was able.

Don't be discouraged, men, if you make all the improvements and she seems unwilling to respond. Years of hurt feelings can't be repaired overnight. You be the one to start. Show her that she comes first in your life, and she won't be able to resist you.

When your wife is doubtful of your love, she'll demand things.

When she knows you love her unconditionally, she won't care what else she owns.

When you *are* a loving husband you will *produce* a pleasing wife.

"Whatsoever a man soweth, that shall he also reap. . . . Let us not be weary in well-doing, for in due season we shall reap if we faint not" (Galatians 6:7,9).

REMEMBER: If you want heaven at eleven start before seven!

14

🪷

WHAT ABOUT THE
OTHER WOMAN?

In the past we dear Christian ladies have tried to avoid considering the possibility of the OTHER WOMAN. While *Cosmopolitan* is constantly concerned with the coquette, we have assumed that if our husband passes the cup on Sunday, he will pass up the cutie on Monday. As we have buried our heads alternately in the sink and the Scriptures, we have believed that our stable, substantial mates would appreciate our devotion to housework and mothering, and not expect us spiritual women to be sex kittens as well. We figured if we got meals on the table and suits home from the cleaners, we were holding our own. Sisters, that's not enough anymore.

With the blatant acceptability of "afternoon delights," sexual siestas seem to be replacing the salami sandwich. While we expect our husbands to be above this kind of thing, it is possible that a man who is upright today may be lying down tomorrow.

But those are worldly men, you say. Could this happen with my good pillar of the church? With Christian leaders openly leaving their wives for fresher fruits, the answer is an unfortunate yes. It could happen to the best of us.

The difference between a man of the world and of the Lord is that the latter has to come up with a scriptural excuse. I've heard some very creative approaches to infidelity.

Tim stated, "The Lord wants my joy to be full but my wife leaves me empty. How can it be wrong for me to love another woman when it seems so good and I don't feel guilty about it? Surely if the Lord disapproved He would give me a guilty conscience."

Ken, a Christian entertainer, asked his wife to participate in group sex. When she recoiled in horror he said, "It's scriptural— that's what David and Solomon did with all those women."

Jack explained that it was all right to leave his wife Ann and five children for his secretary because he was not a Christian when he married Ann; therefore, he was not truly married to her at all in God's sight. This line of reasoning gave him assurance that it was acceptable to start life afresh with the Lord's blessing, and he didn't seem to care that this theory would leave his five children fatherless.

The most colorful spiritual excuse for straying came from a beautiful but bewildered woman. Shirley came up to me after a seminar and told me this true and unbelievable tale. She had recently found out that her husband, an elder in the church, had been "visiting" certain women while their husbands were out of town. When she confronted him with this knowledge, he admitted that he had done more than converse, but he knew his actions were God's will for his life. He had looked at her in a condescending way and explained, as if to a spiritual simpleton, that God had given him a special talent to satisfy women whose husbands were unfulfilling. He was only exercising his gift and establishing a ministry to miserable women. What a gift! Surely more fun than the gift of helps or compassion. What a ministry! Sure to sweep the country and make believers out of skeptics.

The most amazing angle to this story is that he had made this service sound so sincere and acceptable. His wife looked up at me and asked, "Is this *really* a spiritual gift?"

What can we women do?

The best defense is a constant offense, for none of us is immune. The lazy and lethargic mate can become a lunging Lothario under proper provocation.

We must ask ourselves this question: If he wanted someone to light up his life, what kind of flame would he find? What would the *other woman* have that I don't have? What would she do that I don't do?

Amazingly, most men choose women who are just like we used to be before they wore us down trying to remake us. It's hard for a mother surrounded by screaming children to look as sexy and serene as the secretary who spent a quiet hour on her makeup. It's wrong for a man to reject a wife who has struggled through poor times and put up with the quirks of his mother just as he makes it to the top and can travel to Tahiti.

But who said life was fair? We must assess ourselves and take preventive measures.

1. What would the other woman have that I don't have?

How about *looks?* Have you given yourself a critical exam lately? Or have you taken for granted that he'll accept you as you are just because he should?

One woman with a pretty face but a chubby body couldn't figure out why her husband was always staring at other women. I asked, "Has he ever mentioned your weight?"

"Oh, yes," she replied, "but I didn't think it mattered that much."

When a woman is heavy and out of shape she is communicating to her husband that she doesn't care enough for him to look good. When she wears rollers at home and fluffs her hair for her friends, he feels second-rate.

So many women I talk with are candidates for a *McCall's* makeover, but so many wait until he's left before disciplining themselves into action. What about your *looks?*

What about your *brain?* Is it in gear? Do you know what's going on in the world? Do you show interest in your husband's business or work? Do you entertain friends once in a while? Can you tell the difference between the stock market and the stockyards? Do you know the margin of profits from the margin on a typewriter? So often the man climbs up the business ladder and the little woman never catches up. He's in a board room all day and a bored room all night.

So how about your *brain?* Is it on high or just on simmer?

What about your *attitude?*

Are you a delight to come home to or are you devoid of a positive thought? Do you greet him at the door with a kiss or a complaint? One man told me, "My wife has not said an encouraging or cheerful word in years." One said, "I couldn't please her if I gave her the entire State of California." Another said, "Her head is full of long lists of my failures."

If your husband were open for a new option, would she be slim and shapely? Would she be coherent and articulate? Would she be positive and cheerful?

Whatever he might desire in a new woman later he'd rather have in you *now*. Think about it.

2. What would the other woman do that I don't do?

Sometimes a woman who is attractive, intelligent, and successful gets jilted for what appears to be a vastly inferior replacement. It doesn't seem to make sense, but a man may leave a woman who has everything, including the admiration of the Christian community. As he slinks off with the second soprano in the church choir, people ask, "What does he see in her?" The answer is not what he sees in her but what she sees in him. The answer lies in **HOW SHE MAKES HIM FEEL**. She sees possibilities, she see virility, she sees a real man. His superwife is so busy being wonderful that she has little time for him. She is such a star that he feels inferior and left out. She is so happy receiving praise that she never thinks of giving it.

What would the other woman do that I don't do? She would encourage him. She would look at him as if he were the most important person in the world. She would take time to focus on *him,* not just on the family and friends. She would be loving, warm, and romantic.

If there's something your husband wants you to do, he's probably mentioned it before. Were you listening? Were you willing? Ask your husband what he'd want if he could choose another woman, and then keep quiet while he tells you. Why not become the *other woman* yourself and eliminate the chance for competition? It's better to *be* the other woman today than to *see* her tomorrow.

3. Where would they meet that I can't match?

The typical lover's rendezvous is held in a haven of beauty with bowers of flowers. Soft music sets the mood and serenity floats over the satin sheets. How does this compare to your bedroom? Does your husband have to trip over an ironing board to get to the bed? Does he have to fold up laundry to find the sheets? Are there cobwebs over the stereo? Are there piles of old magazines in the corners waiting for your attention? Are your dirty clothes draped over the chairs on their way to the washer? Is there hair all over the sink and toothpaste on the mirror? Is there a dead rose in a bud vase and a yellow philodendron gasping its death pangs?

Recently some friends and I visited a home where the hostess took us on a tour. The house had been in rundown condition when they bought it, and she and her husband had been busy renovating it. We all appreciated their work, but when we got to the master bedroom we all gasped in unison. It was breathtaking. The wallpaper was in apple green with little white flowers, and the headboard and chairs were white wicker. Baskets of ferns hung by the windows, and a ceramic cat slept next to a pot of yellow chrysanthemums. The furniture was not expensive, and they had done the work themselves, but the effect was so inviting that we wanted to settle right in. As we all stood commenting one girl said, "I'm redoing my house also, but I'm leaving the bedroom till last because no one ever sees that."

What a mistake! When the bedroom is left till last we communicate to our husband that our friends are more important than he is. One Christian speaker told me that her bedroom is always a mess because she does all her studying and correspondence in there so it won't show. The living room is lovely, but the bedroom is a clutter. How about your bedroom? Is it a restful, relaxing retreat for you and your husband?

If MGM wanted to make a movie in your town, would they choose your bedroom for the love scenes?

What If It Is Too Late?

We all dread the day when our husband tells us it's all over, when he packs up his pants to move in with our best friend, when a bosomy ballerina dances on stage and they plan to pirouette off into the wings of life forever.

He will make typical statements:

"I don't think I ever loved you."

"I don't think you ever loved me."

"She *really* loves me."

What are you to do?

Before a man comes home to make the fatal announcement, he has analyzed all of your possible reactions. He already feels guilty and he doesn't know how he got himself into this mess. He is hopeful that you will validate his decision by reacting in a predictable way. He wants either a quick agreement—we don't love each other so let's make a peaceful settlement—or a violent screaming scene, which will justify his actions and show you to be immature and unstable, as he has already told the Other Woman that you are.

What is a wife in this position to do to change her husband's mind and hold the home together?

Don't

1. Don't believe it's the end.

While the situation seems hopeless at the moment, if you handle it well it may be a time of meaningful and open communication. For once your husband has caught your undivided attention. Listen to him. Ask him where you've failed him. Ask him for specific needs where you've neglected him.

2. Don't jump on the defensive.

The automatic response is to tell him what a rat he is and how all your faults really stem from his bad behavior. This reaction guarantees a fight in which you both tear each other to shreds. It takes two to create a problem, and you must have had something to do with his desire to leave. Listen; don't argue.

3. Don't review the men in your past.

When we women are hurt, we want to hurt back, so we try to equal his story. One man told me he would have gone back to his wife but after she told him in detail of an affair she'd had, he rejected her for good. Don't turn this into a True Confessions hour or you'll wipe out all hope.

4. Don't believe everything he says.

He wants you to agree that there never was any love between you and that there is no hope for a reconciliation, but don't allow yourself to accept this. He has to say the worst things he can come up with about you and your marriage to convince himself that it's all right to leave. Underneath he's no doubt a decent man who in the past has been critical of other men who have left their wives. He didn't plan this and he has to dump on you to justify his actions. Don't retaliate.

5. Don't run off and get a lawyer immediately.

Many women I've counseled made the mistake of running to a lawyer immediately, proving to their husbands that a separation was the best plan for both. If he goes, there is nothing you can do to stop him, but don't you make the first move if you have any hope of keeping the marriage together. When he is serving you with divorce papers, you will need some legal counsel.

6. Don't attack the Other Woman.

Any attack you make causes him to rise in her defense and move against you. One woman I talked with had gone to the Other Woman's apartment, climbed up a fire escape and through a window, and filled the bed with carpet tacks. One let air out of the Other Woman's tire, and one had a thornbush delivered to her office. While these may be cute pranks, they'll infuriate your husband and effectively cut off any hope for reconciliation.

7. Don't turn your children against him.

Never rant to the children about their adulterous father and the slut he's sleeping with. As he becomes aware of what you're saying, he will attack you back in front of them and vicious war will ensue. Also, you will have so hurt your husband's reputation with the children that if he should return he will have great difficulty establishing respect again. And remember, even though he may never return, he will always be the children's father!

8. Don't say things you'll regret later.

Sometimes in the heat of battle we dig way down to find the most insulting words imaginable and dump them on our partner. Once these hurts are out we can never recall them. Later, when we try to make up, we find ourselves faced with an unpleasant review of our own caustic comments.

9. Don't tell your friends about the affair.

Although our impulse when hit with rotten news is to run and tell all our friends so they can commiserate with us, this is usually a mistake. The more people who know the less chance there is of getting back together. Men hate to be the object of gossip, even if they deserve it, and your husband will appreciate a tongue held in restraint. You never have to retract words you never said.

10. Don't get the whole church to pray for him.

A man who is committing adultery is already out of fellowship with God. He has feelings of guilt, even if he won't admit it, and the catalyst for divorce is his hearing that the church is praying for him as a fallen sinner. I know one man who found out the saints were interceding and tore through the house ripping up his wife's Bibles in a rage. He divorced her and never went to church again. Instead, you pray. You pray diligently, and perhaps share your prayers with a trusted friend.

Do

1. Do know that God is on your side.

Isn't that a comfort? God is never in favor of breaking up one of His families. This thought is completely contrary to His nature and His Scripture, and He will work with you to restore your marriage. God wants to heal this rift and bring you both back together, but He will need your cooperation.

2. Do let your husband know that you love him.

Although the news is shocking and your instant reaction is one of revulsion, keep telling him you love him and will fight for him. This will stun him, as he has already decided that you don't love him and perhaps even that you'll be glad to have him leave. He doesn't think you care enough to fight for him, but be warmly persistent: You do love him and you will hang in there no matter what. Underneath his refusal to believe this will be the fresh thought that there might be some hope for your marriage after all. Keep feeding this possibility, as it may be the best thing you have going for you.

3. Do let him know that you understand.

If you can agree that he had some reason to look around, you have made a big step in the right direction. You will surely never win by calling him adulterous and pointing out his immorality and sin. If he thinks you could and would forgive him, he is more apt to reconsider his future.

4. Do ask God to show you specific weaknesses.

As you go to God in prayer, ask Him to show you specific areas in your life that have caused this to happen. Don't waste prayer time on shaping up Harry; use it to beg God for His mercy in your life and His revelation to you of your innate weaknesses.

One woman I suggested this to asked, "What if I pray to improve and work hard remaking myself and lose him anyway?" I thought that this was an interesting fear, since we can never get worse while getting better! Once God has shown you the specific areas where you have failed your husband, go to him, review them with him, and ask him to forgive you. I know this idea is contrary to what the world is telling us today, but it is consistent with God's plan for our lives. He wants us to examine ourselves and ask forgiveness no matter what our mate has done. Don't give general comments such as—

> "I'm sorry I've been awful."
> "Forgive me for not being a good wife."
> "I'll try to do better if you'll come back."

Be specific:

> "I'm sorry I was lazy and never got up to make your breakfast."
> "I'm sorry I gained ten pounds with each baby and never took it off."
> "I'm sorry I complain about every move you make."
> "I'm sorry I'm never home when you call because I'm down at the church so much."

Ask God to show you specific areas of your weakness, and then confess them to God and your partner. If God shows you one which seems insignificant to you, don't say, "Oh no, God. Surely that little thing is no problem." It's quite possible that this little thing is just what's irked your husband for years.

5. Do be patient with him.

It is only natural that we look for a quick change. We feel that if we've confessed our errors he should come right back and forget the Other Woman instantly. But men are not apt to move so fast. It took years of eroding to get to this point, and it may take a long time for him to believe that you are willing and able to change.

Proverbs 25:15 says, "Patient persuasion can break down the strongest resistance and can convince even rulers" (TEV).

6. Do include him as the children's father.

Many women want to throw the straying husband out and refuse to let him in the door until he repents; however, meeting with the children will remind him of his responsibilities. Do everything in your power to make yourself and your home attractive; make his visits positive and not times for complaining, and let him know that he is still your husband and that the marriage bed awaits him when he returns, both physically and emotionally, but not before. If there are no changes and he is verbally abusive to you, you may need to cease any visits inside the house.

7. Do look at this as a growing period.

While your husband is preoccupied, use this time in the pursuit of positive improvements. Thank God for lonely hours when you can study His Word for direction, when you can open your mind to new ideas, when you can exercise and improve your eating habits. Remember, God promises that all things work together for good for those who love the Lord and are called according to His purpose (Romans 8:28). The problem itself may not be good, but God can redeem your time in the midst of it.

8. Do maintain a sense of humor.

Although you may feel like crying all the time, pray for a light touch and a pleasant word. A man is more apt to return to a bright wife than a sniveling woman. Surely the Other Woman is smart enough to make life fun for him, so why not try yourself to look at the whole scene with a sense of humor? It can't hurt.

9. Do pray for the Other Woman.

It is only natural to hate the Other Woman even if she's your best friend—in fact, *especially* if she's your best friend—but a root of bitterness grows quickly into a hostile spirit that may ruin your life. Don't give her that much control over you. Ask God to remove your hostile feelings and work out His will in her life. Don't rant about her to your children. Don't let your mind be fixed upon her. Don't waste time following her around and checking on her daily routine. Give her happily to the Lord, for He has plans for her. In Proverbs God speaks often of the adulterous woman.

> The lips of another man's wife may be as sweet as honey and her kisses as smooth as olive oil, but when it is all over, she leaves you nothing but bitterness and pain (Proverbs 5:3,4 TEV).

> You will be able to resist any immoral woman who tries to seduce you with her smooth talk, who is faithless to her own husband and forgets her sacred vows. If you go to her house, you are traveling the road to death. To go there is to approach the world of death (Proverbs 2:16-18 TEV).

Give the Other Woman into God's hands, and you become what He has in mind for you.

10. Do work to become pleasing to the Lord.

Focus your attention on what God is trying to tell you in these adverse circumstances. He never allows anything to happen to us that we cannot learn from or that will not lead to some good end. Practice pleasing the Lord, for He is husband to the husbandless. Do all things heartily as unto the Lord. Don't spend your time seeking worldly pleasure or heading out to singles bars; use this period in your life to seek God's perfect will for you, for—

197

When you please the Lord, you can make your enemies into friends (Proverbs 16:7 TEV).

Even though the world is promoting infidelity, it will never be God's norm.

Your situation may look hopeless now, but God is able.

Every test that you have experienced is the kind that normally comes to people. But God keeps his promise, and he will not allow you to be tested beyond your power to remain firm; at the time you are put to the test he will give you the strength to endure it, and so provide you with a way out (1 Corinthians 10:13 TEV).

Remember, you can't but God can!

15

ALL WE LIKE SHEEP HAVE GONE ASTRAY

No good Christian woman gets up in the morning, looks out the window, and says "My, this is a lovely day! I guess I'll go out and commit adultery." Yet I've talked to many who did. No good Christian man wants to abandon his family for a clandestine relationship. Yet the Other Woman is a national problem.

A few years ago I would never have thought that the subject of adultery was anything to mention in a Christian book. I was brought up to believe that nice girls and boys from good homes didn't even think about such things. As a teenager I not only didn't succumb to temptations but I didn't even know there were any. I got married two weeks before my 25th birthday, innocent and pure as the driven snow. I hadn't even read a dirty book.

In my 44 years of marriage I've been propositioned once by a shirt salesman who won me by the toss of a coin as I walked through the lobby of a hotel while attending the League of Women Voter's national convention. I sent him back to play with his shirts. I was once locked in an office by an interior decorator who wanted to dance with me at high noon while we were picking out light fixtures, and I once had to draw the drapes on a cement contractor who was peering in my bedroom window while pouring a patio. Hardly the material needed to write a racy novel!

Then how did I begin to speak on the subject of adultery? Several years ago I wrote a lesson on forgiveness and used the story of David as an example. As I studied David I found a good man who got into trouble, much like Eve (a good woman who didn't mean to go astray).

David was a spiritual giant who knew the Scriptures and taught them to others. He was handsome, talented, musical, poetic, and regal, yet he violated three of the ten commandments. He coveted his neighbor's wife, committed adultery, and plotted the murder of her husband. When the enormity of his sin engulfed him, he cried out to God for forgiveness.

When I finished sharing this message with some women at a weekend retreat, the reaction was surprising. Worried women sought me out in dim corners to confess their various adulteries. I listened wide-eyed to their tales. One woman was having an affair with the organist, who had fashioned a bed from a blanket thrown over cases of old hymnbooks. On Wednesday afternoons they cuddled on the cartons in a small storage space behind the organ pipes.

Another well-meaning woman went over to help a bereaved widower with his housework. As she put some new jungle-print sheets on his bed, he showed up to help her and tried to tangle her up with the tigers.

I soon shifted the lesson on forgiveness to a message called "How Good People Get into Trouble." In 2 Samuel chapter 11 we see how David, a man after God's own heart, went astray. Perhaps you've followed these same steps.

Verse 1 tells us that it was the time of year when kings go forth to battle, but David sent Joab and the troops while he stayed home in Jerusalem. David knew what he was supposed to do but he didn't feel like doing it. David was above the menial tasks of life. He was made for better things than this. David's first step toward trouble was:

1. David wasn't where God wanted him to be.

Has that ever happened to you? Have you ever gone where you knew God didn't want you to be? We wouldn't get into trouble if we stayed where God wanted us to be.

> But that's so dull,
> doing the expected and the right.
> Why not play around,
> just for tonight?

With television making the world look like one vast Love Boat of beautiful people peering at life through rose-colored portholes, we begin to feel left out.

> Same old Fred?
> Try another bed.

The first step to trouble is when we leave God's will for our life and create our own. David stayed home when he should have gone to work. Since he was loafing around all day, he wasn't tired at night. He didn't have television to amuse him with old movies, so he took a walk on his roof. What a good idea! As a fiddler played romantic music, David's eyes wandered over the edge of the roof, and lo and behold there was a beautiful woman taking a bath (verse 2).

If David had been at battle, where he belonged, he would not have seen Bathsheba at her nocturnal ablutions, but he had taken the first step, which then led to the second.

2. Temptation appeared.

Religious people like to feel that temptation comes dressed in a red suit with a pitchfork and wears a big sign saying "sin," but that's not true. Temptation comes attractively packaged or, as in Bathsheba's case, with nothing on at all, which apparently was attractive packaging!

When we are truly believing Christians and know that God has a plan for us, He works to keep us out of trouble. Even if we're not in the right place at the right time and even if temptation does appear, God gives us an opportunity to back out before it's too late.

David inquired after the woman and found out that this vision of loveliness was married (verse 3). God had given David many women, but he knew better than to take the wife of his next-door neighbor. But forbidden fruit is always the sweetest, so David ignored the second chance that God gave him and he sent for Bathsheba, the wife of Uriah. David coveted his neighbor's wife.

3. David committed adultery.

David didn't set out to get into trouble. As the spiritual leader of his country he knew what God expected of him, but he didn't go where he was supposed to be. Then temptation appeared and he jumped at the opportunity. When he was through with Bathsheba he sent her back to her house. He didn't even take her out for breakfast! He just sent her home (verse 4).

Then came the call, the words which most philandering males dread to hear: "Guess what David—I'm pregnant" (verse 5).

4. David was struck with guilt.

What's a man to do? Since David is king, he has nothing to fear. He'll think of a way out to ease his conscience.

As so many of our government officials have felt, "I'm really above the law. I make it, I can break it."

David comes up with Plan A: bring Bathsheba's husband home from the battle, send him into his wife, and David's troubles are over (verse 6). How simple! David is proud that he thought of this because it would be a little embarrassing to have Uriah come home next year and find an unexpected baby.

Notice how friendly David is with this common soldier, a man so insignificant that even though he and Bathsheba had lived next door for years, David didn't even know their names. When Uriah comes in, no doubt amazed that he has been brought before the king, David asks, "How's the war going?" (verse 7). They pass the time of day as old buddies and then David sends him on his way. "Go home to your wife, and as a reward for your devotion to duty I'm sending along a prime-rib dinner for two" (verse 8).

Oh noble David!

At last a good night's sleep. David's troubles are over. How easy it is to overcome problems when you're the king! But morning is dawning and David is yawning when his servants come in with the morning paper and the news that Uriah never went into his house. There must be some mistake. Any full-blooded soldier brought in from weeks in the trenches would be thrilled to spend the night with Bathsheba. But not Uriah.

David can't believe his ears, so he sends for Uriah. Picture David in his bathrobe trying to talk calmly: "Why didn't you go home last night?"

Uriah answers, "With all my friends still encamped on open fields, I'd be a traitor to go in and enjoy the pleasures of my home and wife. I will not do this thing!"

Who's noble now? David had not counted on a man of principles. David would like to shake him and send him home, but he must stay calm. He asks Uriah to stick around another day, and David begins to plot out Plan B.

5. The cover-up got David into deeper trouble.

As with Watergate, the act was bad but the cover-up was worse. Have you ever told one little lie only to be forced into many larger ones to protect the first? When we knowingly disobey God's plan for our life, we are headed for trouble. David's trouble got deeper and deeper and he had to institute Plan B: If Uriah's too nice to go home to Bathsheba sober, let's get him drunk (verse 13). Why, David is that you? Is that our spiritual leader planning to get Uriah drunk?

Why, yes, it is. David had an intimate palace party with his pal Uriah, and when the decent man was drunk David sent him home to his wife. Now good King David's woes are over, but look: He "went not down to his house." Uriah drunk is more noble than David sober! Plan B has failed.

Now David is desperate, so he comes up with Plan C: Have Uriah killed in battle. David would never murder—we all know that—but he *does* need to get Uriah out of the way. If only Uriah had gone along with Plan A or B he would not have been put in position C! It's really his own fault for being so above it all.

So David wrote a letter to Joab: "Set Uriah in the forefront of the hottest battle and retire from him, that he may be smitten and die" (verse 15). In his own hand David wrote the kiss of death for poor Uriah. I'm sure it wasn't easy. David didn't have a thing against Uriah, yet he issued the death warrant on an innocent man to cover up his own sin.

To save postage and get it there faster, David sent the letter in Uriah's own hand (verse 14). How could you, David? Then the news came back, "Uriah the Hittite is dead" (verse 24).

David's troubles are over! He's home free!

Bathsheba mourns the loss of her husband (verse 26), and David, wanting to do things properly, waits till the period of mourning is past before he marries her to live happily ever after.

David got away with it. Because he was in a position of authority he was able to manipulate circumstances to his advantage so that no one would be the wiser.

But the Bible says, "The thing that David had done displeased the Lord" (verse 27).

Have you ever done something you knew was wrong, worked cleverly to cover it up, and rejoiced that you had won? Yet underneath your heart told you that the thing you had done displeased the Lord.

David thought he had the victory—a beautiful new wife and a baby boy.

6. David got caught.

God sent Nathan the prophet to tell David this story (2 Samuel 12):

> There were two men in a city, one rich and one poor. The rich man had many flocks and the poor man had only one little pet lamb that was like his own daughter. When the rich man had company, he didn't want to use his own herd so he took the poor man's only lamb and killed it for dinner (paraphrased from verses 1-4).

When David heard this story he was furious and said, "As the Lord liveth, the man that hath done this thing shall surely die!" (verse 5).

Nathan replied, "Thou art the man!" (verse 7).

7. Although David was guilty, God forgave him.

Nathan then explained how God had loved David as his favorite son and had taken him from a little shepherd boy and made him king, and if that had been too little, God would have given him more (verse 8). David broke God's heart and he had to be punished, but Nathan said, "The Lord hath put away thy sin; thou shalt not die" (verse 13).

8. David was punished.

The baby died, David's children rose up against him, and his wives were given to his neighbor.

How *do* good people get into trouble?

1. They aren't where God wants them to be. Are you?
2. Temptation comes along.
3. They commit the sin.
4. They feel guilty.
5. The cover-up gets them in deeper.
6. They eventually get caught.
7. God forgives.
8. But they are punished.

Does the Bible have any advice about all this?

Yes.

David gives it himself in Psalm 51, written after his visit with Nathan. David knew he had sinned, and he cried out to God.

Have you yielded to temptation? Have you stepped into trouble with your eyes wide open? "All we like sheep have gone astray; we have turned each one to his own way" (Isaiah 53:6).

Perhaps you've strayed from the straight and narrow. Perhaps you ladies joined the choir to sing hymns and found some new notes that struck responsive chords. Perhaps you men counseled a frustrated damsel in distress and helped her a little too much.

What do you do when you've already strayed?

Try David's advice. Follow David's example (Psalm 51).

1. Ask God for mercy.

David says, "Have mercy upon me, O God, according to thy loving-kindness" (verse 1). When we ask for mercy this means that we know we don't deserve God's forgiveness, but we also know that He loves us enough to give it. We are never more appreciative of love than when we know we don't deserve it. This principle applies to your relationship with your partner whom you have hurt.

You beg for mercy, knowing you don't deserve it.

Your partner, through the love of God, forgives you.

You are so grateful for undeserved forgiveness that you love more deeply than ever before.

Your partner responds and the healing begins. Don't expect instant miracles, for the hurts are deep.

2. Admit your mistake.

"For I acknowledge my transgressions, and my sin is ever before me" (verse 3). David has a guilty conscience and he can't get his bad behavior out of his mind. He knows that to be rid of this black cloud hovering over him he must openly acknowledge his mistakes, and he does. Notice that he does not add a "however," as we are apt to do.

"I know I was wrong; however, anyone married to you would have done the same thing." God wants us to admit that we have sinned and not try to water down the act with howevers.

Our mate needs to hear the same words from our lips as David spoke if we hope to reconcile our marriage. It takes a mature person to admit the complete blame for the problem without casting a few howevers of correlating responsibility on his partner.

3. Tell the truth.

"Behold, thou desirest truth in the inward parts" (verse 6). God wants to hear the truth out in the open. David knew he had been deceptive. In coming clean with our partner we do not need to add details that will ruin the possibilities of recovery and will make the whole scene so vivid that our mate will never get it out of his or her mind. The aim is to heal, not to hurt. We should "tell the truth in love."

4. Be willing to change.

"Wash me ... cleanse me ... purge me ... hide thy face from my sins, and blot out my iniquities. Create in me a clean heart" (verses 2,7,9,10). David felt dirty from his sin. He asked God to wash him clean. Once we have asked for mercy, admitted our mistakes, and told the truth, we have taken care of the past. Now it's time to clean up ourselves, get our head straight, and live right.

To start, ask your partner to *share* with you all the things you should do differently, and write them down without argument or defense.

At this point do not make deals, such as "I'll do this if you'll do that." Be mature. This is *your* sin that has to be dealt with even if you feel your partner contributed to it. *You* make plans on restructuring your life and pleasing your partner. To insist that your mate change at this moment of your sin is only a childish way to ease your guilt and keep you from shouldering the blame. Be willing to make all the improvements, and let God work in your partner's heart in due time. Chances are that if your mate sees genuine shifts in a positive direction, he or she will more easily forgive and forget and will also want to improve.

5. Restore fellowship with God and your partner.

"Renew a right spirit within me" (verse 10). When we openly disobey God's clear rules for our life, we fall out of fellowship with God. When we realize our errors and confess our sins, we are restored. How uncomfortable we are when we have a wrong spirit within us and how deeply we desire to be renewed and have spiritual fellowship with God and our partner!

"Cast me not away from thy presence, and take not thy Holy Spirit from me" (verse 11). David asked God to renew him, to give him a right attitude. He begged God not to cast him out and not to remove the power of the Holy Spirit from him. (David had seen what happened to Saul when God took his power away. He had seen the deep depression, the irrational moods.) David knew that God had used his life greatly and lifted him up to the top position in the land, not on David's merits but on God's mercy.

6. Ask for the joy of the Lord.

"Restore unto me the joy of thy salvation, and uphold me with thy free Spirit" (verse 12). David had known what it was like to have fellowship with God. He had known the joy of the Lord, and he wanted it back. When we have openly sinned, as David did, and wounded our partner deeply, we cannot expect instant improvement or miracle cures. It takes time and trust to rebuild a relationship. But when we ask for the joy of the Lord, He will give it to us and it will begin to shine its healing rays on the hurts.

7. Thank God for your broken spirit.

"O Lord, open my lips, and my mouth shall show forth thy praise" (verse 15). David knew that he could bring sacrifices to God in repentance, or he could lay a lamb on the altar, or he could give money. He also knew that God is not impressed with our material possessions and our gifts but with our attitude. So often we find it easier to do with money and gifts what we won't do with our hearts. When we've hurt our partner or a friend, we'd rather send flowers than display a truly repentant spirit. Yet the Bible says, "The sacrifices of God are a broken spirit; a broken and a contrite heart, O God, thou wilt not despise" (verse 17).

How beautiful is a broken spirit, how appealing a man who has given up his will to God!

How touching is a contrite heart that cries out, "not my will but Thine!"

Never be ashamed to give up your pride and let down your walls of defense. Only then can the sun shine in.

Can any good come from our mistakes? Can God do anything with sinners such as we are? David answers these questions. He promises God that he will make good use of the lessons he has learned.

8. Teach others from your mistakes and bring them to the Lord.

A person who has never been wrong and is self-righteous is unattractive to others, but one who is willing to admit his sin and the depth of God's forgiving power has much to share with others. When I was young and cocky, thinking I could control my destiny, I had no compassion for people with problems. I felt that mistakes were a sign of weakness, and I respected only strength.

Once I suffered through the loss of my two sons, after doing everything humanly possible to heal them, I knew what heartbreak was and I could feel for others.

Once I was brought to my knees with a broken spirit, I was open to the claims of Christ and I was restored. The Lord Jesus gave me a new life to use for His glory.

David tells God, "When this is over, I'll teach others about You and many will be converted."

Why not make the best of your worst? What problem are you involved in right now? Follow David's good advice.

1. Ask God for mercy.
2. Admit your mistake.
3. Tell the truth.
4. Be willing to change.
5. Restore fellowship with God and your partner.

6. Ask for the joy of the Lord.
7. Thank God for your broken spirit.
8. Teach others from your mistakes and bring them to the Lord.

There is no pot so black that God can't shine it up and use it for His glory!

16

☙

WHAT IS
COMMUNICATION?

According to the dictionary, communication is a sharing of ideas, an exchange of information, a mutual participation. Using this basis, communication is *not* a monologue, a tirade, or a deaf ear.

Communication needs at least two active people, one who talks and one who really listens.

For a radio to communicate it needs a transmitter and a receiver. A commentator can talk his head off, but he doesn't communicate until at least one person turns on his radio and listens.

My brother, Ron Chapman, is the number one communicator on Dallas radio, but he is not content just to be funny, articulate, and informative each morning. He wants to be sure that someone is *listening.* And he is not content to have just one person listening; he wants more people to tune in to him than to any other personality in the area. Every time the surveys are taken Ron Chapman is on top of the ratings, and that's where he wants to stay.

It's easy for us to follow this logic from a performer, but most of us go through life settling for only half of what we want, and never really communicating at all.

When Did Our Communication Break Down?

We are usually attracted to someone who communicates with us on the same wavelength. We have mutual interests. We love to hear about the other person's activities, we enjoy sharing on verbal and emotional levels. We think that if we marry, we will live and communicate happily ever after.

What went wrong? When did our communication break down?

1. One talks so much that the other quits listening.

This happened in our marriage. By the time Fred came home at night I had eight hours' worth of experiences to share with him. At first he listened, but after a while he turned off his receiver.

The true Sanguine has more to say than anyone needs to hear, and a Melancholy listener feels that much of the monologue is trivia. When Fred and I began to put our communication back in order, he begged me to boil the story down to the facts. This spoiled some of my fun but at least he would listen, and I realized that he did not need to know the entire genealogy of each person I mentioned.

When Marita was dating her future husband, Chuck, he gave me a hilarious impersonation of Marita. As soon as he picks her up she starts with the exciting details of everything she's done since he saw her last. She continues through the ride to the restaurant, the waiting in the lobby, and half through the dinner. She then takes a deep breath and says, "How are things with you, Chuck?" He replies

"Fine," and she starts again, never to stop until she bids him good-night.

As Chuck told me this tale he concluded, "I spend $30 on the evening and all I get to say is 'fine.'"

Sometimes we talk so much that we close communication.

2. My opinion doesn't matter.

Before marriage we at least appear interested in each other's opinions because we are each putting our best mouth forward. One of our early and painful lessons comes when we find that our opinion doesn't really matter. Whichever partner is the more domineering begins to proclaim policy, and the other realizes quickly that to offer an opinion leads to argument.

There are two possible outcomes. You can both fight over every problem, communicating at top volume to ears who have turned off the sound, or one of you can shut up, giving the other the life-long attitude that he is always right because you don't buck him on anything.

Each solution leads to complete breakdown of meaningful communication. Fred and I played this game. As soon as we came back from our honeymoon, he put me on a training program. We no longer communicated as equals but as teacher-pupil. He laid down edicts and I obeyed in shock. The alternative was to go home to Mother and admit that I was a failure. I became afraid to offer opposing opinions, and soon I became a rubber stamp to his every whim even though I was steaming underneath.

One day his mother asked me why I had allowed him to go into a business venture that failed, and I replied, "I thought it was better to keep our marriage together than to try to buck him in business."

Some couples may look peaceful, but they have no meaningful communication because one partner is transmitting to a dead receiver.

3. I know you'll prove me wrong.

It is very difficult for a person with *feelings* to communicate with someone with *facts*. Very early in our marriage I found that Fred was very big with statistics. I wanted him to spend time with me and the children, but he was in mad pursuit of expanding his business. He was always going to get things under control next year, and then he would get acquainted with us. Next year never came. As I would plead for attention and pour out my *feelings*, he would cut me off with *facts*. I had to look at so many projections of profits on big ledgers that after a while I gave up communicating. I knew that if I brought up a *feeling* he would quickly douse it with a *fact*.

Looking back at this period of our life, Fred now agrees that he stifled me with statistics because he didn't want to hear my opinion. He always won the battle, but he lost a close relationship with me. After failing at some projects I had opposed, he began to listen to my opinion. Now he won't make a major decision without seeing how I *feel* about it.

4. I'm afraid of your reaction.

When we are dating we all feel free to converse because we know the other person will receive our words open-mindedly. He or she wants to get to know us and listens with attention. But as we begin to function in the closeness of marriage, we find negative reactions to some of our favorite subjects. The more fearful we become of pushing our partner in an adverse direction, the less we communicate. Because we are afraid of a bad reaction, we tend to share our true feelings only with outsiders who will listen. Sometimes this person is of the opposite sex and one who hangs on our every word, making us feel we've married the wrong person.

5. I'm afraid you'll correct me.

When Fred and I were first married and I would tell entertaining stories at parties, he would correct me. This was a surprise to me because my brothers and I had always supported each other's humor no matter how far it might stray from the truth. We rehearsed clever lines on current events that we knew would be brought up in an evening, thus appearing to be more witty than we actually were. We put a premium on quick response and play on words and we were considered the life of the party.

When I left this supportive system for a critical partner, I was stopped in my tracks and stifled in my conversation. Fred would correct the time of day, the color of the carpet, and the quotes I gave of others. I didn't realize at the time that Fred felt my creative statistics were lies and that he felt morally obligated to tell the truth. His factualizing of my humor, however, led me in the opposite direction, and I learned to keep quiet when Fred was around so I wouldn't be humiliated.

This natural reaction leads to trouble, for the person who is afraid of being corrected by his mate will seek out others who find his wit appealing, and they are not so hard to find. On every corner there is someone looking for a friend.

When Fred and I finally dealt with this problem and he saw what his search for the truth was doing to my personality, he agreed to let me relax in his presence and have fun in whatever way I wanted without fear of correction. As he took off the pressure, I came closer to the truth. Now Fred responds joyfully to my stories even when he's heard most of them before.

6. I'm afraid you'll laugh at me.

Before marriage we laugh *with* our partner but afterward we laugh *at* them. Somehow we feel that it shows our superiority if we can scoff at the statements and actions of our mate. How many times have you seen a husband berate his wife in public? How many times have you seen a wife ridicule her husband's humor? After we are the victim of cutting comments and we know our mate is making fun of us, we cease to communicate or we attack more frequently, hoping to win a futile game.

When did your communications break down? Did one of you talk so much that the other quit listening? Did you find that your opinion just didn't matter? Were you proven wrong with facts every time you tried to discuss a meaningful issue? Did you become afraid of your partner's reaction to touchy subjects—afraid you'd be corrected, afraid of being laughed at?

All of these genuine concerns push us further apart, and some of our marriages deteriorate into two people living under the same roof but with not much in common. We are no longer exchanging ideas but merely passing the salt.

What Barriers Have I Built?

Robert Frost once wrote, "Something there is that does not love a wall." In marriage no one loves a wall, and yet many of us are as busy as beavers building barriers which effectively block out our communication. We find an abundance of building materials which construct emotional walls as real in our lives as the old-fashioned bundling boards were for the Puritans. Something has come between us.

Depression	Anger		Joking	Silence
	Interruptions		False Agreement	
Defensiveness		Ridicule		

1. Interruption

Sanguines, who don't ever want to listen, use the technique of interruption and quick answers to effectively block communication.

The partner mentions that the garage is a mess. The Sanguine jumps right in without even knowing his reason for bringing up the subject. "I know it's a mess. I'll clean it tomorrow. I'll throw all your tools in a box and move the bikes out to the breezeway. When you come home tomorrow night, you won't recognize the place, and you'll never have to ask me about the garage again!" And he never does. He soon learns not to bring up any topic which she will jump on, and as he thinks it over, that's almost every topic. Those of us who are Sanguine don't think we're interrupting. We just feel we're helping you out, adding color to your plain thoughts.

Interruption cuts off any dialogue and turns it into a monologue. Some Sanguines, such as me, finish people's sentences, making two-way conversation obsolescent.

I thought the concert was . . .
absolutely breathtaking. They deserved the standing ovation.

After lunch let's go . . .
to Macy's. The exact place we should go. The sale is sensational and you'll love the bargains.

In school today . . .
you ripped your dress. I can see right off what you were doing. Why do I even put a decent thing on a child like you?

Harry came into the office . . .
to ask for money again, I presume? If that bum ever came to see you for any reason but squeezing another nickel out of you I'd drop dead.

Be my guest!
Interruption and the finishing of others' thoughts is an excellent way to eliminate any future communication.

2. Depression

One young man said to me, "If I say something that doesn't hit her right, she goes into an instant depression. It's like a black curtain drops down between us." For some people the cloud of gloom is constantly on call, and it will come out the minute a displeasing thought pulls the trigger. Melancholies use this as a threat to their partner. If you bring that subject up again I'll get depressed. Since the mate will do anything to prevent a week of gloom, he soon learns to avoid anything that will cause trouble. The Melancholy person uses this method to control conversations, and soon the communication becomes superficial and safe but no longer sincere.

The threat of depression is a quiet deterrent to any open exchange of ideas.

3. Anger

"Don't you ever say that again. You know that makes me furious!" And if you didn't before, you know now. No one wants to stir up anger in another person, and the angry person knows that. Because he knows that, he is in a strong position to weed out any topics he doesn't want sprouting up around him. After demonstrating his volatile temper, he lets you know you had better take no chances with him. After a while he doesn't have to blow up; he only has to threaten: "You're getting too close"; "Watch what you're saying"; "You know that upsets me."

The Choleric temperament resorts to anger and may announce ahead of time when he is in a terrible mood. The husband stalks in at night and yells, "This has been the worst day of my whole life." This tells the wife and children not to bring up any controversial subject, to keep the conversation innocuous, and not look too happy or bright. It's a fine line and provides many family hours of tension and fear.

The angry mother manipulates her children into submission by screaming at them in front of their friends. This fear so frightens them that they are desperate to please and can be brought into line by the slam of a door.

While anger is the loudest block to communication and definitely deters disagreements, the person who uses this tool is ultimately unloved and unaccepted, and both mate and children are always looking for some way of escape, some haven to run to, some way to come in from the rain of torrential tirades and temper tantrums.

Anger works, but you'll be a lonesome victor.

4. False agreement

The Phlegmatic wants peace at all costs and tends to agree quickly to something he doesn't want, in order to save a fight. The partner assumes that because he said yes he meant it and proceeds with the illusion of agreement. One man I counseled said, "I'd rather pretend my marriage is all right than talk about it, as change might be worse."

There are many marriages that appear smooth on the surface only because one person builds a facade of agreement while feeling henpecked underneath. After a while the family ignores him and makes decisions without him. He has effectively eliminated any exchange of ideas, and things tend to go on around him but not with him.

Agreeing quickly does save arguments, but it removes a person from the mainstream of activity and excludes any contribution to the conversation. As one Choleric wife told me, "He's nothing but a piece of furniture!"

5. Joking

When Sanguines sense that someone is approaching a touchy subject, they tend to turn the whole thing into a joke. They find that if they can turn a potential difficulty into humor, they can avoid any meaningful conversation in an inoffensive way. They can skirt the issue quickly and get people's minds diverted into a colorful story which is so much fun that no one would ever want to get back to the subject at hand. For years I employed this tactic with Fred, until he gave up trying to discuss serious matters with me. Although I've tried to improve, it takes years to rebuild a bad reputation.

While playing around can postpone any meaningful discussion, the person who resorts to this tactic may end up as a joke himself and the last laugh may be on him. In the bedroom the Sanguine wife often uses a piercing humor to cut off her Melancholy husband's advances, leaving him feeling isolated and depressed for days.

6. Ridicule

Before I began to work on the negative areas of my life I used to major in making fun of others. My brothers and I had a knack for this and we used to do parodies of the peculiar customers who came into the store. While these takeoffs were done to amuse ourselves on rainy days, they did have a lasting and damaging impact, because my automatic defense when the conversation approached any condemnation of me was to throw out a sarcastic barb which would stun the opposition and bring laughs from the crowd.

Once I began to work on my relationships with people, I realized that ridicule is never a positive experience for anyone. While the audience might respond, the person hurt would retreat, and I learned that ridicule is a permanent barrier to friendship and communication. Anytime we get a laugh at the expense of even one person, we have made a major mistake.

7. Defensiveness

Some people have minds like lawyers and have a case ready for the first person who tries to get close to their heart. You never ask them the why of anything because they will tell you more than you ever wanted to hear. Whatever happened, it wasn't their fault, and if you question their judgment they will attack you with a string of statistics that make you look stupid. They build strong walls around themselves that will resist any outside attack and then wonder why they're standing alone in the fort.

Defensiveness is a solid barrier to heartfelt communication, for people grow weary of trying to tunnel under, dig through, or climb over the wall. Take the wall down and listen. It might even be a compliment.

8. Silence

Since silence is intangible it's hard to get a handle on and impossible to fight with. It just won't sit up and respond, yet it's one of the greatest barriers to communication. How can you talk with a statue? How can you exchange ideas with a wife who became an instant deaf-mute? How can you converse with a husband who's encased in a soundproof newspaper?

Some people feel that as long as they keep their mouths shut they surely can't be to blame for any problems. Sometimes they keep quiet so long and the partner gets so frustrated that a minor incident will trigger a massive explosion. The Quiet One then says with a sigh, "It takes so little to get you upset."

Silence seems so inoffensive, but it effectively halts any two-way communication. One Phlegmatic man told me his wife hit him across the face when he hadn't done a thing. I called her over and asked, "Did you hit this man?"

"Yes, I did!"

"Why"

"I just wanted to see if he was still alive!"

What barriers have you built to block communications? Have you walled yourself away from your mate so there is no mutual participation? Can you talk to your hairdresser more freely than to your husband?

Ask yourself these questions:

1. Do I interrupt and finish sentences for others?
2. Do I drop into depression as a defense?
3. Do I get angry if people don't see things my way?
4. Do I pretend to agree just to shut them up, and resent it inside?
5. Do I make a joke out of serious subjects in order to avoid facing them?
6. Do I make fun of others and ridicule them in front of people?
7. Do I jump to my own defense before anyone can plead a case?
8. Do I clam up and refuse to talk when the subject gets too close?

If you have answered yes to even a few of these, you have trouble communicating. You may be verbal and vivacious, but if you use any of these blocks you are walling yourself away from a true exchange of ideas with those close to you. Sit down and discuss this problem with your mate. See which one of you uses which kind of block.

Why Have I Built These Walls?

We all have some areas within us that are private property, and we tend to fence them in. Sometimes we announce early in marriage:

"There are certain things I do not wish to talk about."
"Don't ever bring that up again!"
"I will not discuss sex with you."
"I don't wish to talk with you about my family."
"I don't believe you and it's too late now anyway."

If either one of you has said anything like these statements, make this the subject of your next conversation.

Ideally, thoughts similar to these will stimulate positive reactions and open channels of communications which have been blocked up for years. To be successful, however, you must not be defensive, argue, or condemn. No matter what your partner says, be willing to reply, "I'm so glad to know how you really feel."

Guidelines to Effective Communication

It is absolutely essential that couples talk things out with each other if they wish to have a rich, deep, and meaningful marriage.

Hugh Boudreau, a Baltimore marriage counselor, said, "The inability to converse shows up in 85 out of 100 couples visiting marriage counselors. The inability of husbands and wives to talk to each other is our number one marriage problem."

Women: This Is What A Man Wants:

1. Sincerity

This word comes from the Latin *sine cera,* meaning "without wax." Back in the Roman days, when disreputable people made an urn to sell, if it did not come out smoothly they would fill in the cracks with wax to fool the purchaser into thinking it was perfect. But artisans who did outstanding work would proclaim their pieces to be *sine cera*—without any fillers.

When we women converse we tend to fill in the cracks with excuses and with blame put on others, but our husbands would like sincere statements. When we communicate with them they would like us to be sincere vessels with no guile, artifice, or fillers.

Are you ready to talk to your husband openly, hiding nothing, with no excuses? Can you be, perhaps for the first time in your married life, sincere and clear without exaggerating or manipulating?

2. Simplicity

Originally this word meant "without a fold." It referred to garments which were made simply, with nothing to hide. How many of us women can approach our men with the simple facts? How many can wear garments without folds of deception, without ruffles of exaggeration, without pleats of endless details, without pockets of concealment?

Those of us with poor marriage relationships, with husbands who flinch when we begin to talk, have probably never stated a simple fact to a man who desires an open heart, a clear statement, an honest answer, an uncomplicated truth. We have covered and concealed. We have drenched them with details and drowned them in trivia. Can we begin to make simple statements without any folds?

3. Sensitivity

To possess this quality we must be aware of and tuned in to the other person's feelings. As women we must be sensitive to our partner's needs and not approach him with our problems when it is clearly not the right time. So often we store up complaints in a bottle all day and when our husband walks in we take out the stopper and let him have it. When this deluge becomes a constant style of communication, our mates stop coming home or arrive with plugs in their ears.

If we could only pray for a sensitive spirit and try to discern their desires before we dump, we would have much better reception. Feed them and let them know you love them before emptying the wastebasket on them.

4. Stability

Many men tell me they are afraid to bring up any meaningful subject to their wives because they fall apart. Men don't like weepy women, and if a woman employs this type of barrier to communication often enough, her husband will withdraw.

Men like to approach problems from an organized, businesslike point of view, and they respect a woman who is stable and serene even under stress.

Some girls grow up getting their way through emotions. They have temper tantrums and make a scene, and the family gives in. When they marry they use the same tactics on their husbands, and the men wonder what they have on their hands.

These little-girl tricks are unbecoming to a mature woman and contrary to the stability that a man wants in a wife.

Men: This Is What A Woman Wants:

1. Attention

All of us crave attention so much that if you won't listen to our heartfelt pleas, we will find someone who will. It's not just *your* wife who is trying to get you to pay attention. We all want men who look at us as if we were intelligent, listen to the details we delight in dropping, and respond to what we really said. An occasional "uh huh" is not enough. We want you to put down the paper and pick up our hands. We want you to look *at* us eye-to-eye, not *through* us to the Washington Redskins, or the wallpaper.

If you want to communicate with us, pay *attention* to what we say but don't feel we need *answers*. Fred finally understands that when I cry out my problems to him, I only want him to listen and commiserate. I don't want him to prescribe a cure. I already know the answer; I just want an audience.

Somehow men find this pattern illogical. They feel that if we tell all our misfortunes of the day we are asking for help. We're usually not.

When I lost my car in the seven-story parking garage, I didn't need a lecture on the little numbers and letters painted on the walls. When I told Fred I fell up my office stairs, I didn't need to hear how clumsy I am and that my heels are too high. When I suffer through a whole day with the neighbor's two dogs yelping incessantly I don't get spiritual when Fred smiles and says, "Love thy neighbor as thyself."

To communicate with us, listen to us and love us. Don't preach or teach. Only answer if we ask and even then proceed with caution.

2. Agreement

If you men want to open up communications, try to agree with us in some area quickly. This will unnerve us and give you an immediate advantage. Because most of you love to argue with us and put us down, we are stunned by a man who agrees with us on anything. Arguing builds up barriers between us. Agreement tears them down. You don't need a wall when you're both on the same side.

This simple principle of agreement, when applied, will be a blessing in your marriage. Amos 3:3 says, "Can two walk together except they be agreed?"

In the past Fred found something wrong with everything I said. He was so predictable that I would carry on mock conversations in my mind with him. As soon as I would hear him disagree, I would file that thought away in the reject pile, never to be dealt with again. What a big pile of resentment I built up, a barrier to communication! Now he listens to the end of what I'm saying and at least agrees with part of my message.

3. Appreciation

The dictionary tells us that appreciation implies "A just estimation of a thing's value, an understanding." Oh, how we women want to be looked upon as something of value, and how we want to know that you understand what we are trying to say!

To understand, you have to listen, put yourself in our place, and hope you catch our drift. We won't always be logical and we won't think as you do, but we do want to be appreciated and understood.

Often philandering females will give me the excuse "My husband never understood me, but when I met Steve Studley I could tell he understood." He probably didn't understand her much better than her husband, but he encouraged her conversation and made her feel intelligent, and she just knew he understood. Let us know you are so grateful to be married to us and we will do almost anything you want.

4. Appointments

When you men sense that there are some communication problems in your marriage, take the leadership and set aside some special time to converse. George Vandeman in *Happiness Wall to Wall* says, "Marriage partners who will not listen are already experiencing a separation of interests. Where there is no dialogue, there is emotional divorce."

The majority of the couples Fred and I counsel with don't hate each other but are just emotionally divorced. They stopped communicating somewhere along the line and neither side did anything about it. Don't let this happen to you. Don't wait for your wife to come in hysterical; plan relaxing times when you can get away together and communicate. Don't take friends or relatives along. Don't go on a tour with 24-hour activities. Go to a quiet motel and renew acquaintances. Go over the topics in this chapter and find out where your communication went astray.

Some couples who do not force themselves to sit down and discuss their poor communication never know until it's too late where they missed out.

One couple had a simple problem that they had not solved. They didn't want to break up their marriage, but each thought the other didn't love him. When I listened objectively, I found a Sanguine wife who said "I love you" 20 times a day but did no housework and forgot to wash his socks. He was a Phlegmatic man who never said he loved her but quietly did all the housework. Each one was communicating a message that the other didn't understand. She said "I love you" but did nothing. He said nothing but did her work. Using their own standards, each one had concluded that the other was not in love. Once they had an interpreter, they saw their simple mistake.

Who knows what little irritants you could clear up if you tried? Make an appointment with your wife and learn to communicate.

Often we don't make it so easy for our partners, and we let them play guessing games until they smash into the concrete corners that we have walled up in our lives.

One day I was visiting in a small town, and as I drove down the street to the home where I was staying, I noticed one yard with a big sign on it that said "Private Property—Keep Out." A big ugly dog was chained to the sign, and my curiosity was aroused. What's different about this house? What kind of people live there? What made them put up the sign and send out the dog? No other house on the street attracted my attention except the one labeled "Private Property." I asked my hostess about it and she told me the couple there hated children and put up the sign to let people know this. "The strange thing is," she said, "That all the children are drawn to that yard. They walk as close to the property as they dare, they throw things at the dog, and they ruin the place on Halloween."

By putting "Private Property" on their lawn, this couple had aroused the curiosity and attention of all who passed by. We always want to know about whatever is off-limits.

What is your Private Property?

1. For some it's **The Past.**

One adorable little woman said to me at a retreat, "When we got married my husband told me not to ask about his past. I was so in love with him that I agreed to never question him, but now I can't stand it any longer. We're drifting apart and I know it's because he's holding something back. What could his past have been?" The poor girl couldn't get this nebulous past out of her present. She had to break through the wall and find out what was in *the past.*

If there is something in our past which we do not wish to discuss we should not mention it, as the thought automatically arouses curiosity. It is never advisable to bring up sordid experiences and give the gory details of any negative activity, for the mind makes an instant image that may never be erased. Either be clear about your past or don't mention it. Teasing isn't fair.

2. For some it's **The Big Secret.**

A woman visiting in my home asked to take the Personality Profile. When I looked at her scores they seemed contradictory, and I asked if she was playing a role in life. She flinched and I knew I had hit against some Private Property. As she resisted my questions, I could tell I was getting closer. There was something inside that no one knew. Finally she began to cry and she told me, "My husband and I are the pillars of the church but I know he leads a double life. When he's out of town he picks up other women in bars and I'm scared to death that someone will find out. I keep covering up for him and he won't let me mention it or talk about it. He pretends it isn't true and there's no honest communication between us. If anyone ever finds out in the church, we'll all be a disgrace."

This dear woman was living a lie. Her husband was pretending that all was well and she was playing a frightening role for the world. Many of us build thick walls to hide the Big Secret, and this action keeps us from communicating honestly with anyone.

3. For some it's **Money.**

"Don't ask what I do with the money."
"Don't nag me about the bills."

"Can't you ever be content with what you have?"
"You're more interested in my money than in me."

These and similar statements cut off communication about money. No matter what question you need answered, you don't dare ask about it until the gas is shut off and the phone disconnected. No matter who writes the checks, you need to both know the state of your bills, budget, and investments.

4. For some it's **The Children.**

"The children are your problem."
"I have enough hassle at work, so don't tell me the trouble you've got with the kids."
"I earn the money; you run the children."
"You go to the school. You see the principal. Do you think I have time for junk like that?"

Statements such as these are cover-ups for irresponsibility and insecurity. They signal *Private Property* to the mate but they mean, "I don't wish to bear my part of raising the children and I haven't any idea of what to do with them, so I'll let you worry about their problems. That way I won't show my ignorance and I'll be able to lay all the blame for their failures on you."

Many men have such pride that they do not want to touch any area in which they are insecure and uncertain, so they refuse to talk about it. This puts an impossible job on the mother and prevents her from even expressing her ideas. She cannot bring up any dilemmas from diapers to discipline to drugs. She's left holding the fort alone, deserted by the one who should be in command and defeated by mutiny among the troops.

5. For some it's **The Real Me.**

"If he knew what I'm really like he'd hate me."
"If I ever exposed my inner thoughts she'd leave."

Many of us never learn to communicate at all with anyone because we are hiding the *Real Me*. Somewhere along the line we have picked up the idea that we aren't worth much. Perhaps our parents told us we were dummies. Perhaps a teacher asked us why we weren't smart like our sisters. Perhaps we told our mothers our inner feelings and they were shocked and said, "Never tell anyone anything like that again!"

Whatever the cause, many of us have become what other people wanted us to be, and we have walled up our real selves behind a friendly facade.

One woman on the verge of a nervous breakdown told me, "As a child I played the perfect role my mother demanded. As a teen I hid anything my family didn't sanction and appeared to be a good girl. When I married I had to change the rules to suit a new leader, and now I'm so confused that I don't know who the real me is or even if there is one."

So many times when we try to conform to the roles that others expect of us, we lose our identity. This became clear to me several years ago when Fred said of our daughter Marita, "She is so adorable, so fresh and free and fun."

I replied quickly without thinking, "She's just like I was before you made me over."

This comment led to an unexpected conversation where we discussed how often men are attracted to certain traits in a woman and when they get her home they try to remake her to be the perfect wife, and she then loses the very personality which drew them to her in the first place. I realized that I still had some resentments over the reconstruction Fred had done on me during those first 15 years, and I wondered how much of the Real Me had resurfaced since Fred removed the pressure. Gratefully, we were able to discuss these thoughts openly, and Fred in a warm and loving manner encouraged me again to be the *Real Me*. At this point in my life, because we've talked through so many of our issues, we both feel free to be exactly who God made us to be. No more pretense. No more walls. No private property.

6. For some it's **Anything That Demands Action.**

Some of us are extremely resistant to any new thoughts that might suggest a change. We have walled up our will and we refuse to discuss anything that would require new effort. I often ask women with marriage problems, "What would your husband like you to do differently?" Usually the husbands have made their wishes known—lose weight, fix your hair, stay home once in a while, clean up the house, make the beds, quit complaining. Yet so few women will discuss these areas openly because talking about the solution would demand some actions.

One woman told me, "The problem isn't that I'm a messy housekeeper; it's that he's not spiritual." I explained that he might get more spiritual if he were sitting in a clean house.

So many of us put "Private Property" signs on sections of our lives where we don't want to make an effort to change.

Recently a woman named Betty brought me her friend Teri, a new believer who needed instruction. As the three of us talked over lunch, I sensed that Betty had more problems than Teri. Betty told me how Teri is, how she gets up early each day, how she cooks a big breakfast for the family, how she does her housework quickly, and on and on.

"As for me, I never seem to get anything done. My house is a mess and my three little girls are as sloppy as I am."

When asked her why she was unable to keep her house in order she replied promptly, "I'm on the phone all day counseling women with marriage problems."

I warned, "If you don't shape up your home, you might have some marriage problems of your own."

Her whole countenance fell and she said, "My husband keeps mentioning what a mess the place is and how neat his sister's home is. One day last week he told me if I didn't clean the house, he was going to leave, but I pretended he was joking and wouldn't discuss it."

Here sat a saint of the faith busy saving other people's marriages but refusing to see the dangers in her own. As her husband cried out clearly to her, she walled up any mention of the subject that would demand action on her part.

Ask yourself, "What Private Property am I protecting?"

1. Am I covering up my **past** and not willing to share my childhood, my family, my ambitions, my hurts, and my defeats with my partner?

2. Am I eaten up inside because I'm hiding a **big secret** that needs to be dealt with?

3. Am I unable to discuss **money** problems and work them through without becoming emotional?

4. Am I unwilling to cooperate on raising the **children** and am I putting the blame for failures on my mate?

5. Am I afraid to let anyone get to know my **real self** or am I not sure who I really am?

6. Am I an expert at avoiding **anything** that demands **action?**

Let's pause at this point and assess our communication problems. Remember, it takes two to communicate, and one must lead. As a start, find a time when you and your mate can discuss your mutual problems. If your partner is open, ask him or her to read this chapter in order to help you with your shortcomings. Never ask anyone to read something because *he* needs it, but only because *you* need *his* help.

Ideally both of you should make lists of areas where you have failed yourselves and each other. If getting this organized will scare off your mate, prepare informally in your head.

Before bringing up your problems, be sure it is not a time when his attention is preoccupied or when he's racing to get out the door. Women seem to have a gift for choosing the wrong moment to begin a deep discussion.

If you have difficulty in starting a conversation in a positive direction, here are some sample sentences.

"We used to communicate well before we were married; when did this break down? Where have I failed?"

"I read a book that made me realize for the first time that I have kept us from communicating well by my interrupting, depression, and anger. I want to work on this area in my life. Will you help me?"

"There are certain things in my life that I haven't wanted to discuss. I was afraid you'd laugh at me or like me less if I was straightforward with you. I'm hopeful now that you will listen and still love me."

Don't expect instant euphoria, as your partner hasn't heard these thoughts before and he's not sure you mean business. Be prepared for him to tell you, "It's about time you realized that you are the problem in our marriage." Agree with him and then move on. When you take the blame a decent man will soon own up to his part of the marriage problem.

17

🌺

How Can I Check
My Ability to Communicate?

O n the following pages we have shown some of the communication problems of the different personality types. Read these over and see if they shed new light on your family's difficulties. Then take the two marriage surveys for both husbands and wives. We have been using these surveys in our marriage classes for years and have found them to be very helpful in opening up meaningful communication.

The Sanguine

The Popular Sanguine loves to talk but doesn't enjoy listening and often interrupts what the other person is saying. The Sanguine hates bad news and will quickly change the subject and derail the entire sentence before it even gets on track if he or she senses some critical words in the speaker's mind. If a negative thought does leak out, the Sanguine will make a joke of it, leaving the other person, often a serious-minded spouse, in a depression. *There's no point in ever trying to discuss anything of importance*, the spouse thinks. This pattern of behavior is a natural cover-up for the Sanguine's refusal to get involved in problem situations. The Sanguine doesn't mind being thought stupid as long as he or she is smart enough to avoid responsibility and criticism.

The best way to communicate serious truth to the Sanguine is to make an appointment: "Tomorrow night after dinner we need to discuss our overdrawn bank account." The thought of facing stark reality will so frighten the Sanguine that his or her defenses will be down by tomorrow night. (It also gives this person time to return unnecessary purchases and find money left in coat pockets or used as bookmarks in several novels!) Don't allow Sanguines to sidetrack you or make light of the situation. They have short memories, are easily distracted, and hate accountability, but understanding their weaknesses will change a hopelessly frustrating experience into a positive one.

If you are Sanguine, with a desire to have fun and a tendency to run from bad news, realize that it's time to grow up, face the truth, and actually listen to what others have to say. As Fred says, "When you're talking, you're not learning anything. You already know what you're saying." So listen and learn!

The Melancholy

The Perfect Melancholy is the opposite of the Sanguine. Sanguines talk whether or not they have any great truth to share; Melancholies keep quiet, even when they have the correct answer! Their thoughts are so deep that their partners have to reach way down inside and pull them out. Fred used to say, "If you really loved me, you would know what I'm thinking." This statement puts an unfair burden on the other person, who has no clue as to what the Melancholy person is thinking. This game proceeds like a TV talk show:

Sanguine: What's the matter with you?
Melancholy: Nothing. (This is always the answer.)
Sanguine: There is something wrong!
Melancholy: There is nothing wrong with me.
Sanguine: Yes, there is! Tell me! You're driving me crazy! (Sanguines can't stand suspense.)
Melancholy: If I tell you, you'll laugh at me.
Sanguine: No, I won't laugh.
Melancholy: Yes, you will. You always do.
Sanguine: No, I promise I won't laugh. Tell me.
Melancholy: I was hurt when you said I don't have a sense of humor in front of the pastor.
Sanguine: That's the funniest thing I've ever heard. How could you be upset at the truth?
Melancholy: I'll never tell you anything ever again.

Does any of this sound familiar to you? Both parties have to repair this communications breakdown:

- The Sanguine has to listen and not scoff or laugh.

- The Melancholy has to say what's bothering him or her early on without torturing the listener.

- The Sanguine has to apologize for his or her thoughtlessness.

With these parameters in mind, let's replay that conversation:

Sanguine: What's wrong with you?
Melancholy: I was just brooding over the comment you made in front of the pastor.
Sanguine: What did I say?
Melancholy: That I have no sense of humor.

Sanguine: I realized afterward that I shouldn't have said that. I'm really sorry.

Melancholy: Thank you for saying you're sorry.

How much simpler it is when each person communicates clearly and courteously!

The Choleric

The Powerful Cholerics are the most difficult to communicate with because they are always right. They see little reason to discuss various approaches to the situation when there is obviously only one way to handle this thing: their way. "If you'd just do what I tell you to do, when I tell you to do it, we'd get along just fine." That's true if we are living with a group of robots. Press a button and off they go, preprogrammed to do it your way. But what if a Choleric is living with real people who are intelligent and who feel their way is worth a listen?

If you live under the domain of a Choleric, you might use this approach:

"I'm so glad to live with someone who is always right and who is always fair. Because you are a just person, I want to tell you something, insignificant though it may be, and see what you think about it. I don't want an answer right now. Mull it over and I'll check with you on Monday."

This approach appeals to the Choleric's strength of being right and fair. Not needing an answer now keeps the Choleric from an instant cut-and-dried solution that ends any further communication. Instead, this gives him or her time to process the information and evaluate your opinion.

If you are the Choleric, realize that even though you are usually right you need to allow others to express opinions without making them feel stupid. If you are courageous, you will ask your family, "When I talk to you do you feel I'm putting you down?" Watch the look of panic as they evaluate whether they dare to speak the truth and risk reprisal. Encourage them to talk to you even if you don't feel you need their opinion. Because one of your weaknesses is being too impulsive and acting before thinking things through, you will be doing yourself a favor to let people finish their sentences. Other people will respect you more when you have paid attention to their opinions. It's much better to have people do it your way because they want to, not because you've intimidated them. And remember, it's hard to love someone you're afraid of.

The Phlegmatic

The Peaceful Phlegmatic is the easiest person to get along with because he or she wants to have peace and avoid conflict. Phlegmatics are the best listeners, they don't interrupt, and they have balanced opinions. Things don't have to go their way. These traits are essential in a marriage where the other partner is Choleric! The problem comes when the Choleric has been the sole deciding force in the relationship for so long that the Phlegmatic wouldn't dream of uttering a word. One of two things happens: Either the Phlegmatic feels worthless and retreats into a cavern of silence, or the Choleric says, "What do I need this person for anyway? My spouse hasn't had a decent opinion in years!" Either way this marriage can deteriorate into meaningless phrases like "pass the salt."

To avoid this ultimate boredom, this Phlegmatic has to risk giving an opinion, even if it breaks the peace for a few minutes, and the Choleric has to listen and realize that the Phlegmatic might have a credible thought.

If you are the Phlegmatic, realize that if you answer "I don't care" whenever you're asked whether you want coffee or tea, after a while no one will ask. You'll just be handed a cup and told to "drink it." If you are the one relating to the Peaceful Phlegmatic, push them a little to force them into making a decision and then respect their wishes. If you don't, they will become nothing more than robots.

One other element in dealing with Phlegmatics is to realize they have an underlying will of iron; while they may say "Yes" on the surface they may be saying "That'll be the day" underneath. The Phlegmatics' subtle way of control is procrastination. They think, *If I wait long enough, someone else will do it.* Again the solution takes two. The Choleric has to discuss what should be done instead of giving orders that make the Phlegmatic quietly rebellious, and the Phlegmatic has to move into action instead of postponing the inevitable and angering the Choleric.

Here are some additional quick communications tips for each of the four personalities:

> Popular Sanguine: Learn to listen, don't interrupt, don't laugh everything off. Accept the fact that life is full of strife. Grow up, face reality, and don't expect others to protect you forever.

> Perfect Melancholy: Don't take everything personally. Don't make your partner play Twenty Questions to get an answer. Realize that life may not be quite as bad as it seems at the moment.

> Powerful Choleric: Don't expect everyone to want to do it your way. Don't assume you know everything. Let people offer opinions without cutting them off or putting them down. Don't get angry if others disagree. They might be right.

> Peaceful Phlegmatic: Speak up, make decisions, move into action, say what you mean. Don't procrastinate and expect others to do your work. Be willing to take a risk. You probably have the best idea of all.

No matter what your personality is, you can now recognize where other people have communication difficulties and help them out. It takes more than one person to have an intelligent two-way conversation. With this in mind, we'll devote the rest of this chapter to communication with the person who is probably closest to you: your spouse.

Communication Survey, Part 1

How well do you and your partner communicate? Communicating is not just talking. Most couples are able to talk without ever sharing their deepest feelings with each other. They hesitate to express their hurts and their pains and their discouragements because they fear they will either trigger an avalanche of rebuttal or be made to feel stupid. Some partners fear sharing their joys and achievements lest they tap into their mates' feelings of low self-worth and end up feeling guilty that they are happy.

Communication in marriage is the ability or freedom to express feelings, thoughts, or ideas to each other with the confidence that they will be openly received. In a healthy marriage an exchange of positions can be offered without any fear of rejection or retribution.

To see how well you understand each other's feelings and accept the need to share, start by answering the 25 questions that follow. The wife should answer only the questions for wives, and the husband the questions for husbands. Fill out your answers without looking to see how your partner responded.

Part 1 for Wives

Remember: Change is inevitable. Growth is intentional.

Directions: Each statement should be scored 0-4 according to this scale:

The statement applies:

   0—Almost never
   1—Seldom
   2—Sometimes

3—Much of the time
4—Almost always

1. My husband is generally available to listen to me when I want to talk. _____

2. I am generally available to listen when my husband wants to talk. _____

3. My husband is sympathetic and understanding when I want to share some deeper feelings with him. _____

4. I am sympathetic and understanding when my husband wants to share some deeper feelings with me. _____

5. My husband does not generally have to weigh his words carefully to keep me from getting angry or upset. _____

6. I do not generally have to weigh my words carefully to keep my husband from getting angry or upset. _____

7. My husband and I usually have interesting things to talk about with each other. _____

8. I am generally satisfied with my husband's efforts to please me sexually. _____

9. My husband is generally satisfied with my efforts to please him sexually. _____

10. We are generally able to discuss our feelings about sex quite openly. _____

11. My husband is my best friend. I feel free to share my hurts and frustrations with him. _____

12. I feel free to share my feelings with my husband even when they don't agree with his. _____

13. We generally do not interrupt each other. _____

14. My husband rarely belittles me or puts me down in front of other people. _____

15. I rarely belittle my husband or put him down in front of other people. _____

16. My husband generally does not criticize or correct me. _____

17. I generally do not criticize or correct my husband. _____

18. I help my husband feel good about himself, and I let him know he is valuable and important to me. _____

19. My husband helps me to feel good about myself and lets me know I am valuable and important to him. _____

20. We generally discuss family problems and questions together and then reach decisions on which we both can agree. _____

21. My husband understands and respects my desire for occasional privacy and times to be alone. _____

22. My husband is generally quick to apologize when he has offended me. _____

23. I am generally quick to apologize when I have offended my husband. _____

24. We are generally able to discuss our spiritual walk with the Lord with each other. _____

25. I feel I understand fairly well what my husband desires from me emotionally. _____

Today's date: _____   Total _____

Part 1 for Husbands

Remember: Change is inevitable. Growth is intentional.

Directions: Each statement should be scored 0-4 according to this scale:

The statement applies:

- 0 - Almost never
- 1 - Seldom
- 2 - Sometimes
- 3 - Much of the time
- 4 - Almost always

1. I am generally available when my wife wants to talk. _____

2. My wife is generally available to listen to me when I want to talk. _____

3. I am sympathetic and understanding when my wife wants to share some deeper feelings with me. _____

4. My wife is sympathetic and understanding when I want to share some deeper feelings with her. _____

5. I do not generally have to weigh my words carefully to keep my wife from getting angry or upset. _____

6. My wife does not generally have to weigh her words carefully to keep me from getting angry or upset. _____

7. My wife and I usually have interesting things to talk about with each other. _____

8. My wife is generally satisfied with my efforts to please her sexually. _____

9. I am generally satisfied with my wife's efforts to please me sexually. _____

10. We are generally able to discuss our feelings about sex quite openly. _____

11. My wife is my best friend. I feel free to share my hurts and frustrations with her. _____

12. My wife feels free to share her feelings with me even when they don't agree with mine. _____

13. We generally do not interrupt each other. _____

14. I rarely belittle or put my wife down in front of other people. _____

15. My wife rarely belittles me or puts me down in front of other people. _____

16. I generally do not criticize or correct my wife. _____

17. My wife generally does not criticize or correct me. _____

18. My wife helps me to feel good about myself and lets me know I am valuable and important to her. _____

19. I help my wife feel good about herself, and I let her know she is valuable and important to me. _____

20. We generally discuss family problems and questions together and then reach decisions on which we both can agree. _____

21. My wife understands and respects my desire for occasional privacy and times to be alone. _____

22. I am generally quick to apologize when I have offended my wife. _____

23. My wife is generally quick to apologize when she has offended me. _____

24. We are generally able to discuss our spiritual walk with the Lord with each other. _____

25. I feel I understand fairly well what my wife desires from me emotionally. _____

Today's date: _____   Total _____

INSTRUCTIONS: Compare your scores individually on each of the questions you have just answered. If each of your totals equals 100, you understand each other well. Anything less means you have something to talk about! A score of two or more points on any particluar question should be discussed as soon as possible. A discussion means listening to what your partner is saying and feeling. There are no rights or wrongs to feelings, and therefore *you must allow your partner to express his or her feelings, without interrupting, without correcting, without criticizing, and without disagreeing.* Anything less will stifle meaningful communication.

If you are not able to discuss these statements with each other due to anger, disagreement, or unwillingness, you may both benefit from the help of an effective and objective counselor.

Important Note: Before proceeding with your line-by-line discussion, read the following important guidelines from Philippians 2 (NKJV):

> Verse 3: "Let nothing be done through selfish ambition ... but ... let each esteem others better than himself."

> Verse 5: "Let this mind be in you which was also in Christ Jesus, who ... "

> Verse 7: "Made Himself of no reputation, taking the form of a servant."

And read through the following three rules of communication.

The Three Rules of Communication

Rule one: You must allow your partner to express his feelings, without interrupting, without correcting, without criticizing, and without disagreeing. Anything less will stifle meaningful communication.

Rule two: Never make "you" statements: "You said ... " or "You glared at me" or "You got angry" or "You made me feel stupid."

Instead, make "I feel" statements: "I felt hurt" or "I feel I'm not worth anything to you" or "I feel stupid." Everyone has feelings. Some people (such as Fred at one time) have so deeply suppressed their past hurts that they appear to have no emotions at all. They sit stone-faced, responding to nothing. Their natural feelings are dead.

Everyone has a right to have feelings and emotions. Even Jesus had deep feelings; Scripture frequently describes His expressed emotions. (For an interesting study on Jesus' emotions, start with these verses: Matthew 26:37-39; John 11:35, 38; 12:27; 13:21; and Hebrews 5:7.)

Rule three: Absolutely avoid using the two instant blockade words: *Always* and *Never.* The moment you say to your partner, "Yes, but you always . . ." you force him or her to put up an immediate wall. He begins to plan how to refute your untrue and unfair statement. Now instead of listening to you, he is planning the counterattack! Meaningful communication has been stifled. There is no longer the sense of freedom that feelings, thoughts, and ideas will be openly received by the other person.

Make an agreement now with each other that when one of you unintentionally breaks one of these three rules, the other person can stop you by immediately saying, for example, "Wait a minute. You just interrupted me. Please let me finish and then I'll listen to you."

It is neither spiritual nor wise to hide or suppress your real feelings. However, it is also neither wise nor spiritual to dump them on someone else in an explosion of anger or rage. Emotions must be appropriately expressed, without bringing pain or hurt to someone else. Going patiently and caringly through the communications exercises in this book and following the three simple rules—

1. No interrupting
2. No "You statements"
3. No blockade words

—will enable each of you to express your feelings appropriately and in a healthy manner.

Virtually every couple struggles with being able to express honest concerns and hurts to each other without erecting block walls that shut off all sharing. You are no different in your marriage relationship. The difference is how soon you learn to deal with the problem. We struggled for years until we learned the three basic rules, then how to listen to each other, and then how to "hear" how the other felt. Finally we got to a point where it was safe for us to express our own feelings without fear of retribution, and we eventually learned how to encourage and edify each other (see Ephesians 4:29). Now we are actually able to express anything we wish to each other. (We still consider the time and emotions of the moment, so we don't dump thoughtless words that will hurt.) After 44 years of marriage, we have learned how to enjoy each other, how to have fun with each other, how to be in love! One of the most profound steps forward came when we learned to communicate.

Paul said in Philippians 4:11, "I have learned in whatever state I am, to be content (NKJV)." Even Paul had to work at it. He had to *learn,* and it didn't come easily or naturally. Learning to communicate may take a long time, especially if you have spent years establishing unhealthy patterns. Do not expect an overnight miracle, but begin working at it. The habit patterns that were established years ago are not quickly broken. The hurts that have been inflicted over the years are not instantly released and healed. Healing is not an event; it is a process.

The communications survey you completed earlier in this chapter will enable you to discover those areas of your relationship in which walls have been erected. The pages will do the talking, rather than your throwing emotions at each other. A score of two or more points on any particular question will clearly show you both that you have very different viewpoints on the same issue. Take time to find out why. Begin by accepting the possibility that some of the differential may be due to the way you have acted, or reacted, in the past. You, as well as your partner, may have been responsible for slamming the door shut and blocking all healthy communication.

Agree together now to reopen that door. Look at each other from a new perspective. Think to yourself, *What have I done to you that has caused you to shut me off? What can I do to make you feel safe in expressing your real feelings to me? Can I also express my innermost needs to you without fear of having the door slammed again in my face?*

This survey is a valuable tool if you will use it. It will help in building your marriage to the level of intimacy that God intended for it to be. Now you are ready for Part 2 of the Communication in Marriage Survey.

Communication Survey, Part 2

Once again there are separate surveys for husbands and for wives. Complete your own list without "spying" on your partner's answers; if you prefer, write your answers on a separate piece of paper.

When you have each finished your pages, making sure that you complete all five sections to the best of your ability, make an appointment with your mate. Take time to share with each other what you have written and what you feel. The same three basic rules still apply: Don't interrupt, don't give "you" messages, and don't say "never" or "always."

Part 2 for Wives

A. The two personality weaknesses in my husband that I would most like to see strengthened are:

1. _____

2. _____

B. The two personality weaknesses in me that my husband would like to see strengthened are:

1. _____

2. _____

C. The three major emotional needs I want my husband to meet for me are:

1. _____

2. _____

3. _____

D. The three major emotional needs that my husband wants me to meet for him are:

1. _____

2. _____

3. _____

E. Three things in our marriage that I do not feel my husband and I can discuss are:

1. _____

2. _____

3. _____

Part 2 for Husbands

A. The two personality weaknesses in my wife that I would most like to see strengthened are:

1. _____

2. _____

B. The two personality weaknesses in me that my wife would like to see strengthened are:

1. _____

2. _____

C. The three major emotional needs I want my wife to meet for me are:

1. _____

2. _____

3. _____

D. The three major emotional needs that my wife wants me to meet for her are:

1. _____

2. _____

3. _____

E. Three things in our marriage that I do not feel my wife and I can discuss are:

1. _____

2. _____

3. _____

To maintain the progress you have made, resolve now to redo the survey in three months: Right now, set aside a night on your calendar for that purpose. And protect that date, for it is very important to both of you. Don't let any other less essential activity steal away your "progress report." You may be thrilled at how much better you are doing, although you will probably see some areas that still need improvement. Redirect your attention and effort on those areas. You will be glad you did!

Changing Yourself

When couples seek marriage counseling they must both be willing to listen, to change, and to resist placing the blame on the other person. We have met with couples after seminars who wanted to prove to us that the fault was the other person's. Occasionally they try outshouting each other in a desperate attempt to win. When this happens in front of an innocent person who is trying to help, imagine what this spouse is like at home! When each partner is trying to win, they both lose.

In his book *Feeling Good: The New Mood Therapy,* Philadelphia psychiatrist David Burns says that frequently in marriage problems one member of the couple is "resistant to change ... very angry, perceiving him or herself as a victim and blind to his own role in the problem.... The price of intimacy is giving up anger and hostility."

Although Dr. Burns doesn't say so, we know that without the power of the Holy Spirit in our lives, giving up anger and hostility is difficult. Yet we agree with his statement that we will never achieve intimacy in our marriage relationships until we give up anger and hostility. There is little hope that we can communicate effectively and lovingly when we are angry. Often our hostility comes from childhood issues and is not the fault of our mates.

Choleric Betty knew she could be happy if only she had a different husband. As she told us, "Even the pastor admits that Joe is boring." A letter came from her a short time ago expressing how enlightening it was to read *Personality Plus* and find out there were other people like Joe and her.

"Now that I see Joe is a genuine Phlegmatic, a balanced and low-key person, I've started to look at him differently," she wrote. "I realize that two of me might be too much for one marriage. When I told Joe that I found out what kind of personality he had and that it was all right, he almost fell off the couch!

" 'I didn't think you felt I had any personality,' he said.

"I told him I didn't used to think so but I had begun to realize that different isn't wrong. A big smile came over his face and he's been beaming ever since. He even sent me flowers at the studio and signed the card *Personality Plus!* Can you believe it?"

We *can* believe it because we get letters every day telling us how lives have been changed by understanding the personality differences.

We got another letter from Betty later telling us that she and her husband had done the Communication Surveys. She told us that two months earlier she would not even have tried to do anything with him where he had to talk.

"Now that I understand my personality, I realize that I never gave Joe a chance," she said. "As soon as he would start a sentence I would jump in and finish it. No wonder he didn't say much.

"When I read your first rule on communication and found out that I should let my partner express his feelings without interrupting or correcting, I realized I had *never* done that. I was so impatient to get to my words that I cut his off. He had learned to sit quietly and say nothing. It was easier than trying to buck me. I took it that he had nothing to say and was boring.

"Now that I'm biting my tongue, I've found that he still has the dry Phlegmatic sense of humor that I loved when we were dating. He's really not all that dull. There may be other women out there like me. Please tell them to encourage their husbands and let them talk. By nighttime some of these men are too tired to fight. Joe is so happy with what the Communication Surveys taught us that he's giving them out to people at work. (I called your office and ordered some.) He's become somewhat of a counselor on his own. Will miracles never cease!"

Isn't it amazing to see what a simple little exercise can do to change a marriage? The secret is in *doing* it. So few people will take the time to sit down and exchange ideas in a positive setting. They'll watch TV, go shopping, do aerobics, visit friends, and chauffeur children, but they will not face their marriage issues. They use the old excuse "We've tried it before and it didn't work."

Take the time to understand your personality and to exchange feelings by using the communication survey. Who knows—this could be a major milestone in your marriage.

As Betty said, "I've read a lot of books, but I always used them to straighten out other people. Now I'm beginning to work on myself, and Joe is delighted."

18

🪷

BUILD UP RELATIONSHIPS AND TEAR DOWN WALLS

In our family we have all memorized Ephesians 4:29: "Let no corrupt communication proceed out of your mouth, but that which is good to the use of edifying, that it may minister grace unto the hearers." We call this our communication verse, and it ultimately became the foundation verse for my book *Silver Boxes*. As a family we reduced the verse down to three little words, "Is it edifying?" Let's see what this verse means.

Let no corrupt communication ...

Any curt, cutting, caustic comment is corrupt. Any sarcasm, slander, or swearing is corrupt. The Bible tells us that we are to use no corrupt communication.

... proceed out of your mouth ...

When we are in control of our senses, we can stop damaging words before they get out. Some of us Sanguines get our mouths in motion before our brain is in gear, and we live to regret it. We must train ourselves to think before we speak. Once the words are out, we can't stuff them back in; they are intangible and elusive.

On Marita's fourth birthday she received four talcum powder mitts. No child needed that much powder, so I put them away. The following Sunday we had company, and while the adults lingered over dessert the children went to Marita's room to play. After a while a little girl came out ghostly white from head to toe. Only her eyes stood out. The mothers all ran to see what had happened. The children had found the four talcum mitts and they had powdered each other completely. Every particle of powder was out of the mitts and the room was a mist of white. No matter how we tried, we could never have gotten that powder back in the mitts, and for months when we walked on Marita's carpet little puffs of powder appeared.

Many families have done the same with words. We've covered each other with angry barbs and sarcastic accusations. We've hit each other with demeaning phrases and we can't get them back. No matter how we try to apologize, those words are out there floating loose. We can't stuff them back in our mitts, and when we tread on certain subjects those words come up as dust between our toes.

Don't let any corrupt communication proceed out of your mouth. In Mark 7:15 Jesus tells us that it's not what goes into our body that defiles us but what comes out of it. For from the inside, from a man's heart, come the evil ideas which lead him to do immoral things and to say unkind, vicious, and slanderous words.

...but that which is good to the use of edifying...

Edifying means to build up. Does everything that comes out of your mouth build up those to whom it was directed? Or do many of your comments tear down the listener? Our words are to be good and to build up those around us.

Our daughter Lauren visited a Christian family for a few days, and when she came home she said, "There was something missing there." As we discussed what it might be, she realized that while they were nice people they never encouraged one another. The parents constantly complained to each other and nagged the children. The communication was tearing down and not building up. "I guess I didn't appreciate how you two speak to us until I saw how sad their life is without compliments and encouraging words; they don't even try to practice 'Is it edifying'!"

Proverbs 25:11 tells us, "A word fitly spoken is like apples of gold in pictures of silver."

... that it may minister grace to the hearers.

To minister means to serve and grace means a favor, so we are to serve up favors to those who hear us. When we give gifts to our friends we always buy the best we can afford. We want people to think of us as generous and thoughtful. Yet how often do we realize that each word we give is a gift? It is presented to someone. Are your words wrapped up in a silver box, or do they come in a plain brown wrapper?

This verse, Ephesians 4:29, was life-changing to our family as we were raising our children. When any one of us would say something unkind, some sentence that did not do a favor, we were each allowed to ask, "Is it edifying?" By checking each other, we learned to be kind and complimentary.

Does your home exemplify this teaching? Galatians 5:15 in The Living Bible says, "If instead of showing love among yourselves you are always critical and catty, watch out! Beware of ruining each other." How easy it is to ruin each other with critical words! How much easier it is to destroy a marriage than to build it up!

Have you ever read *Silver Boxes—The Gift of Encouragement?* It has become a classic. Once you have read it, you'll want everyone you know to have it, so they too will give out words that are like gifts, little silver boxes with bows on top.

Am I Talking Through a Hole in the Wall?

Some of you may have spent so many years building your walls of interruption, depression, anger, false agreement, joking, ridicule, defensiveness, or silence to fence off your own area of Private Property that it would take King Arthur and his entire court to knock down your fortress. You have learned how to fend off invaders with your weapons and you've successfully kept your mate at a distance. You communicate on your terms on your topics at your time. You've established a pattern and you don't know how to change.

In the last three chapters you've learned a few facts:

- To communicate we need a transmitter and a receiver.
- We need to be tuned in to the right wavelength.
- We need to be static-free, clear of anything that hinders our reception.
- We must have our transmitter off in order to hear.
- We can't send and receive at the same time.

You understand the principles but you don't think you have the power to put it into practice—and you're right. On our own we can't change our pattern of behavior, but in Romans 12:1,2 we learn that when we present our bodies, including our minds and our mouths, to the Lord, He will transform us. He will give us the ability to communicate on a positive level. We need to plug ourselves into a dependable power.

We can try to break down the barriers to communication with our own hands, but we will fail. "All we like sheep have gone astray; we have turned each one to his own way" (Isaiah 53:6). When our own way leads us into trouble, when our marriage is falling apart, we little sheep need help. When a wall has come up between us and we're talking through the cracks, we need a carpenter to take it down. We need Jesus. Paul tells us in Ephesians 2 that we have walked a worldly path, that our conversations have been in the flesh, that we are by nature angry children, and that without Christ we have no hope, but that God is rich in mercy and He loves us. Through Christ Jesus He has brought those of us who were far off unto Himself.

"For he is our peace, who hath made both one and hath broken down the middle wall of partition between us" (Ephesians 2:14).

When Fred teaches his lesson on communicating, he demonstrates the ability of Christ to break down our walls by this little triangle.

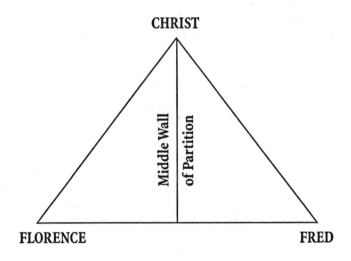

You see Fred and Florence far apart, with a wall between us. We know it shouldn't be there, but it sneaked up in the night and we are on opposite sides. At the very top of the wall is Jesus Christ, who says, "Come unto me."

As Fred looks up he begins to climb. His eyes are not on me and my nasty behavior but on the Lord. As he prays, he rises up until he reaches the top and is one with the Lord. If I refuse to budge and want to wallow in my miseries, Fred doesn't have to worry. His peace is in the Lord, who has promised him, "If I am lifted up I will draw all men to me." As I sense that Fred is at peace, that he is not going to fight with me but is loving me unconditionally in spite of my bad behavior, I begin to soften and start scaling my side. The closer I get to Christ, the closer I get to Fred, until we are all three at the top and the wall is gone.

As Fred teaches, "My peace does not depend on my partner's behavior but on my relationship with the Lord." Where are you sitting today? Are you and your partner on opposite sides of a wall? Is there a middle wall of partition between you? Are you tired of talking through a hole in the wall? It takes one person to start the upward climb. Shouldn't it be you?

Look Up

Thou wilt keep him in perfect peace whose mind is stayed on thee, because he trusteth in thee (Isaiah 26:3).

Know that when you look up to the Lord and trust Him to straighten out your problem with your partner, He will. You are responsible for your own behavior, not your partner's. Do what you know is right, and let the Lord pull up your mate.

Lift Up

If I am lifted up ... I will draw all men unto me (John 12:32).

When you lift up the Lord and not yourself and your opinions, you take the pressure off your partner and allow the Lord to work. He will, in His own time and way, draw your partner to Himself.

Light Up

He is our peace, who hath made both one and hath broken down the middle wall of partition between us (Ephesians 2:14).

Now, 44 years later, we still work on our communications. Some of the habit patterns that were established in the earlier years did not easily dissolve. Fred's critical and correcting spirit left emotional scars that did not simply disappear one day. Fred has worked diligently to do his part to remove all traces of the wall that he built. I have done the same. Today Fred and I travel constantly, all over the world, helping couples tear down walls, lift up the Lord, and love each other. We are together 24 hours a day, seven days a week, and we are having the best time of our lives. We're not merely pretending to *like* each other, because now we truly *love* each other. What an amazing difference there is, because we did what we are suggesting to you. Was it worth it? The answer is a resounding yes! Should you keep trying? Without a doubt!

As you allow Christ to lift you both up to the top, He makes you one again. He reunites you with a peace that passes all understanding. He breaks down the middle wall of partition between you. No longer are you each huddled in darkness on opposite sides of the wall, but you are together, on top, in the light!

19

PRAYER CHANGES PEOPLE

Continually restate to yourself what the purpose of your life is. The destined end of man is not happiness, not health, but holiness. Holiness means unsullied walking with the feet, unsullied talking with the tongue, unsullied thinking with the mind—every detail of the life under the scrutiny of God.

—Oswald Chambers, *My Utmost for His Highest*

Why are you here? What is your purpose for living? These are questions I (Fred) frequently asked myself before I became a Christian in August of 1966. Before then I had not a clue as to why I was on this earth. Life had not been particularly good to me; for most of my first 37 years I had been plagued with doubts and discouragement even though I worked hard to overcome these barriers and become "a success." And what did I think I needed to do to become a success? Build a business, make a substantial amount of money, live in a nice house, have a loving wife and children I could be proud of, gain personal recognition, and leave this world a somewhat better place than I found it.

Look at my list of goals. Check those that apply to you and add any others that you believe indicate success.

_____ Build a business.

_____ Make a substantial amount of money.

_____ Live in a big house.

_____ Have a loving wife and children I could be proud of.

_____ Gain personal recognition.

_____ Leave this world a better place than I found it.

_____ _____

_____ _____

When I review what I once thought success meant, I am struck by how materialistic and self-centered I was, with the exception of the last item on the list. And even this has self-centered overtones because I also wanted to be remembered and recognized for what I accomplished. Perhaps a statue or a publicly displayed painting would help people remember me when I was gone! I am reminded of a poem I once saw that said if you want to see how big an impact you will have on the world, stick your hand in a bucket of water, then take it out. The mark that remains in the water is your mark on the world. This does tend to give one a sense of humility and finiteness! But realistically, if our purpose in life is to make our mark on the world, aren't we doomed to disappointment? After all, they toppled Lenin's statue in Red Square.

Lenin? Lenin who? How quickly they forget once we are gone!

So what *is* our purpose in this world as Christians? Again and again Scripture gives us the clear answer:

Let your light so shine before men that they may see your good works and *glorify your Father which is in heaven* (Matthew 5:16).

You have been bought with a price; therefore *glorify God in your body* (1 Corinthians 6:20 NASB).

Whatever you do, do *all to the glory of God* (1 Corinthians 10:31 NASB).

With one accord you may with one voice *glorify the God and Father of our Lord Jesus Christ* (Romans 15:6 NASB).

Whoever speaks . . . whoever serves, let him do so as by the strength which God supplies, so that *in all things God may be glorified through Jesus Christ* (1 Peter 4:11 NASB).

These Scriptures tell us we are put on this earth as Christians for one thing and one thing alone: to glorify our Father in heaven. Our lives are not our own; we have been purchased with a price. Everything we do or say is to bring honor and glory to the Lord. As Oswald Chambers wrote so eloquently in *My Utmost for His Highest,* "The purpose for which [we are] created is that [we] may be God's servant, one in whom God is glorified," and "There is only one relationship that matters, and that is your personal relationship to a personal Redeemer and Lord. Let everything else go, but maintain that at all costs, and God will fulfill His purpose through your life."

The Relationship That Matters Most

To help you evaluate how well you are letting everything else go so you can concentrate on the "one relationship that matters," write the number that best describes your response now, *today*, to each verse in the following evaluation.

0 = Rarely
1 = Sometimes

2 = Often

3 = Most of the time

Don't be afraid to write a 3 if your answer really is "most of the time." But also be honest enough to give yourself a zero if you rarely do as this verse directs you. No one is going to check up on you. Your answers are for you alone to help you assess your current spiritual commitment.

_____ 1. Seek ye first the kingdom of God and his righteousness (Matthew 6:33).

_____ 2. Do not lay up for yourselves treasures upon earth ... But lay up for yourselves treasures in heaven (Matthew 6:19,20 NASB).

_____ 3. Devote yourselves to prayer, keeping *alert* in it with an attitude of thanksgiving (Colossians 4:2 NASB).

_____ 4. Accept one another [including your spouse], just as Christ also accepted [you] to the glory of God (Romans 15:7 NASB).

_____ 5. Be kind to one another, tenderhearted, forgiving each other, just as God in Christ also has forgiven you (Ephesians 4:32 NASB).

_____ 6. Husbands, love your wives, just as Christ also loved the church and gave Himself up for her (Ephesians 5:25 NASB).

_____ 7. Do nothing from selfishness ... but ... regard [your spouse] as more important than [yourself] (Philippians 2:3 NASB).

_____ 8. Rejoice always; pray without ceasing; in *everything* give thanks (1 Thessalonians 5:16-18 NASB).

_____ 9. Whatever is true, whatever is honorable, whatever is right, whatever is pure, whatever is lovely *...let your mind dwell* on these things (Philippians 4:8 NASB).

_____ 10. Discipline yourself for the *purpose of godliness*; for bodily discipline is only of little profit, but godliness is profitable for all things ... for the present life and also for the life to come. (1 Timothy 4:7,8 NASB).

_____ 11. Let no unwholesome word proceed from your mouth, but only such ... that it may give grace [a favor] to those who hear (Ephesians 4:29 NASB).

_____ 12. Lay aside every encumbrance, and the sin which so easily entangles us, and ... run with endurance the race that is set before us, fixing our eyes on Jesus (Hebrews 12:1,2 NASB).

Now add up all your responses and enter your total score:

_____

The maximum score on your spiritual evaluation is 36. How did you rate yourself? If you were a little too hard on yourself, go back and recheck your answers. On the other hand, if you gave yourself a higher score than you deserve, go back and correct that as well. Be honest with yourself. The objective is to help you see how deeply you are committed to becoming like Christ and how effectively you are working to have that "mind in you which was also in Christ Jesus" (Philippians 2:5).

That should be our goal, our purpose in life. As we become more and more like Him, we take into ourselves more and more of His nature and characteristics. Our friends begin to see the difference. Our family members start to feel more relaxed and comfortable around us. They begin to see a new kind of spouse and parent, one whose life radiates the love of the Lord Jesus.

Did you end up with a total score below 20? A score in this range indicates that living for the Lord and making Him preeminent in your life is probably not your highest priority right now. Other things are capturing your time and attention. They may all be "good" things. They may not be bad or evil. But they may not be the *best* things you could be focusing on. You now have the opportunity to decide what will be the centerpiece, the focus, of your life in the future. Where will you be spiritually a year from today? Write down your answer in the space below.

I determine today that a year from now I will

_____

_____

_____

_____

If your total score falls between 21 and 30, you are clearly making a conscientious effort to become the person that God intends you to be. You can see for yourself where your lower scores were and gain insight into the areas where you need to apply some extra attention and effort.

Scores between 31 and 36 don't mean you're almost perfect. So don't pat yourself on the back just yet! Let the Lord Jesus tell you when He is well-pleased with you. But scores in this range do help you see that you are moving in the direction He desires for you.

"The abiding characteristic of a spiritual man is . . . the one concentrated *passion* of the life is *Jesus Christ*," wrote Oswald Chambers. "Never allow anything to deflect you from insight into Jesus Christ. It is the test of whether you are spiritual or not. To be unspiritual means that other things have a growing fascination for you" (from *My Utmost for His Highest*).

How to Become More Spiritual

As Christians we understand that we are to make the Lord the first priority in our lives. But the question is always, How do we actually do that? How do we find time for Him in our day? You may be saying what I said a few years ago: "My day is already so full that I don't even have time for myself."

Sometimes it's not easy to change old habits, even when we know how important it is to make the change. But there is one certainty, no matter how busy our days are, no matter how pressured we already feel our lives are: *We must make time for the Lord.* We must make Him the first priority in every day of our lives.

There are at least three constants in our lives. One is aging and eventually death. Another is change, or uncertainty. The third is time: We all have the same 24 hours in every day and, to varying degrees, the discretion to determine how we use that amount of time.

If we are to be the spiritual leaders in our homes, if we are to fulfill our God-ordained function of responsibility as Scripture directs us, we must make a commitment. We must find a minimum of 30 minutes a day when we can be alone with God. Our goal should be an hour, but we can start with a more modest objective. Look over your daily schedule. When can you set aside at least 30 minutes to spend with Him? It might mean getting up a half-hour earlier and then retreating to the quiet spot you have set aside for your daily communion.

There are two essential elements of the Christian's daily life. Both are equally important, but tragically most people omit them completely from their daily lives. These two essentials are Bible study and prayer.

1. Bible Study

How much time have you actually spent in Bible study, not in church or in a group but in *personal* Bible study, in the past seven days? Count up the actual number of minutes or hours you have spent in undistracted prayer with your Father in heaven during these same seven days. The minutes or hours you come up with will probably closely correlate to your score on the spiritual assessment. Men, why do we so often allow our wives to surpass us in Bible study, in seminars, in personal growth—and then expect them to recognize and accept us as their spiritual "head"!

I would like you to know that I too struggled for many years with these same conflicts. The theoretical idea of Bible study was never really a problem for me; I enjoyed studying, learning, and growing in my knowledge of God's Word. The problem was actually finding the time to do it. Too frequently the pressures of my daily schedule, the "tyranny of the urgent," would crowd out my best intentions; weeks, maybe months, would go by before I realized I had been skipping my daily Bible study.

2. Prayer

While Bible study is something I've always enjoyed, the other daily essential, prayer, was a different matter for me. It never seemed to come easily, perhaps because no one ever taught me how to pray. Too often when I would sit at my desk to pray my mind would begin wandering. Other times I would start to pray and then just doze off. I tried praying in a corner. I tried praying on my knees. I tried praying standing up. I tried praying in the car while driving to work. Nothing seemed to work. Because prayer seemed to be so unmeaningful, I pretty much stopped praying except at appointed times.

Until about ten years ago I could count up on one hand the number of meaningful times of prayer I had experienced in my whole Christian life! All that has changed, and now I often speak on prayer, sharing what I've learned. I begin by asking, "How many of you, like me, have struggled with prayer? Do you find that your mind wanders or you doze off, and then because prayer seems not to be meaningful to you, you find yourself not praying very much?" No longer am I stunned at the number of hands raised in response to my questions—usually a full 80 percent of the audience! So I know this is a common problem. It is particularly a problem for people who have suffered childhood victimization. Among those of us who have been violated it is almost universal!

Ten years ago all I needed was one hand to count the times when prayer had stirred my heart. But today? There have been too many times to count! Sometimes it is daily, one wonderful day after another. I admit that some days my prayer time doesn't seem to be as dynamic as on other days. But that isn't the issue, for I am still maintaining my daily prayer contact with my Father in heaven. I look forward each day to the time we spend together. Bible study is still rewarding and insightful; now prayer is too. What has made the difference? It's a practice I began ten years ago.

At first glance what I am about to tell you may seem incredibly simple. But I assure you that if you do what I suggest consistently, with your heart and mind open to God's presence, it can change your life.

Ten years ago I began, at the Lord's direction, to write down my daily prayers. I've done it almost every day since then. I simply write a letter to my Lord in heaven, sometimes addressing Him as "Dear Lord Jesus" and other times as "Dear heavenly Father." There are times when I don't address Him at all; I just start writing to Him. The words and the form are not important. What is important is that I come into His presence to talk to Him, praise Him, worship Him, confess to Him, ask of Him, and to intercede before Him for someone else. Over the last ten years I have spent an average of 30 to 40 minutes in communion with Him each day. There have been many times when we have spent well over an hour together.

Until March 1993, I used a standard-size 8½" × 11" spiral notebook. (Later I'll tell you what I use now.) Writing on both sides of the page, 200 pages or more per notebook, I have filled 13 notebooks. I call them my "prayer closet." I always have my current notebook with me, and wherever I am, whenever the time presents itself, I sequester myself away and spend personal, private time with the Lord.

The Blessings of Daily Written Prayer

Writing your prayers does many things for you. In my life, the most obvious thing it has done is bring me the healing power of the Lord. All the old issues I struggled with for so many years have been cleansed away. Today when I speak on how prayer can change your life, there are always people who come up to me later and tell me the phenomenal changes that have occurred in their lives, too, as they have written their prayers.

Writing your prayers is also an important discipline; by dating your prayers you can see very quickly if you have missed any days. Second, it helps you focus your mind on the Lord and prevents your thoughts from wandering. Writing also helps keep you alert, in accordance with Colossians 4:2: "Devote yourselves to prayer, keeping alert in it with an attitude of thanksgiving" (NASB).

It also helps protect you from the flaming missiles of the evil one, who is very happy when Christians are not praying. Inevitably he tries to attack us as we endeavor to submit ourselves to the Lord and draw closer to Him.

Most amazingly, as I write my prayers, I have learned to hear God's still, small voice. When I do I write down exactly, word for word, what He has said to me!

This describes only a fraction of the many blessings I have been given by coming to my heavenly Father in daily written prayer. If you are interested in further understanding of written prayer I suggest you read my book *The Promise of Healing.** The final section is devoted to various practical aspects of making written prayer, or prayer journaling, as it is also called, a rewarding part of your daily journey with the Lord.

Perhaps the most significant benefit of daily written prayer is a totally changed life! For verification that it has changed *my* life, you could ask my wife. She lives with me. She sees that the suppressed anger that once raged within me is gone. She no longer sees a critical spirit in me. Now she not only enjoys being with me, but she misses me deeply on those few occasions when we're apart. Jesus said, "I have come to heal the brokenhearted, to set the captive free" (paraphrase of Luke 4:18). He has done that for me through written prayer simply because I was obedient to His offer to "come unto me, all ye that labor and are heavy laden, and I will give you rest" (Matthew 11:28). God also kept the promise made in Isaiah 26:3: "Thou wilt keep him in perfect peace whose mind is stayed on thee." Writing my prayers enables me to keep my mind focused, or "stayed on" Him.

I will never forget an experience that happened just a few years ago when I started to write my prayers early one morning. I had begun my prayers with an inspiring time of Bible study. Then I started to write. I wrote and wrote, covering about 4½ pages. I didn't have any particular issues that morning to discuss with my Father; I was just enjoying our fellowship. When I finished after an hour and 20 minutes of writing I felt uplifted, encouraged, and filled with God's spirit. Then I decided to read over again, for a second blessing,

---

* Fred Littauer, *The Promise of Healing* (Nashville: Thomas Nelson, 1994; originally published as *The Promise of Restoration* by Here's Life Publishing in 1990).

the prayers I had just written. How long do you think it took me to read what I had just spent well over an hour writing? Just about four minutes!

Then I heard a voice speaking to me. It sounded so clear in my mind that I will never forget the exact words I heard: "You're wasting your time writing your prayers. Think of how many more people you could pray for if you prayed orally." It sounded logical and seemed valid, but immediately I heard another voice, a different one, saying, "No, I want you to continue writing your prayers, for all the time you are writing your mind is stayed on Me!" There was no question whose voices I heard. The second was clearly the Lord, countermanding the voice of satan.* He was trying to separate me from what the Lord was using to bring me closer to Him. I don't know about you, but as for me and my house, we will serve the Lord! I will not listen to the evil one.

I have continued to write my prayers almost daily since that time. I say *almost,* for there have been days when I've missed this communion. I have learned how important it is, however, to *not miss,* because if I miss but one day, it seems quite easy to miss another. And if I happen to miss two, well, missing just one more will be okay, won't it? No, it won't! That's just what satan is watching for. He wants me to miss; then he knows I may become vulnerable so his fiery darts are more apt to sneak through my spiritual armor.

Maintaining Daily Discipline

I have developed a little system that helps me maintain the daily discipline of writing my prayers. It may also help you maintain good habits and can be used just as effectively to help you break bad ones. Each day in a small pocket diary I write down the number of days in a row I have spent time with the Lord in written

---

* Satan's name is not capitalized because he deserves no honor.

prayer. There have been days when I wasn't able to get to my prayer time until late at night because of the complexity of our schedule that day.

Now I will not allow myself to get in bed until I have had at least some time with the Lord. I'll admit I'm apt to be sleepy, and my prayer time may be a little shorter than usual or less intense than I would like, but I still take a moment to bring my spirit into communion with God. It's not that God needs to hear from me; it's that I need that time with Him, and I can't afford to miss even one day. Tomorrow might be just as hectic, and then I would have missed two days!

As I see that little number growing each day on my weekly diary, I don't want to have to go back to zero and start all over. It really works to give me that edge that I need in self-discipline. And the results speak for themselves!

In March of 1993 I succumbed to the temptation of buying a laptop computer. Even though I was basically "computer illiterate," I began learning how to write my daily prayers on my computer. I'm still not a typist, but I'm getting there, gradually. I'm picking up my writing speed. Now instead of getting cramps in my arms I sometimes get them in my shoulders! Writing my prayers on my laptop computer has proved to be just as effective as handwriting, and it gives me many additional technical advantages. It has now become my new prayer closet where I pray to my Father who hears me in secret and rewards me openly (see Matthew 6:6).

We are all well aware that there are many Scriptures that command us to pray. We know that prayer is for our benefit, not God's. The Lord doesn't need to hear our prayers, but He likes to hear from us. He wants to hear from us. Jesus Himself in His earthly ministry frequently slipped away to a private place to pray to His Father. In the Garden of Gethsemane on the night before His crucifixion, Jesus went a little ways away from Peter, James, and John and said to them, "Remain here and keep watch with Me."

When He returned about an hour later, what were they doing? They were sleeping! He was about to give His life for them, and they couldn't even stay awake to stand watch while He prayed! His words to them are still important for us to understand today: *"Could you not keep watch for one hour?"* (Mark 14:37 NASB). Is Jesus saying something to you at this very moment about keeping watch with Him for just one hour? Perhaps just one hour a day? His very next words to these three disciples are equally significant for us, His disciples today: "Keep watching and praying, that you may not enter into temptation; the spirit is willing, but the flesh is weak" (Matthew 26:41; see also Mark 14:38 NASB).

How profound His words are for us today! Indeed, our spirit is willing but there is so much temptation around us. It is so easy to stumble—not only to stumble into sin, but far more frequently to stumble out of our daily prayer fellowship with Him. Make no mistake—satan prowls about like a roaring lion, seeking whom he may devour (See 1 Peter 5:8). It is a foolish general who does not keep his or her perimeters well-armed and guarded. It is a foolish Christian who does not keep his or her spiritual defenses on full-time alert as well—always vigilant, ever ready to discern the infiltrations of the enemy. Those flaming missiles will come as surely as the darkness descends at the end of each day.

Staying consistently close to the source of our spiritual power enables us to know exactly where our shield of faith is so that we can reach for it in time to protect ourselves and our family from the enemy's attacks! Our Father expects us to be the *protectors* of our families, protecting them physically and emotionally; and certainly as spiritual leaders we are to protect them spiritually as well. To do this we need to know the strength of our spiritual power, and we need to know how to exercise it.

Could You Be Your Own Marriage Counselor?

What can you do for yourself?

1. Take an objective look.

Since our first thought in negative situations is to straighten out others involved, we seldom think of looking at ourselves. Our friend came to me with her marriage problems. She claimed she wanted help but her husband Charlie refused to go to a counselor. One day she came to me in tears: Charlie had agreed to go for help.

"Why are you crying?" I asked. "Isn't this what you've been waiting for?"

"I don't understand," she replied. "The minute he said he would go I got upset."

What was this woman's reason for tears? Now that Charlie was willing to seek help, she was miserable. As long as he refused to go, she could content herself that he was the problem. But once *he* was willing *she* had to examine herself and be ready to change. It's always easier to blame others than to straighten up ourselves.

Understanding the four basic Personalities is an excellent tool for self-examination. Even in the brief form given in this book, you can find your strengths and work to accentuate them, and identify your weaknesses and pray to overcome them. By being aware of the different kinds of natures that people have, you can more easily accept those who are not like you. It was such a relief to Fred and me to know for the first time that we weren't out to get each other. Because I was Sanguine and wanted to have fun didn't mean I was a nitwit. Fred comments, "On the contrary, I now recognize and respect the brilliant mind which works like a computer that God gave to Florence. Because she is different, I always thought she was wrong. I thought I needed to help her become 'perfect' like me. Now I love and appreciate the beautiful woman that God created. He was pleased with what He created just the way He created it. Now I have learned to be pleased He created her to be the bright, sparkling, and spontaneous Sanguine that she is."

Because Fred was serious and purposeful didn't mean he was morose. As we began to see ourselves as different and often opposite in personality, we saw two people whom God could use in His divine plan. We were able for the first time to look realistically at our own weaknesses and want to improve ourselves rather than each other.

It is always easy to want to shape up other people, but we cannot counsel ourselves until we are able to evaluate our own lives from an objective point of view. Read *Personality Plus* and *Your Personality Tree* for further information on understanding yourself, your mate, and your family.

2. Check your maturity.

Since placing the blame on others is a very natural emotion of self-preservation, we tend not to reach full maturity. We make excuses and we rationalize around our failures instead of being willing to admit our faults and take responsibility for our actions. I spent my whole life knowing that I could be happy if only my circumstances would improve. When they got better I raised my goals, always hoping for that mythical day in the future when all the pieces in my lifetime puzzle would fit together. That has never happened, but I have learned in whatever state I am, therewith to be content.

We are to grow up to Christ, who is our Head. We are to aim to become like Him. Only a mature person can step back, take a look at his life, and see where it needs to be changed. If you haven't already done it, go back and take the maturity tests in Chapter 8.

3. Study the cure for marriage problems.

While the steps given for "The Cure" seem simple, we have seen them work in many lives. The key to any advancement lies in a personal desire to improve the situation. We have to be willing to be willing. We have to look at the heart of our problems and not just go sell the cows. When both sides of a marriage case are willing, any pair can be pulled back together. When only one side is willing, it's possible but more difficult.

When neither side is willing, it takes a miracle. But God specializes in hopeless cases. He wants us to confess our sins to Him and ask Him to remove them from our lives. He wants us to see the good qualities in our mate that attracted us to him or her in the first place and stop focusing on the negatives. When we are ready, the Lord will give us the ability to forgive our partners and put the problems of the past behind us.

You can be your own marriage counselor if you will prayerfully follow these steps. Remember, you are only held accountable for your own life, not that of your partner, and if he or she does not improve at all you can be content in knowing that *you* are in the center of God's will. As Christians, we have the unique gift of being able to have inner peace and God's joy no matter what our circumstances may be (John 14:27; 15:11).

4. Learn to communicate.

When you can sit down peaceably with your mate and discuss your differences, you can solve any disagreement. Ask yourself what barriers you have used to prevent a meaningful exchange of thoughts. What Private Property have you been protecting? What cutting comments have you thrown to hurt your partner? Are you willing to concentrate and listen to what your partner has to say? Can you sit still and not interrupt? Can you hear complaints and not get defensive?

If you can communicate honestly and helpfully with your partner, you can solve your own marriage problems.

It is possible to be your own counselor if you can take an objective look at yourself, not lay the blame on others, be willing to change, forgive and forget, see your partner's good points, and communicate openly.

When Do We Need Outside Help?

When we are so clouded by emotion that we can only see our own side.

When we know the fault is our partner's and could prove it in any court of law.

When we are willing to change only if our partner shapes up first.

When we might try to forgive, but know we could never forget.

When we can't see anything good about our mate, and the feeling is mutual.

When we can't even speak without screaming.

When we don't think we can live another day like this.

What Kind of Help Do We Need?

When seeking help, it is best not to go to friends, as you put them in an awkward position. If they tell you the truth you'll hate them, and if they don't tell you the truth they can't help you.

Some pastors are excellent counselors, and those who are not able to get involved can usually recommend an objective Christian who is competent. If you have some scriptural knowledge you will have enough discernment to know whether the advice given is biblically sound. If a counselor suggests that you have an affair or prescribes any kind of sexual perversions, flee quickly. Unfortunately, there are some people in the psychology field today who take strange pleasure in suggesting unnatural acts to weak women or desperate men, so beware.

In the final chapter of my book *Blow Away the Black Clouds*, I teach how to counsel a depressed person. I have learned that everyone with a marriage problem is somewhat depressed, for depression is a feeling of hopelessness when we know we can't make it on our own.

Once you and your mate have completed the material in this book and have been able to talk openly about your past problems, you should invite a few couples into your home and begin to study with them. So many need help but don't know where to turn. You may provide that help by leading them to the Lord and then going through this material with them. Let them know you have had marriage problems; use your difficulties as examples and then show them solutions. There is no better way to continue improving than to teach others how to change.

When Fred and I first started teaching the Sunday school class on marriage, we had no experience and we were not psychologists. Yet people's lives were changed and many went on to help others as well.

When you are willing, the Lord is able.

21

IS THERE ANY HOPE?

Gail and Jay were full-time Christian workers on the staff of a large organization when I met them. Gail was a very tall, strong, attractive woman of 22, and Jay looked like the typical college football player. She was a Choleric and he was an easygoing Phlegmatic.

Gail heard me speak at a conference and asked if she could bring a mixed-up friend to see me. After we dealt with her friend, the woman said, "Gail's not very happy herself."

The friend left and Gail told me she was furious at Jay because he wanted to buy a sports car, which she felt was foolish and impractical. As she sputtered on, it was apparent that Gail and Jay didn't see eye-to-eye on anything.

She thought he was strong when she married him because of his size, but now she felt he was weak. "He can't make a decision without thinking for days, and when he makes it he's wrong. I know

I'm supposed to be submissive, but he doesn't have much will, and I can get things done while he's thinking about it. He's supposed to be out on the campus each day but he forgets his appointments and some days he never leaves the house."

The more she talked the worse Jay became, until there was nothing good about Jay at all. Soon she admitted that she was ready to leave him if he didn't shape up.

The next day Jay came to see me. "I don't know why Gail thinks I'm weak. I lift weights every day!"

Jay told of a wife who wanted her own way, tried to hurry him and push him around, and thought he was dull and unspiritual.

"Do you know what she does if I don't let her have her way? She throws herself on the floor and has a temper tantrum."

I instantly pictured this tall young woman kicking and screaming on the floor.

"What do you do when this happens?"

"I just stand there and look down and say, 'Gail, please don't do that.'"

I suggested that the next time this took place he should tell her firmly to grow up and stop this childish behavior and then leave the room until she ceased. It's no fun to have a temper tantrum with no audience.

He came back pleased. "She stopped crying when I left."

I explained that lifting weights was not the kind of strength he needed. I suggested that they both begin by learning to identify and understand their God-given personality differences. I told him he had to show strong leadership in their marriage, become dependable in his ministry, and learn to make decisions.

When Gail returned I asked her about her temper tantrums, and she shamefully admitted that she had behaved this way all her life. "It worked with my mother, and when Jay wouldn't do what I wanted I tried it on him."

Choleric Gail had to back off on her controlling nature, grow up and stop her tantrums, and accept Jay the way he was. When I gave her some practical suggestions, she bucked me because she knew that everything was Jay's fault.

Gail and Jay needed help. They were blaming each other like little children. Gail was so upset over her problems that she couldn't think straight. Jay was utterly bewildered by this overpowering woman and thought lifting weights was the answer. They couldn't communicate without screaming, and their Christian ministry was disintegrating.

Is There Any Hope?

Within a few weeks many changes took place with Gail and Jay. I explained how different their personalities were, and they began to understand each other. Lights went on! I showed them what it meant to mature, and they began to grow up. I went over the steps in the Marriage Cure, and they followed them with success. I mediated their conversations until they could communicate without me.

Later they asked if they could do something for me to make up for the time I had spent with them, and I said, "Yes, put your story in letter form and let me print it to give hope to others."

Here is Gail's letter, and yes, there is hope.

Dear Florence,

I finally put down some of the basic changes in our lives since you counseled with us.

I didn't really believe in Jay or his abilities, so I didn't ever build him up because I felt that this was being a hypocrite. I felt that the way to make him a good husband was to tell him in detail all he'd done wrong that day and how he could improve. I earnestly prayed for Jay to change in these areas of weakness, especially in his stubbornness. He wouldn't do a thing I told him to do. To me, all our friction would be easily done away with if Jay would simply follow the solutions I had outlined for him. It all seemed so clear to me.

For example: In our work on the campus, we called students and made appointments in order to meet together and go over some principles to help them grow in their Christian life. Well, Jay would try to keep all these appointments in his head, without writing anything down. Needless to say, he would forget appointments or forget from one week to the next who he had seen and what he had gone over with them. I felt that it was my God-given duty to make him more efficient. But in spite of all my nagging and temper tantrums, Jay didn't become more organized; he became less organized.

It was the same story in our financial situation. Nothing I could say or do changed Jay in the least.

In our family spiritual relationship the same problem was repeated. I would remind him that he was my spiritual leader . . . "Right?" "Right!" "Well, why aren't you leading? You're going to be held accountable before God for never teaching me from the Word in a family devotion." So poor Jay would get out a book with some poem or lovely thought for the day. This was not up to par with what I wanted, and I let him know how I felt. I would say, "Jay, why don't we ever have a devotion out of the Bible?" To my amazement and bewilderment, in all three of these areas Jay never changed.

All three of these examples stem from the same basic root problem: I did not trust God and believe that He loved me enough to take care of changing the man I had married. I didn't realize that God was sovereign enough to not let anyone or anything ruin my life. I could never have said, "God, he is your child. Do what you want in his life." I was not submissive to Jay because I was not submissive to God. God's love and acceptance of me wasn't real. I didn't rest in God's protective care of my life. I felt it was up to me to see that my life wasn't ruined.

Meanwhile, Jay and I argued all the time. I tried to hurt him with words and eventually he tried to hurt me too. We both realized *that we were unhappy and not making our marriage work. I had been a Christian a year (which I thought was a long time) and we had been married three months.*

*We were sent to a brand-new campus that was one hour from any other staff to begin the work. I thought of asking our director's wife for help, but when I mentioned any problem of any nature to her, she wouldn't even let me finish my sentence before she was telling me to "confess." Also, they both made it clear that they thought Jay was not the spiritual tiger he should be. This added to the pressure I put on Jay to improve, because I wanted us to look good in their eyes. I was afraid to go to anyone for help because I felt they would ask Jay and me to leave the staff or think we were unspiritual. The fact that we **were** unspiritual and that God knew it didn't seem to dawn on me.*

But God knew what He was doing in allowing us to experience all these pressures, because I finally became so desperate that I was more concerned about our marriage than our ministry. I came to you for help that first summer because I felt that you were straightforward and didn't try to spiritualize things. You were practical. Also, I thought I'd never see you again and wouldn't have to worry about facing you after telling you all my problems. You came right to the heart of the problems . . . ME!

This shocked me. I had never thought I was wrong to nag Jay, because I thought my motives were pure. I would make him a man of God. You helped me see things from a different perspective—God's. It was God's responsibility to change Jay, not mine. I was not called into Jay's life to be the "Junior Holy Spirit." Then you went over what I was called to do in Jay's life. I was to be an encouragement. I was to build him up and give him a relaxed, accepting type of home atmosphere. This, you said, was being a true helpmate because I would be helping, not hindering, the Holy Spirit to change Jay's life.

I didn't know that there were practical, constructive things I could do and still be submissive. My mind didn't have to be in neutral, and that came as a surprise to me.

Also, besides looking at things from God's point of view, you helped me to see Jay's side of things. How did I learn how to do things? I learned by trying and making mistakes. You asked me, "How is Jay going to learn to be a good staff member, to handle your money, and to be the spiritual leader you need?" The only way was by my relaxing in God and letting Jay go. He needed to try, to make mistakes, to learn. So what if the lights go off! He'll learn to pay the electricity bill on time. It was amazing to see Jay respond to encouragement. He would ask my opinion and really listen. I got the results I could never have gotten by nagging. As Jay felt more and more secure and felt more like I respected and admired him, he changed tremendously.

As Jay and I talked about all of this later, he explained what my changes of attitude and action did for him. He told me that, for example, my harping on having a family devotion caused him to feel like he wasn't my spiritual leader, and so why even try? If his own wife didn't believe in him, what was the use? Then I began to tell him what I liked about the "nice thoughts for the day" and how much I appreciated him and what he had just taught me. I would tell him what a wonderful spiritual leader he was and how I looked forward to each time he taught me, instead of complaining because he didn't do it often enough. He said that this made him come before God and say, "Lord, Gail thinks I'm her spiritual leader and You know I'm not. Please change me so that I won't disappoint her."

All this time I thought he would get a big head if I constantly encouraged him, not knowing that this would only spur him on. I didn't realize that he already knew his shortcomings and felt terribly inadequate. All that my belittling did was paralyze him as far as change was concerned. But when I told him that I believed in him, he felt like maybe he wasn't such a loser and maybe God could use him.

He didn't feel threatened by someone who seemed to be able to do everything while he felt inadequate in everything. He now felt free to ask and learn how to be a good staff member and manager of our money. He knew that I wasn't going to pick up the ball if he dropped it. This made him realize that in **reality** he was my leader, and not just in my words. This forced him to get help and read and learn, because I wasn't going to do it for him.

As I stepped out on faith, God changed my heart. At first I would tell the Lord over and over, "Lord, I don't *feel* like Jay's my leader, but You say he is. So by faith I'm going to tell him how much I appreciate that devotion or that idea he presented, even though my feelings aren't that way." Gradually God began to make it real in my life. I began to really *feel* respect for him. The things I said to encourage him became real in my emotions. Also, I began to notice the good qualities in his life that were far superior to mine. Now he manages our money much better than I ever could. He has learned all of this because I let go of him and gave him the freedom to change or not.

I found that, when my mind was busy dwelling on the positive, it was easier to relax and be understanding. I used to have fits because Jay took so long to make a decision. But now I've come to cherish that quality in him, because I realize the reason it takes him so long is that he is weighing all the pros and cons, finding out God's leading in the matter, weighing other people's opinions, etc. All of this is because he loves me and realizes that his decision is going to affect my life. Therefore he wants to be sure he does the right thing. This is a big change in attitude for me from feeling that he was just wishy-washy or indecisive.

Finally, I discovered that treating him with respect and building him up causes him to treat me the same way in return. We have experienced such closeness and real joy in being together that it's hard to believe. One of the most rewarding times came when Jay told me that I was truly his best friend!

Thank you for all your love to us.

In Christ's Love,
Gail

Yes, there is hope!

APPENDIX A

Personality Profile Test
and Scoring Sheet

PERSONALITY PROFILE

DIRECTIONS: In *each* of the following rows of *four words across*, place an X in front of the *one* word that most often applies to you. Continue through all forty lines. *Be sure each number is marked*. If you are not sure of which word "most applies," ask a spouse or a friend, and think of what your answer would have been when you were *a child*. (Note: Definitions of test words are found in Appendix B.)

STRENGTHS

1	Adventurous	Adaptable	Animated	Analytical
2	Persistent	Playful	Persuasive	Peaceful
3	Submissive	Self-sacrificing	Sociable	Strong-willed
4	Considerate	Controlled	Competitive	Convincing
5	Refreshing	Respectful	Reserved	Resourceful
6	Satisfied	Sensitive	Self-reliant	Spirited
7	Planner	Patient	Positive	Promoter
8	Sure	Spontaneous	Scheduled	Shy
9	Orderly	Obliging	Outspoken	Optimistic
10	Friendly	Faithful	Funny	Forceful
11	Daring	Delightful	Diplomatic	Detailed
12	Cheerful	Consistent	Cultured	Confident
13	Idealistic	Independent	Inoffensive	Inspiring
14	Demonstrative	Decisive	Dry humor	Deep
15	Mediator	Musical	Mover	Mixes easily
16	Thoughtful	Tenacious	Talker	Tolerant
17	Listener	Loyal	Leader	Lively
18	Contented	Chief	Chartmaker	Cute
19	Perfectionist	Pleasant	Productive	Popular
20	Bouncy	Bold	Behaved	Balanced

294

WEAKNESSES

21	____ Blank	____ Bashful	____ Brassy	____ Bossy
22	____ Undisciplined	____ Unsympathetic	____ Unenthusiastic	____ Unforgiving
23	____ Reticent	____ Resentful	____ Resistant	____ Repetitious
24	____ Fussy	____ Fearful	____ Forgetful	____ Frank
25	____ Impatient	____ Insecure	____ Indecisive	____ Interrupts
26	____ Unpopular	____ Uninvolved	____ Unpredictable	____ Unaffectionate
27	____ Headstrong	____ Haphazard	____ Hard-to-please	____ Hesitant
28	____ Plain	____ Pessimistic	____ Proud	____ Permissive
29	____ Angered easily	____ Aimless	____ Argumentative	____ Alienated
30	____ Naive	____ Negative attitude	____ Nervy	____ Nonchalant
31	____ Worrier	____ Withdrawn	____ Workaholic	____ Wants credit
32	____ Too sensitive	____ Tactless	____ Timid	____ Talkative
33	____ Doubtful	____ Disorganized	____ Domineering	____ Depressed
34	____ Inconsistent	____ Introvert	____ Intolerant	____ Indifferent
35	____ Messy	____ Moody	____ Mumbles	____ Manipulative
36	____ Slow	____ Stubborn	____ Show-off	____ Skeptical
37	____ Loner	____ Lord-over-others	____ Lazy	____ Loud
38	____ Sluggish	____ Suspicious	____ Short-tempered	____ Scatterbrained
39	____ Revengeful	____ Restful	____ Reluctant	____ Rash
40	____ Compromising	____ Critical	____ Crafty	____ Changeable

NOW TRANSFER ALL OF YOUR X's TO THE CORRESPONDING WORDS ON THE PERSONALITY SCORING SHEET AND ADD UP YOUR TOTALS.

Created by Fred Littauer

PERSONALITY SCORING SHEET

STRENGTHS

	SANGUINE	CHOLERIC	MELANCHOLY	PHLEGMATIC
1	Animated	Adventurous	Analytical	Adaptable
2	Playful	Persuasive	Persistent	Peaceful
3	Sociable	Strong-willed	Self-sacrificing	Submissive
4	Convincing	Competitive	Considerate	Controlled
5	Refreshing	Resourceful	Respectful	Reserved
6	Spirited	Self-reliant	Sensitive	Satisfied
7	Promoter	Positive	Planner	Patient
8	Spontaneous	Sure	Scheduled	Shy
9	Optimistic	Outspoken	Orderly	Obliging
10	Funny	Forceful	Faithful	Friendly
11	Delightful	Daring	Detailed	Diplomatic
12	Cheerful	Confident	Cultured	Consistent
13	Inspiring	Independent	Idealistic	Inoffensive
14	Demonstrative	Decisive	Deep	Dry humor
15	Mixes easily	Mover	Musical	Mediator
16	Talker	Tenacious	Thoughtful	Tolerant
17	Lively	Leader	Loyal	Listener
18	Cute	Chief	Chartmaker	Contented
19	Popular	Productive	Perfectionist	Pleasant
20	Bouncy	Bold	Behaved	Balanced
Subtotals				

Weaknesses

#	SANGUINE	CHOLERIC	MELANCHOLY	PHLEGMATIC
21	Brassy	Bossy	Bashful	Blank
22	Undisciplined	Unsympathetic	Unforgiving	Unenthusiastic
23	Repetitious	Resistant	Resentful	Reticent
24	Forgetful	Frank	Fussy	Fearful
25	Interrupts	Impatient	Insecure	Indecisive
26	Unpredictable	Unaffectionate	Unpopular	Uninvolved
27	Haphazard	Headstrong	Hard-to-please	Hesitant
28	Permissive	Proud	Pessimistic	Plain
29	Angered easily	Argumentative	Alienated	Aimless
30	Naive	Nervy	Negative attitudes	Nonchalant
31	Wants credit	Workaholic	Withdrawn	Worrier
32	Talkative	Tactless	Too sensitive	Timid
33	Disorganized	Domineering	Depressed	Doubtful
34	Inconsistent	Intolerant	Introvert	Indifferent
35	Messy	Manipulative	Moody	Mumbles
36	Show-off	Stubborn	Skeptical	Slow
37	Loud	Lord-over-others	Loner	Lazy
38	Scatterbrained	Short tempered	Suspicious	Sluggish
39	Restless	Rash	Revengeful	Reluctant
40	Changeable	Crafty	Critical	Compromising

Subtotals | | | |

GRAND TOTALS

Appendix B

Personality Test Word Definitions
(Adapted From Personality Patterns by Lana Bateman)

STRENGTHS

1. **ADAPTABLE.** Easily fits and is comfortable in any situation.
   ADVENTUROUS. One who will take on new and daring enterprises with a determination to master them.
   ANALYTICAL. Likes to examine the parts for their logical and proper relationships.
   ANIMATED. Full of life, lively use of hand, arm, and face gestures.

2. **PEACEFUL.** Seems undisturbed and tranquil and retreats from any form of strife.
   PERSISTENT. Sees one project through to its completion before starting another.
   PERSUASIVE. Convinces through logic and fact rather than charm or power.
   PLAYFUL. Full of fun and good humor.

3. **SUBMISSIVE.** Easily accepts any other's point of view or desire with little need to assert his own opinion.
   SELF-SACRIFICING. Willingly gives up his own personal desires for the sake of, or to meet the needs of, others.
   SOCIABLE. One who sees being with others as an opportunity to be cute and entertaining rather than as a challenge or business opportunity.
   STRONG-WILLED. One who is determined to have his own way.

4. **CONSIDERATE.** Having regard for the needs and feelings of others.
   CONTROLLED. Has emotional feelings but rarely displays them.

COMPETITIVE. Turns every situation, happening, or game into a contest and always plays to win!

CONVINCING. Can win you over to anything through the sheer charm of his personality.

5. **REFRESHING.** Renews and stimulates or makes others feel good.

   RESPECTFUL. Treats others with deference, honor, and esteem.

   RESERVED. Self-restraint in expression of emotion or enthusiasm.

   RESOURCEFUL. Able to act quickly and effectively in virtually all situations.

6. **SATISFIED.** A person who easily accepts any circumstance or situation.

   SENSITIVE. Intensively cares about others, and what happens.

   SELF-RELIANT. An independent person who can fully rely on his own capabilities, judgment, and resources.

   SPIRITED. Full of life and excitement.

7. **PLANNER.** Prefers to work out a detailed arrangement beforehand for the accomplishment of project or goal, and prefers involvement with the planning stages and the finished product rather than the carrying out of the task.

   PATIENT. Unmoved by delay, remains calm and tolerant.

   POSITIVE. Knows it will turn out right if he's in charge.

   PROMOTER. Urges or compels others to go along, join, or invest through the charm of his own personality.

8. **SURE.** Confident, rarely hesitates or wavers.

   SPONTANEOUS. Prefers all of life to be impulsive, unpremeditated activity, not restricted by plans.

   SCHEDULED. Makes and lives according to a daily plan; dislikes his plan to be interrupted.

   SHY. Quiet, doesn't easily instigate a conversation.

9. **ORDERLY.** A person who has a methodical, systematic arrangement of things.

   OBLIGING. Accommodating. One who is quick to do it another's way.

   OUTSPOKEN. Speaks frankly and without reserve.

   OPTIMISTIC. Sunny disposition who convinces himself and others that everything will turn out all right.

10. **FRIENDLY.** A responder rather than an initiator; seldom starts a conversation.

   FAITHFUL. Consistently reliable, steadfast, loyal, and devoted, sometimes beyond reason.

   FUNNY. Sparkling sense of humor that can make virtually any story into an hilarious event.

   FORCEFUL. A commanding personality whom others would hesitate to take a stand against.

11. **DARING.** Willing to take risks; fearless, bold.

   DELIGHTFUL. A person who is upbeat and fun to be with.

   DIPLOMATIC. Deals with people tactfully, sensitively, and patiently.

   DETAILED. Does everything in proper order with a clear memory of all the things that happened.

12. **CHEERFUL.** Consistently in good spirits and promoting happiness in others.

   CONSISTENT. Stays emotionally on an even keel, responding as one might expect.

   CULTURED. One whose interests involve both intellectual and artistic pursuits, such as theater, symphony, ballet.

   CONFIDENT. Self-assured and certain of own ability and success.

13. **IDEALISTIC.** Visualizes things in their perfect form and has a need to measure up to that standard himself.

   INDEPENDENT. Self-sufficient, self-supporting, self-confident and seems to have little need of help.

   INOFFENSIVE. A person who never says or causes anything unpleasant or objectionable.

   INSPIRING. Encourages others to work, join, or be involved and makes the whole thing fun.

14. **DEMONSTRATIVE.** Openly expresses emotion, especially affection, and doesn't hesitate to touch others while speaking to them.

   DECISIVE. A person with quick, conclusive, judgment-making ability.

   DRY HUMOR. Exhibits "dry wit," usually humorous one-liners which can be sarcastic in nature.

DEEP. Intense and often introspective with a distaste for surface conversation and pursuits.

15. **MEDIATOR.** Consistently finds himself in the role of reconciling differences in order to avoid conflict.
    MUSICAL. Participates in or has a deep appreciation for music, is committed to music as an artform, rather than the fun of performance.
    MOVER. Driven by a need to be productive; a leader whom others follow; finds it difficult to sit still.
    MIXES EASILY. Loves a party and can't wait to meet everyone in the room; never meets a stranger.

16. **THOUGHTFUL.** A considerate person who remembers special occasions and is quick to make a kind gesture.
    TENACIOUS. Holds on firmly, stubbornly, and won't let go until the goal is accomplished.
    TALKER. Constantly talking, generally telling funny stories and entertaining everyone around, feeling the need to fill the silence in order to make others comfortable.
    TOLERANT. Easily accepts the thoughts and ways of others without the need to disagree with or change them.

17. **LISTENER.** Always seems willing to hear what you have to say.
    LOYAL. Faithful to a person, ideal, or job, sometimes beyond reason.
    LEADER. A natural-born director who is driven to be in charge and often finds it difficult to believe that anyone else can do the job as well.
    LIVELY. Full of life, vigorous, energetic.

18. **CONTENTED.** Easily satisfied with what he has; rarely envious.
    CHIEF. Commands leadership and expects people to follow.
    CHARTMAKER. Organizes life, tasks, and problem solving by making lists, forms, or graphs.
    CUTE. Precious, adorable, center of attention.

19. **PERFECTIONIST.** Places high standards on himself, and often on others, desiring that everything be in proper order at all times.
    PLEASANT. Easygoing, easy to be around, easy to talk with.

PRODUCTIVE. Must constantly be working or achieving; often finds it very difficult to rest.

POPULAR. Life of the party and therefore much desired as a party guest.

20. **BOUNCY.** A bubbly, lively personality, full of energy.

    BOLD. Fearless, daring, forward, unafraid of risk.

    BEHAVED. Consistently desires to conduct himself within the realm of what he feels is proper.

    BALANCED. Stable, middle-of-the-road personality, not subject to sharp highs or lows.

WEAKNESS

21. **BLANK.** A person who shows little facial expression or emotion.

    BASHFUL. Shrinks from getting attention, resulting from self-consciousness.

    BRASSY. Showy, flashy, comes on strong, too loud.

    BOSSY. Commanding, domineering, sometimes overbearing in adult relationships.

22. **UNDISCIPLINED.** A person whose lack of order permeates most every area of his life.

    UNSYMPATHETIC. Finds it difficult to relate to the problems or hurts of others.

    UNENTHUSIASTIC. Tends not to get excited, often feeling it won't work anyway.

    UNFORGIVING. One who has difficulty releasing or forgetting a hurt or injustice done to him, apt to hold onto a grudge.

23. **RETICENT.** Unwilling to get, or struggles against getting, involved, especially when complex.

    RESENTFUL. Often holds ill feelings as a result of real or imagined offenses.

    RESISTANT. Strives, works against, or hesitates to accept any other way but his own.

    REPETITIOUS. Retells stories and incidents to entertain you without realizing he has already told the story several times before; is constantly needing something to say.

24. **FUSSY.** Insistent over petty matters or details, calling great attention to trivial details.

FEARFUL. Often experiences feelings of deep concern, apprehension, or anxiousness.

FORGETFUL. Lack of memory, which is usually tied to a lack of discipline and not bothering to mentally record things that aren't fun.

FRANK. Straightforward, outspoken, and doesn't mind telling you exactly what he thinks.

25. **IMPATIENT.** A person who finds it difficult to endure irritation or wait for others.

INSECURE. One who is apprehensive or lacks confidence.

INDECISIVE. The person who finds it difficult to make any decision at all. (Not the personality that labors long over each decision in order to make the perfect one.)

INTERRUPTS. A person who is more of a talker than a listener, who starts speaking without even realizing someone else is already speaking.

26. **UNPOPULAR.** A person whose intensity and demand for perfection can push others away.

UNINVOLVED. Has no desire to listen or become interested in clubs, groups, activities, or other people's lives.

UNPREDICTABLE: May be ecstatic one moment and down the next, or willing to help but then disappears, or promises to come but forgets to show up.

UNAFFECTIONATE. Finds it difficult to verbally or physically demonstrate tenderness openly.

27. **HEADSTRONG.** Insists on having his own way.

HAPHAZARD. Has no consistent way of doing things.

HARD TO PLEASE. A person whose standards are set so high that it is difficult to ever satisfy them.

HESITANT. Slow to get moving and hard to get involved.

28. **PLAIN.** A middle-of-the-road personality without highs or lows and showing little, if any, emotion.

PESSIMISTIC. While hoping for the best, this person generally sees the down side of a situation first.

PROUD. One with great self-esteem who sees himself as always right and the best person for the job.

PERMISSIVE. Allows others (including children) to do as they please in order to keep from being disliked.

29. **ANGERED EASILY.** One who has a childlike flash-in-the-pan temper that expresses itself in tantrum style and is over and forgotten almost instantly.

    AIMLESS. Not a goal-setter with little desire to be one.

    ARGUMENTATIVE. Incites arguments generally because he is certain he is right no matter what the situation may be.

    ALIENATED. Easily feels estranged from others often because of insecurity or fear that others don't really enjoy his company.

30. **NAÏVE.** Simple and child-like perspective, lacking sophistication or comprehension of what the deeper levels of life are really about.

    NEGATIVE ATTITUDE. One whose attitude is seldom positive and is often able to see only the down or dark side of each situation.

    NERVY. Full of confidence, fortitude, and sheer guts, often in a negative sense.

    NONCHALANT. Easy-going, unconcerned, indifferent.

31. **WORRIER.** Consistently feels uncertain, troubled, or anxious.

    WITHDRAWN. A person who pulls back to himself and needs a great deal of alone or isolation time.

    WORKAHOLIC. An aggressive goal-setter who must be constantly productive and feels very guilty when resting, is not driven by a need for perfection or completion but by a need for accomplishment and reward.

    WANTS CREDIT. Thrives on the credit or approval of others. As an entertainer this person feeds on the applause, laughter, and/or acceptance of an audience.

32. **TOO SENSITIVE.** Overly introspective and easily offended when misunderstood.

    TACTLESS. Sometimes expresses himself in a somewhat offensive and inconsiderate way.

    TIMID. Shrinks from difficult situations.

    TALKATIVE. An entertaining, compulsive talker who finds it difficult to listen.

33. **DOUBTFUL.** Characterized by uncertainty and lack of confidence that it will ever work out.

DISORGANIZED. Lack of ability to ever get life in order.

DOMINEERING. Compulsively takes control of situations and/or people, usually telling others what to do.

DEPRESSED. A person who feels down much of the time.

34. **INCONSISTENT.** Erratic, contradictory, with actions and emotions not based on logic.

    INTROVERT. A person whose thoughts and interest are directed inward, lives within himself.

    INTOLERANT. Appears unable to withstand or accept another's attitudes, point of view, or way of doing things.

    INDIFFERENT. A person to whom most things don't matter one way or the other.

35. **MESSY.** Living in a state of disorder, unable to find things.

    MOODY. Doesn't get very high emotionally, but easily slips into low lows, often when feeling unappreciated.

    MUMBLES. Will talk quietly under the breath when pushed, doesn't bother to speak clearly.

    MANIPULATIVE. Influences or manages shrewdly or deviously for his own advantage, will get his way somehow.

36. **SLOW.** Doesn't often act or think quickly, too much of a bother.

    STUBBORN. Determined to exert his own will, not easily persuaded, obstinate.

    SHOW-OFF. Needs to be the center of attention, wants to be watched.

    SKEPTICAL. Disbelieving, questioning the motive behind the words.

37. **LONER.** Requires a lot of private time and tends to avoid other people.

    LORD OVER. Doesn't hesitate to let you know that he is right or is in control.

    LAZY. Evaluates work or activity in terms of how much energy it will take.

    LOUD. A person whose laugh or voice can be heard above others in the room.

38. **SLUGGISH.** Slow to get started, needs push to be motivated.

    SUSPICIOUS. Tends to suspect or distrust others or ideas.

SHORT-TEMPERED. Has a demanding impatience-based anger and a short fuse. Anger is expressed when others are not moving fast enough or have not completed what they have been asked to do.

SCATTER-BRAINED. Lacks the power of concentration, or attention, flighty.

39. **REVENGEFUL.** Knowingly or otherwise holds a grudge and punishes the offender, often by subtly withholding friendship or affection.

RESTLESS. Likes constant new activity because it isn't fun to do the same things all the time.

RELUCTANT. Unwilling or struggles against getting involved.

RASH. May act hastily, without thinking things through, generally because of impatience.

40. **COMPROMISING.** Will often relax his position, even when right, in order to avoid conflict.

CRITICAL. Constantly evaluating and making judgments, frequently thinking or expressing negative reactions.

CRAFTY. Shrewd, one who can always find a way to get to the desired end.

CHANGEABLE. A child-like, short attention span that needs a lot of change and variety to keep from getting bored.

Other Books by
Florence and Fred Littauer

HARVEST HOUSE PUBLISHERS
Blow Away the Black Clouds
How to Get Along with Difficult People
It Takes So Little to Be Above Average

WORD PUBLISHING
The Gift of Encouraging Words
Silver Boxes (also available in Spanish and Polish)
Dare to Dream (also available in French, Spanish, and Polish)
Raising Christians—Not Just Children
Hope for Hurting Women
Looking for God in All the Right Places
Wake Up, Men
Wake Up, Women (also available in Indonesian)
Your Personality Tree (also available in Spanish, Indonesian, and Polish)

THOMAS NELSON PUBLISHERS
Freeing Your Mind from Memories That Bind (also available in Spanish)
The Promise of Healing
I've Found My Keys, Now Where's the Car? (also available in Polish)

FLEMING REVELL-BAKER BOOKS

Putting the Pieces in Place, with Marita Littauer
Personality Plus (available in 11 other languages)
Personality Puzzle (also available in Indonesian)
Put Power in Your Personality
Testing . . . 1 . . . 2 . . . 3

CREATION HOUSE
Touched by the Master

If you wish to receive information on all of the Littauer books, engage Florence for your church or business, or find out when there will be a CLASS or any of the other Littauer Seminars in your area, please call or write to:

CLASS
1611 S. Rancho Santa Fe Road
Suite F2
San Marcos, CA 92069
(760) 471-0233

Other Good
Harvest House Reading

THE MARRIAGE MAKER
by John and Teri Nieder

What is the hidden power of becoming one? How can the Holy Spirit make a difference in your marriage? John Nieder, host of the popular radio broadcast "The Art of Family Living," and his wife, Teri, offer a refreshing look at marriage's most often-neglected resource—the Holy Spirit. Thoughtful questions and devotions at the end of each chapter make *The Marriage Maker* both practical and inspirational. Excellent for personal use or group study.

THE MASTER'S DEGREE
by Frank and Bunny Wilson

Sharing their early years in the school of marriage and the wisdom and understanding garnered along the way, Frank and Bunny Wilson provide "mini-courses" in intimate relationships. Filled with personal experiences and practical learning, this book explores the spiritual, emotional, and physical aspects of marriage, then shows how God views, supports, and participates in every relationship. Includes special sections for husbands only and for wives only.

QUIET TIMES FOR COUPLES
by H. Norman Wright

Designed to stimulate genuinely open communication between husband and wife, each day's devotions makes it easy for couples to share about the deeper parts of their lives.

QUIET TIMES FOR PARENTS
by H. Norman Wright

H. Norman Wright, whose *Quiet Times for Couples* has been on the bestseller list since April 1991, now shares poignant insights on the joys and challenges of parenting. In 366 one-page devotions, Wright delivers the same honest inspiration and encouragement that continues to make his earlier devotional so successful.

Dear Reader:

We would appreciate hearing from you regarding *After Every Wedding Comes a Marriage*. It will enable us to continue to give you the best in Christian publishing.

1. What most influenced you to purchase this book?
   - ❑ Author
   - ❑ Subject matter
   - ❑ Back cover copy
   - ❑ Recommendations
   - ❑ Cover/Title
   - ❑ Other _____

2. Where did you purchase this book?
   - ❑ Christian bookstore
   - ❑ General bookstore
   - ❑ Department store
   - ❑ Grocery store
   - ❑ Other _____

3. Your overall rating of this book:

   ❑ Excellent   ❑ Very good   ❑ Good   ❑ Fair   ❑ Poor

4. How likely would you be to purchase other books by this author?

   ❑ Very likely   ❑ Somewhat likely   ❑ Not very likely   ❑ Not at all

5. What types of books most interest you? (Check all that apply.)
   - ❑ Women's Books
   - ❑ Marriage Books
   - ❑ Current Issues
   - ❑ Christian Living
   - ❑ Bible Studies
   - ❑ Fiction
   - ❑ Biographies
   - ❑ Children's Books
   - ❑ Youth Books
   - ❑ Other _____

6. Please check the box next to your age group.

   ❑ Under 18   ❑ 18-24   ❑ 25-34   ❑ 35-44   ❑ 45-54   ❑ 55 and over

Mail to:

Editorial Director
Harvest House Publishers
1075 Arrowsmith
Eugene, OR 97402

Name _____

Address _____

State _____ Zip

Thank you for helping us to help you in future publications!